FIRST EDITION

Celebrating
Live Theatre
AN INTRODUCTION

D1558386

Written and edited by Mary Kate Caffrey

Framingham State University
University of Massachusetts, Boston

cognella®
academic publishing

Bassim Hamadeh, CEO and Publisher
Michael Simpson, Vice President of Acquisitions and Sales
Jamie Giganti, Senior Managing Editor
Jess Busch, Senior Graphic Designer
John Remington, Senior Field Acquisitions Editor
Monika Dziamka, Project Editor
Brian Fahey, Licensing Specialist
Claire Yee, Interior Designer

First published in the United States of America in 2016 by Cognella, Inc.

Trademark Notice: Product or corporate names may be trademarks or registered trademarks, and are used only for identification and explanation without intent to infringe.

Printed in the United States of America

ISBN: 978-1-63189-052-9 (pbk) /978-1-63189-053-6 (br)

www.cognella.com   800-200-3908

Contents

PART FOUR
Enhancements to Theatre Throughout History— Directing, Technical Support, and the Critic

PART FIVE
Genres and Styles of Theatre from Around the World

DEDICATION

This book is dedicated to Brigid O'Connor, Eamon Caffrey, and my parents, Robert and Mary Lou M. Caffrey, in gratitude for all of their love and support.

The aim of art is to represent not the outward appearance of things, but their inward significance.

—Aristotle

THANKS

Special thanks go to: Dave Nuscher, for copious edits and insightful suggestions all along the way; Yumi Grassia for assistance with translation and correspondence with colleagues in Japan; Dr. Charles Wall, Dr. Barbara Finkelstein, Dr. Deanna Yameen, and the sabbatical committee at Massasoit Community College for granting me a semester sabbatical to complete the final sections of the text; Brigid O'Connor; Karen Perlow; Janie Howland; Frances Nelson McSherry; Sara Pruitt Dahl; Mike Katz; Robert Lublin; Anthony Phelps; Mr. Koike, President of the Theatre Museum, Waseda University, Japan; Richard Grey, BeNT Productions, Clinton, MA; Rieko Ward, Director of Operations, The Japan Society of Boston; Kate Finnegan, Executive Director, KAJI ASO Studio, Boston, MA; Kim Hoff; Elena Ivanova; Virgil C. Johnson; Howard Enoch; Frank Galati; Robert Breen; Nan Withers-Wilson; Dawn Mora; David Mold; J. Paul Marcoux; J.L. Styan; Chandra Pieragostini; Lizza Riley; Monica Tecca; Amy West; Kara Pascucci; Robert Pascucci; Jackie Pascucci; Mary Kearney; Threshold Theatre, Inc.; Richard Toma, Jeanine Kane; Claudia Traub; Kristin Linklater; Robert Chapline; Lisa Tucker; Jess Martin; Mal Malme; Becca Lewis; Moe Angelos; The Five Lesbian Brothers; The Theater Offensive; New Repertory Theater; Shakespeare and Company; Speakeasy Stage Company; The Nora Theater; Underground Railway Theater; The Lyric Stage Company; Actor's Shakespeare Project; Wheelock Family Theater; Boston Midsummer Opera; Central Square Theatre; Boston Playwrights Theater; Triangle Theater; Centastage; The Back Alley Theater; Concord Academy; Emerson College Performing Arts Department; Boston College Theater Department; Northwestern University Department of Theater and Performance Studies; MIT Dramashop; University of Massachusetts, Boston, Department of Performing Arts; Daniel Gidron; Cliff Odle; Ginger Lazarus; Rafael Jaen; Michael Fennimore; Tanya Williams, Orville Wright; Carrie-Ann Quinn; Jeff Miller; Susan V. Booth; Larry Lenza; Amanda Rogers; the many other actors, designers, directors, teachers, playwrights, students, theatre administrators, stage managers, TD's, theatre technicians, board members, crew members, reviewers, and back stage heroes who have touched my life and inspired me over the years; and the dedicated team at Cognella Academic Publishing for all of their support, especially: Monika Dziamka, project editor; John Remington, aquisitions editor; Jamie Giganti, managing editor; Jennifer Bowen Levine, administrative program specialist; Jess Busch, cover designer; Tim Gladson, digital librarian; Brian Fahey, licensing coordinator; Chelsey Rogers, marketing specialist; Arek Arechiga, royalties specialist; and Claire Yee, interior designer.

PREFACE

The goal of this book is to introduce you to the art of live theatre.
Some readers will be moved by this experience to become very active players and participate
as designers, writers, directors, administrators, technicians, or performers. Most readers will
take the knowledge culled from this book and experience a live theatrical production in a new
and exciting way: as a more appreciative and educated audience member. Reading this book
will not make you an expert in any one area of theatre, but it will introduce you to some of
the varieties of live theatre and the many ways in which you may participate and be a part of
this art form. My hope is that you will appreciate what theatre can offer that other art forms
cannot. In this survey text, my intention is to pique the novice's interest and broaden the
scope of the experienced theatregoer through an abridged exploration of numerous aspects
of the art form, shedding light on how theatre began, its evolution across different areas of
the globe over thousands of years, and the ways in which it continues to develop and change.

PART
One
WHY THEATRE?

CHAPTER ONE

Theatre as a Fragile, Delicate—Yet Vital— Living Entity

...You have to come at it (theatre) freshly. ... This is the delicacy and fragility of theatre, it doesn't last. We are such stuff as THAT moment is made, that dream today is made of. Tomorrow's dream is a different one. ... Our world was the world we were in then, that day. ...

Every Hamlet, every year is a fresh Hamlet because that young man is living in that year, not the next year or the year before. And I think that is the strength and beauty of theatre, it has nothing to do with its past, although it rolls underneath it like a surge of the ocean. But actually every actor in the "today-ness" of his work is what brings freshness to the play.

—Director, Janet Suzman, American Theatre Wing Interview

Why do humans need theatre? Theatre is an art form that, like other art forms, allows the human race to reflect on and attempt to work out what it is to be human. In this way, theatre is about connection and reflection. The imperfections and vulnerabilities of life require people to learn, reflect, grow, and change. Theatre is a creative, inventive, expressive way for humankind to do all of these things. Theatre has existed in some manner for as long as human beings have inhabited the earth. Its manifestations have varied from era to era and culture to culture. It may be perceptive, discerning, beautiful, fine, elegant, exquisite, ornamental, or aesthetically pleasing. It is often rife with spectacle, excitement, thrill, sensation, commotion, disturbance, turmoil, and crisis. These similar and contrasting facets of theatre may exist at any moment in any production. Theatre is not a clear and straightforward form of art just as life has never been clear and straightforward.

Perhaps this is not your understanding of theatre. Many people believe that they need to buy a ticket and go into a building in order to say they have ever gone to "the theatre." What those people don't know is that they have most certainly witnessed and even been a participant in a theatrical event. Theatre is IN us and WE are in theatre. Without us, there is no theatre.

What is theatre? Theatre is a performing art. Theatre is alive. At its essence, theatre needs three basic components—an audience, an actor, and a story. These three essentials of theatre are the same no matter where in the world one travels.

Theatre is a unique art form that may incorporate many other art forms. It is unique in a few ways. First, the primary tool or instrument that is used in this art form is the individual. With other art forms, the artist uses himself, but he also uses some kind of instrument or tool to create his art. The painter uses paint and brushes. The musician uses his trumpet. The sculptor uses stone, metal, or clay. One might argue that a dancer or a singer also uses himself as the primary instrument through which he creates his art. This is true. The line between theatre, dance, and singing is a very blurry one. In many cultures, there is no line between these performance traditions. Movement and musical vocalization are the basis of theatre in the performance traditions of many Eastern cultures.

So, what is the difference between singing, dance, and theatre? There are a few differences. The primary difference is something called transformation. In most theatrical styles, the actor is expected to transform himself into the character that he is playing. Some would argue that a dancer does this as well. However, a dancer is deemed great primarily on his ability to perform certain movements with his body. If a person wants to be a professional ballet dancer, his body must meet certain aesthetic standards. A dancer trains only his body. A singer must have a certain vocal aptitude: something that requires both a natural ability to match pitch as well as training in order to optimize that talent. Unlike the dancer or the singer, however, the theatre artist must use both his voice and his body, but he must also transform himself and "be" someone or something other than himself.

Theatre has its roots in ritual. Ritual is a collective ceremony performed by members of a society. Results are usually performed for religious or cultural reasons. Most ancient rituals were meant to summon gods or to influence nature. Our ancestors also performed tribal rituals to honor important life events, such as the changing of the seasons or by marking life passages, such as birth, coming of age, marriage, and death. Early tribal rituals included elements we now consider theatrical—staging, costuming, masks, makeup, dance, formalized speech, chanting, singing, and specific physical props (staffs, spears, skulls) with spiritual qualities that would prove crucial to the staged event. Not all rituals are based in religion, some are secular—changing of the guards, the robes worn by judges and at graduation ceremonies, the lowering of the ball on New Year's Eve, etc.

Religious and secular rituals, which are still enacted all over the globe, are descendants of these ancient tribal ceremonies. Rituals give the events they represent and honor enhanced meaning, grandeur, and authority. Like theatre, ritual is the act of performers recreating, intensifying, and making meaningful the myths, beliefs, legends, and traditions common to the human experience.

Over the centuries, some of the traditions of ritual have remained. However, because theatre is a living art form, it is constantly changing. Throughout history, theatre artists all around the world have constantly explored innovative ways to express their vision. And the goal is always for the performer to share that vision with an audience. Without an audience it is only a rehearsal; it is not a performance.

Why theatre? To answer this question let us look at what one of the first known critics of theatre said about it:

> *Poetry in general seems to have sprung from two causes, each of them lying deep in our nature. First, the instinct of imitation is implanted in man from childhood, one difference between him and other animals being that he is the most imitative of living creatures and through imitation learns his earliest lessons; and no less universal is the pleasure felt in things imitated. We have evidence of this in the facts of experience. Objects, which in themselves we view with pain, we delight to contemplate when reproduced with minute fidelity: such as the forms of the most ignoble animals and of dead bodies. The cause of this again is that to learn gives the liveliest pleasure, not only to philosophers but to men in general; whose capacity, however, of learning is more limited. Thus the reason why men enjoy seeing a likeness is, that in contemplating it they find themselves learning or inferring, and saying perhaps, "Ah, that is he." For if you happen not to have seen the original, the pleasure will be due not to the imitation as such, but to the execution, the coloring, or some such other cause.*

> —Aristotle, *Poetics*

In this passage Aristotle identified two reasons for the necessity of theatre: to learn and to entertain. These two motivations for theatre remain to this day.

LEARNING THROUGH THEATRE

Participating and witnessing the reenactment of an event enables people to attempt to more deeply understand themselves and others. Performing—or participating as an audience member as someone takes on a role in a theatrical production—allows an individual to try things on and feel or experience relationships, actions, and their consequences without permanent ramifications.

ENTERTAINING THROUGH THEATRE

Theatrical performance has the ability to entertain an audience. One of the most integral aspects of entertainment is the fact that there is an audience. This audience turns what might be a private event or activity into a public one. Entertainment is something that humans have always been drawn to. Simply, something is entertaining if it can hold the attention and interest of an audience. The level and significance of the entertainment is determined by its ability to make the audience feel and connect in an emotional way. Oftentimes people associate entertainment with something that gives pleasure or delights. Entertainment is not always delightful or pleasurable; it is something that creates a heightened sense of being alive. Entertainment creates a sense of urgency and energy in the body, which subsequently creates a sense of gratification.

CHAPTER TWO

A Brief History of Theatre
Around the World

As we stated in Chapter One, the roots of today's theatre lie in ritual and celebration. Ancient civilizations created rituals and celebrations to mark milestones in life. Performance has always been an integral aspect of ritual celebrations. These rituals include celebratory elements that we find in present-day theatre. Performance rituals may include costumes, props, music, masks, and impersonation of gods, spirits, animals, humans, and natural elements. No matter what area of the globe you explore, you always seem to find performance traditions that are connected to ritual and celebration. These ritual celebrations around the globe evolved into a theatre that became the venue where humans could give public expression to private feelings.

Theatre is found in many different parts of the world. Each tradition is unique but is also tied to theatre traditions around the globe. All theatre includes some very basic elements. However, each culture's theatre has developed differently due to the values, beliefs, traditions, and accepted behaviors of that culture. There are two main categories into which theatrical performance can be divided. These are the *performance tradition* and the *written tradition*. One or another of these traditions has dominated theatrical performance around the globe throughout history. It is beyond the scope of this book to explore why this might be. But it is important to note that the closer people of various cultural backgrounds get due to technological advances, the more these traditions interweave.

Each tradition has its own merit, value, and importance. Each tradition has lasted for thousands of years, untouched by the other. Each tradition, as has been stated previously, shares the basic elements of theatre. But it would be injudicious for one tradition to dominate, overtake, or even eliminate the other due to a lack of appreciation or understanding of what makes that tradition "theatre." It is important to remember that theatre is a PERFORMING art and not a written art. As the study of drama—and particularly dramatic literature—has moved into the classroom, many have begun to think of theatre as a written play. However, at the end of this book, I hope you will come to broaden your idea of theatre—to understand that the written play is not necessarily "the thing," as Shakespeare's *Hamlet* suggests. Theatre is so much more than words on a page; it is a living, breathing, imaginative art form, which may not even require a written text at all.

The written tradition has dominated Western society since the time of the ancient Greeks. The legacy of theatrical criticism was begun by Aristotle (384–322 BCE) in his work *Poetics*. In this tradition, written play texts are divided into genres, or categories. These categories of drama are used to convey the human experience and reflect social context and universal feeling. In the written tradition, sense is made of a play's emotional impact and point of view. Genre in the written tradition implies the perspective the playwright brings to the subject. It also implies the viewpoint the audience should bring to the production. For example, a tragedy will present a character who will struggle and confront painful and terrifying limitations. An audience experiencing a tragic play will expect to feel sadness, pity, and fear. A comedy may deal with similar subject matter, but the characters will prevail over the odds, and the audience will expect laughter, celebration, and a happy ending. A melodrama will speak directly to the audience's emotions and will stage its deepest anxieties with simplicity, sensationalism, and sentimentality. This genre guarantees that the audience will be appeased by an idealized ending.

The performance tradition has dominated Eastern and Native societies. In these societies, the critical tradition is absent, and theatrical categories tend to develop from the perspective of the artist through historical growth of the form and through cultural and religious influences. For example, the Noh theatre of Japan categorizes works by the nature of the main character. Indian Sanskrit Theatre groups performance types by the dominant moods or feelings that are evoked.

PART

Two

THE ESSENTIALS OF THEATRE—AUDIENCE, STORY, ACTOR

CHAPTER THREE

Audience Expectations and Traditions

AUDIENCE

Trudy

They asked me to explain goose bumps—do they come from the heart?
Do they come from the soul? Do they come form the brain?
Or do they come from
geese? ...

Next, they insisted I take them somewhere
so they could get goose bumps. They were dying to see
what is was like.
I decided maybe we should take in a play.
I got goose bumps once that way.
So we headed back toward Shubert Alley ...

Did I tell you what happened at the play? We were at the back
of the theater, standing there in the dark,
all of a sudden I feel one of 'em tug my sleeve,
whispers, "Trudy, look." I said, "Yeah, goose bumps. You
definitely

*got goose bumps. You really like the play that much?" They said
it wasn't the play
gave 'em goose bumps
it was the audience.*

*I forgot to tell them to watch the play; they'd been watching
the audience!
Yeah, to see a group of strangers sitting together in the dark
laughing and crying about the same things … that just knocked
'em out.
They said, "Trudy,
the play was soup …
the audience …
art."*

*So they're taking goose bumps
home with 'em.
Goose bumps!
Quite a souvenir.*

*I like to think of them out there
in the dark, watching us.
Sometimes we'll do something and they'll laugh.
Sometimes we'll do something and they'll cry.
And maybe one day we'll do something so magnificent,
everyone in the universe will get
goose bumps.*

Every theatrical performance, by definition, must be performed by live actors and have a live audience. If a performance is recorded and shown to an audience at a later time, it is not theatre.

This is a very important distinction. Because theatre is performed in the moment in front of a live audience, that audience has a part in the performance. With a recorded performance—on film, video, or television—those who watch the presentation will never have an impact on it. It will also never change. It will always be the same. A theatrical performance is always unique. You will never see the exact same performance twice. This is because no two moments in life are ever the same. Live events exist only in the moment they occur.

The audience has a very big impact on a performance. There is a palpable energy that is shared by the audience and by those who are creating a production. The energy that is shared influences all those who share in the live event—the audience members, the performers, the technicians, the ushers, et al. Sometimes that energy is shared by the audience with the performers in the form of vocal responses (laughter, gasps, yelling at the players, boos, hissing, responding to what is happening on stage with words or sounds). At other times, the energy is shared in a physical manner (clapping, throwing items at the stage, physically participating with the performers). Whether the interaction between performer and audience is major or minor, that connection shapes the theatrical experience.

WHAT IS AN AUDIENCE?

The audience is a group of individuals. As the performance flows through each audience member's body, mind, and heart, she radiates her individual response to the performance. Each audience member brings her own life experience with her to the theatre. That experience influences how she will respond to the play, how she is moved by the play, what levels of the play she understands, and how the performance will affect her.

The audience is also a group of people. They are in the same space, sharing the same energy, and as that energy radiates around and through them, they become an active part of the performance.

THE AUDIENCE THROUGHOUT HISTORY

Contemporary Western audiences may be surprised to find out that a relatively passive, controlled audience is a somewhat new and unusual phenomenon. Research has shown that, historically, audiences at theatrical events have been very active participants. One reason for this is that theatre has its roots in ritual. The roots of Western theatre lie in the ritual celebrations of the ancient Greeks, dating back to the fifth century BCE. Theatrical performances were a major element of the Festival of Dionysus, the god of wine and fertility. Playwrights would compete each year for prizes awarded to the man who wrote the best trilogy. These festivals were held outdoors in amphitheatres that were carved into the Greek hillside. (See Figure 3.1.) It was a time of celebration, and the celebration honored Dionysus by taking part in those gifts that he bestowed on humankind: wine and reproduction. Based on what historians have discovered, these festivals were meant to give the citizens a good time. The whole community would attend these celebrations. Audiences would be able to move freely about and, if they chose to, could be very close to the stage. The plays were based on stories that everyone knew, so the playwright's skill

Figure 3.1 Ancient Theatre of Epidaurus, Greece, Built 4th Century BCE. Photo: Kate Caffrey, 2014.

was demonstrated through his[1] ability to move the audience through the words, action, and structure of his play. And, if the audience was moved, the response would most likely not be a contained one. This audience had been imbibing, making merry, and philandering for days. When Aristotle writes in his *Poetics* about what makes a good play, he discusses the fact that great plays strike fear and pity in the hearts of an audience. The audience can empathize with a character and actually have an emotional and physical reaction. These reactions are what Jane Wagner's Trudy refers to as "goose bumps."

---

1   All playwrights were men at this point in history.

CHAPTER FOUR

Story

One of the most basic elements required in any production is a story. All theatre is live storytelling. Storytelling is more personal and individual than collective ritual performance. Storytelling usually relies on a single voice, and it often has a single point of view. Storytelling generates elements of characterization—an integral aspect of theatre. Storytellers create character through adjusting their voices and using gestures and facial expressions to reflect the personalities and emotions of the character portrayed in their stories. They craft a structured story and engage their audience through suspense, larger than life details, and a narrative that is both personal and emotionally affecting.

STORY IN PERFORMANCE TRADITIONS

In most performance traditions, the spoken words (if there are any) are not specific and/or communicated through a written text; hence, the distinction between "written" and "performance" theatrical traditions. Usually, there are no (or not many) specific written "lines" or words that must be memorized. Performance traditions rely a great deal on spectacle, movement, imagery, improvisation, vocal inflection, puppetry, music, and improvisation to communicate a story. The stories—and the ways in which they are presented to an audience—are often not written down but are passed down from generation to generation through oral tradition, apprenticeships, and rigorous physical and vocal training programs. Some performance traditions and the stories that go along with them have been lost over the years. This has been due mainly to the oppression of native performance traditions by colonization. Throughout history, countries that have focused on "conquering" and then colonizing have diminished—or even destroyed—the performance traditions native to the culture that has been usurped. The colonizer will bring his own performance tradition and will require that those living in the "new" colony adopt the performance tradition of the dominant colonizer. Because performance traditions are so closely linked to ritual and religion, native traditions are misunderstood and feared. Those traditions, which do not fit into Western ideas of what is "appropriate" or correct, may be forbidden and are, most often and at the very least, unsupported. Most of the countries that have been involved in colonization have culturally espoused the beliefs of the Judeo-Christian vision of life. Many native performance traditions are seen as contrary to these beliefs. What is not understood becomes threatening because it is unfamiliar. Those aspects of life that frighten people will be oppressed and often labeled as "wrong," "illegal," or—at worst—"immoral" or "evil." As the world has become more tolerant and open to differences, some of these performance traditions—and the stories that accompany them—have had a rebirth. Some of the stories and traditions have not survived, however.

STORY IN WRITTEN TRADITIONS

Written traditions in theatre are those with which most students who have been educated in the Western tradition are familiar. When students are learning to read and begin exploring language arts or literature, they will often study a play as one genre of literature. When speaking of literature, other genres include poetry, novels, short stories, essays, etc. When speaking of written theatre, we also discuss different genres (comedy, tragedy, melodrama, farce, etc.) as well as various written styles and "movements" in the written tradition.

When a playwright decides to tell a story through a written play, there are many skills that are required—skills that are different than those utilized by someone who would pen a novel, essay, or short story.

HOW IS A WRITING A PLAY DIFFERENT?

Many artists can move seamlessly between literary genres. However, as in any other art form, there are aspects of playwriting that must be learned and practiced. Throughout western history, the primary focus of theatre has been the written words and how they are structured to communicate the author's vision, message, meaning, and intention.

Most theatre historians agree that the first person to really evaluate the play and give some idea of how to write a "good" play was the Ancient Greek scholar

Aristotle in his treatise *Poetics* written in 335 BCE. Ancient Greece had an active and vibrant theatrical culture. The ancient Greeks believed in competition and in Greek men bettering themselves through education and exposure to various aspects of life. Part of the challenge to educate and better oneself came through competition. The same festival atmosphere that existed around sports, with the original Olympic Games in ancient Greece, existed around plays and theatre. Every year, the ancient Greeks would hold a festival to honor the god Dionysis (the god of wine and fertility) to celebrate life. A major part of the festival was a competition among playwrights. The highest honor went to the playwright who wrote the best group of three tragic interrelated plays. The theatres were outside and active as long as there was light by which the audience could see the players.

The Western written tradition focuses on three major components in the creation of a written text to be performed. These three components are dramatic structure, dramatic character, and dramatic language. All of these elements are influenced by the historical and societal context in which the playwright lives.

Dramatic structure is the form a playwright utilizes to convey a play's events. Story is all the events mentioned in the text. The playwright shapes the story through: plot—structure of events taking place on stage; conflict—dramatic tension caused by struggles and obstacles; and character—defined through the choices made by the individuals in the play to win the central conflict.

Plot is crafted to create maximum emotional impact on the audience. The same story can be told through different plots to focus on a particular theme or perspective. Dramatic structure describes the scope and the structure of the action. It is the framework, or scaffolding, upon which the story is told. It is the way the playwright shapes the action. The dramatic structure of a play describes the scope of the action—what events are included in the action. It also describes the progression of the action—at what point in the series of events does the play begin? New dramatic structures have been created throughout history as playwrights have felt the need to convey new ideas and elicit new reactions from an audience. Some structures have prevailed historically and have, with some adjustments, created a "template" for writing successful plays. The most prevalent dramatic structures are climactic and episodic structures.

Climactic structure, also known as Aristotelian Plot, is a tight-knit form with a limited scope. There are a limited number of characters and the action takes place in one or a few locations over a short time period. There is a late point of attack, meaning that the dramatic action begins at the most heightened and intense point in the action. Climactic structure includes exposition, which reveals prior events. Events come about through cause and effect, with numerous complications that keep the action of the drama moving to a climax of emotional intensity—like the twisting of a coil or rubber band. Once the action has reached this climax, or point of highest emotional intensity, there is a falling action—often referred to as a *denouement* (meaning unknotting in French), in which all loose ends are tied up. When the plot cannot be easily resolved, there is a *Deus ex machina*, which is a dramatic device outside of the main action that brings the play to a final resolution. Deus ex machina means "god from the machine" and refers to a device used in ancient Greek plays. (The device was a crane that lowered a god onto the stage to resolve the plot.)

Episodic structure has an early point of attack, with numerous characters, events, and locations. The dramatic action builds, not through cause and effect but through cumulative tension. This type of structure also includes a main plot, with subplots and parallel plots that echo the themes of and comment on the main plot. Shakespeare used this dramatic structure to great effect in his masterpieces.

Other structures that have been developed when these two structures did not work to communicate the author's message are circular structure—which does not move forward to a conclusion but ends where it begins; serial structure—which includes a series of scenes that are thematically related with no continuity of story or character; and structural variations—in which the writer plays with time, and a play does not proceed in chronological order.

Dramatic characters are the human element of the play. The characters in a written play tend to create significance and emotional interest in the play. Characters are defined primarily by their actions but can also be understood by what they say about themselves and what other characters in the play say about them. Well-crafted characters stay with the audience long after the play is over. Characters in plays have needs that they attempt to fulfill, and drama is created by the obstacles that get in the way of the characters achieving their desires. The characters are then defined by what they do—how they confront the obstacles presented to them in the play. In ancient times and up until the rise of the middle class in the eighteenth century, the lives of the ruling class, deities, and saints were the sole subjects of dramatic literature. As society has changed, plays now often feature ordinary people who are placed in extraordinary circumstances. The essential energy of a performance is created by capturing moments of a character's intense struggle against circumstances. The audience sees these struggles as part of the human condition, which creates a universality and connection between character and audience. Life is struggle; humans are always grappling with the conflict and obstacles to the fulfillment of desires that life presents. A character is defined by the way in which he or she deals with these struggles, the path from desire to fulfillment or disappointment. The way in which a playwright creates a character is intricately influenced by the society and culture in which the playwright lives. Culture determines how we view the human psyche, what elements of humanity are valued, and what behaviors are judged as virtuous or villainous. Characters come in many different flavors, and a playwright will write characters in a way that fits the genre and style of the play. Types of characters you will find in plays include: psychological, archetypal, allegorical, stock, depersonalized, deconstructed, and characters with a dominant trait. As with structure, as the world rapidly changes, playwrights react to these changes by finding new ways to write character to represent changing concepts of people and humanity.

Dramatic language is the playwright's basic tool of expression. This is different than writing a screenplay, in which the basic tool of expression is pictures. Movies were originally called "moving pictures," and the focus of film has been primarily on the picture that is created rather than the words that are spoken. Playwrights write for actors, so the text that is written must be actable, speakable, and capable of inspiring physical expression. Stage language is not everyday language, which would be uninteresting on stage. And yet playwrights know how to craft language so that it sounds both natural and poetic at the same time. Stage language is heightened, intensified, and stylized. Dialogue is the primary form of language that is found in a written play. Dialogue is words that are spoken between characters in the drama. These words are the exposition and reveal the story through what the characters say in the present. Theatrical language has many goals: it must advance the plot; express character; provoke or embody action; compress emotion; and set the mood, style, and tone of the play.

In order to advance the plot, the language must be active. The language tells the story and advances the action, so it must be theatrical. To be theatrical, the language must be addressed to someone. Language in an effective play script is rarely, if ever, passive description. Because a playwright's time is limited—she has an hour or two to actively communicate the message and the story—each line must convey information.

Dialogue is used to shape and rhythmically build the script; for example, building intensity for climaxes and building to punch lines. The rhythmic patterns of a character's dialogue may alter to give both the actor and the audience clues to the character's emotional state. Shakespeare was a master of this technique. He set up a normal structured rhythm of iambic pentameter that dominated the text. At times in his text, a character who has spoken in this rhythm throughout will suddenly begin to speak in a pattern that breaks this rhythm. As the actor scans the text, he will notice this change, which gives him a clue that the character is experiencing an emotional change. The audience members can also hear this rhythmic change in performance, which makes them "prick up their ears" and heightens their awareness of the significance of the words and the actions that they are witnessing on stage. The writer of the drama also uses dialect to advance the plot. Dialect enables the playwright to establish location and create character. A skilled playwright creates each character's unique voice through the use of rhythm, vocabulary, inflection, dialect, and grammatical structure.

Dramatic language also expresses character. Each character has his own unique voice. The way in which a character uses language to express thoughts and emotions reflects his education, values, personality, age, and emotional outlook. The language used must also provoke and embody action. Dialogue implies the need to act and give physical expression to the spoken word. For this reason, plays are most often written in the present tense and focus on what is happening now. The language that the playwright uses must support and trigger gestures and strong physical action. When the dramatic language fails, the text is static, actors are immobile and stationary, and the text is difficult to play.

Dramatic language must also compress emotion and compress a lifetime of meaning into two to three hours. For example, in Shakespeare's *Romeo and Juliet*, Juliet experiences the following events in about two and a half hours: she falls in love; she loses her virginity; she gets married; her cousin is killed; her husband is banished; she fakes her own death; she wakes to find her husband dead next to her; she kills herself; and her actions end an age-old feud between her family and Romeo's family. Most people could not imagine experiencing ONE of these life-altering events in such a short time span, let alone NINE such events. Because the playwright must compress emotion, he uses heightened and emotionally charged language. Words are selected for maximum impact, and emotions and relationships must build quickly.

Dramatic language—its sound, rhythm, and structure—also sets the mood, tone, and style of a drama. Types of language are associated with certain styles and forms of drama. The language of classical tragedy, with its verse and strict metrical patterns, creates a sense of dignity. Verse or poetry is often used in drama. Poetry creates images and metaphor, and the words chosen in poetry give rise to literal and symbolic meanings. Contemporary playwrights struggle with the failure of language and the idea that language does not always communicate the truth. Writers must then find new ways to express ideas. Meaning in contemporary theatre is sometimes created through a collage of sound effects, with no literal narrative that rejects linear sequencing.

CHAPTER FIVE

Actor—Traditions and Training

THE TWO MAJOR FORMS OF ACTING: PRESENTATIONAL AND REPRESENTATIONAL

Presentational—Presentational acting is a heightened theatrical style. It was the only acting style in which actors trained prior to the late nineteenth and early twentieth centuries—which brought the onset of the dominance of realism in Western theatre. Prior to this time, most theatre practitioners considered a theatrical performance a "presentation" only, and actors tended to "show" particular aspects of a character's life rather than make an attempt to "be" that character. This type of acting style is more concerned with what is on the outside and what is presented to the audience. There is little concern for what the actor is experiencing or feeling at any particular moment. The focus is on projecting to the audience in an attempt to make the audience feel, think, believe, and react. The actor–audience relationship is very candid, and the actor will address the audience, either directly by speaking to it or indirectly through a general attitude. The actor employs specific use of language, gesture, looks, or other culturally acknowledged signs that indicate that the character and actor are aware of the audience's presence. Today, actors who perform using a presentational acting style or technique are often referred to as "working from the outside in."

Training for this style of acting focuses almost exclusively on movement and vocal training. Performance traditions make expert use of presentational acting. These traditions begin training performers at a very young age. It often includes explicit training of specific muscle groups to create gestures, facial expressions, and movements of the body that communicate specific ideas and feelings to the audience. Presentational actors also spend a great deal of time training their voices for singing and speaking requirements. In addition, many presentational actors study dance and martial arts to ensure that their bodies remain incredibly strong and flexible. The use of costuming and makeup to create a particular visual image of the character is also very important to presentational actors.

Representational—Representational acting emerged as the dominant style of acting in Western theatre in response to the need for a more realistic acting style. This need surfaced in response to the realistic dramas that arose at the end of the nineteenth and beginning of the twentieth centuries. The subsequent development of film and television led to the predominance of representational acting. This manner of acting is most familiar to contemporary audiences because it dominates television and film acting. Because it is so familiar to contemporary audiences, it is often the standard by which uninformed individuals judge all theatrical acting performances.

The representational actor is said to work from the inside out. He makes every attempt to *be* the character he is playing while on stage or in front of the camera. The actor's primary (if not total) focus is on his partner and on the "reality" of what is happening on the stage. The audience is ignored and the actor is absorbed in the dramatic action. In this way, the audience is led to believe that what is happening on the stage is closer to reality than to a performance, and any aspect of the performance that breaks this sense might sway the audience to judge the performance as inadequate.

Training of actors in this style may begin at any point in the performer's life as the physical and vocal demands are not as arduous as that required of the presentational actor. However, once an artist makes a commitment to acting in the representational style, intensive training of the voice, body, mind, and spirit must begin and must continue throughout his career if he hopes to continue to work. Representational actors also learn how to analyze a character and a scene, and there is more of a focus on given circumstances within the text and imaginary circumstances that the actor creates and uses to *flesh out* the person he will become while on stage. These aspects of character will be brought to the play in an effort to reveal to an audience the character's history and emotional/psychological reasons for behaving in the manner presented in the script. The actor works to makes sense of the character and reveal a tangible authentic human being who can touch an audience. Representational actors spend a great deal of time researching and analyzing a character in an attempt to *live* inside the character when they are performing.

ACTING—TRANSFORMATION

What Does an Actor Do?

An actor is an artist who embraces the thrill of simulation and make-believe. Acting is more than imitating a character. An actor interprets a character and through that interpretation, reveals the metaphor and meaning illustrated within it.

The actor is the living human being who creates the living character(s) in a theatrical performance. The actor simulates a transformation into a character who is separate from and yet a part of himself in the performance. The greatest of actors can make an audience believe that he/she IS that character for the duration of the performance. The production allows the performer and the spectators to *live in the moment* of the performance. At times, actor and audience become so engrossed in the actions, character, space, and time represented in the performance that both can suspend disbelief and experience instinctual emotional and intellectual responses to the events that unfold in the play.

Acting is a fundamental human activity—in other words, we all do it. All human beings are actors to some extent. All humans play various "roles" throughout their lives. As children, we get lost in imaginary play. Children quite naturally engage in make-believe in order to learn, grow, entertain themselves and others, and expand their emotional and intellectual education.

The art of acting on stage is a consciously created and shaped performance and requires much training and skill. Sometimes an actor's skill is so great, his performance so engrossing and moving, that the audience will maintain that the actor has a special gift or talent, one that seems almost magical. In some cultures, actors are held in the highest regard as people who possess special, or even magical, powers. These performers are seen as possessing a gift that makes them something other than human—more connected to the spirit world than tied to the material world. At times, this endowment has been honored and at times, it has brought disdain upon these artists. What cannot be denied is that the human need to act and witness performance has always existed.

Acting is an innate human need. Anthropologists have observed the need for play-acting in all cultures. It is one of the ways that humans communicate with and learn from one another. An actor keeps her audience engaged when she acts out her story. In doing this, she may imitate a living being's voice, facial expression, walk, or gesture. She may attempt to alter her voice and body so that her audience can more fully experience the event she is communicating. An actor does actions that move an audience to experience an event through its mind, emotions, and body. In communicating her event, she will leave out details—those that don't excite or interest the audience. Her story does not imitate events as they actually took place. The storyteller chooses the most exciting and compelling moments and reenacts them. Like all artists, the storyteller must delve into the chaos of the details of an event and bring order. Through this process, she will interpret and find meaning in that event. The actor, like all artists, must be trained to create her art—to bring order to chaos.

Acting exists in all cultures. Styles of acting differ from culture to culture and from century to century. However, all acting has four common elements. These are:

- **Focus and Dedication**—All accomplished actors train in technique. Like a dancer, athlete, martial artist, or anyone else who uses her body as her tool or instrument, an actor in any tradition must commit to daily mental and physical work throughout her career. Acting is a vocation that requires this type of diligent resolve.
- **Movement and Intensity**—Acting is art. It is not real life. It is bigger than real life, and yet it is also real. The actor communicates to her audience visually and orally. She creates with her total being. She connects with her audience through the intensity of her physical and vocal expression.
- **Imagination and a Playful Attitude**—Acting requires an imagination. Most humans are born with an active imagination. An actor must constantly develop her ability to imagine. As we age, this becomes more difficult for some. An adolescent or adult may attempt to control or negate her dreams and fantasies for fear of being considered childlike—or worse. One of the requirements of acting IS being childlike when performing. A child is willing to take risks, is physically and vocally expressive, has a vivid imagination, is curious about the world, is determined to get what she wants, is vulnerable to the world around her, and is very good at reading the moods of the people in her environment. For children, life and learning is play. The mind of a child is incredibly inventive. If an event in a child's life is painful or difficult, she will use her imagination to change that event into something that she can tolerate. She will transfer her feelings onto a toy, drawing, or character she creates. She will then act out the event, using her imagination to explore and understand her feelings.
- **Transformation**—Throughout history, the ability of great actors to morph into another living being has often been perceived as something magical. This capability has been considered by many to be inexplicable because some "brilliant actors" accomplish this feat with seemingly little effort. When audience members witness an exhilarating and emotionally moving performance, they will refer to an actor's "talent" or "gift." This power is an important one. It is easier for some people than others. Some people, due to their natures and life circumstances, find it easier to access this capability. However, most have the means to tap into this gift." Those who do it well are fortunate enough to understand the importance of developing the first three elements of acting noted above: Focus and Dedication; Movement and Intensity; and Imagination and a Playful Attitude.

HOW DOES SHE DO IT?

Training/Technique: Voice, Movement, Styles

Although acting training varies greatly from culture to culture, tradition to tradition, and age to age, all traditions seem to embrace the concept that the actor's body and voice are his instruments. This voice must be able to interpret a dramatic story, bring that story to life through the movements and sounds he makes, and act and react spontaneously to stimuli. For these reasons, the body and voice of an actor must be trained.

The Presentational Actor

Acting training in performance traditions enables the body to achieve amazing—and sometimes seemingly superhuman—physical and vocal heights. The training focuses on making the actor's instrument capable of sustaining a performance that is filled with vigorous activity and spectacle. The training varies from tradition to tradition. In some traditions, technique is passed on through long apprenticeships in which young performers watch masters perform and work hard to reproduce what they have seen. This type of training involves years of observation and practice in which the apprentice hones his ability to imitate the exact movements, gestures, and vocal inflections of the expert and experienced professional.

Some performance traditions have very specific systems of movement, facial expression, gesture, singing, and vocal inflection that are taught rigorously to children from a very young age. Children are identified early—sometimes when they are as young as three years old—as having a gift. They are then trained for years in the codes of performance of the tradition. Once they have achieved a certain level of mastery after years of daily training, they will make their debut performances. If they do well, they will continue to train and perform until they become skilled enough to take on the positions of master performer.

Some performance traditions are passed down through families. In some countries, there are performance families that go back many generations. In these families, training begins early, and children learn at their parents' knee. Oftentimes, a parent will be adept at a particular character type, which is complemented by body type, etc. The child of the maestro will often carry similar talents and physical traits and will, therefore, also train in this character type. In other traditions, the actor will train in all of the types of roles and acquire the versatility to perform in each one.

Some actors in the presentational tradition create and then breathe life into what may be seen by others as an inanimate object. Puppeteers must use the inanimate puppet with which they work to create and project character, action, and emotion. These artists convey their performances through the instruments of performing objects, often in addition to their own bodies and voices. If the puppeteer is seen, his physical gestures often mimic the movements of the puppet.

Training for puppeteers includes training the voice and body. Most of this training teaches movement and mime to help the performing artist understand his own physical actions and centering. This training allows the puppeteer to convey physical expression through a performing object. Puppeteers also participate in special workshops and courses of study that teach the performer the art of manipulating a variety of performing objects. Some of these skills are easy, and some are extremely difficult, requiring a great deal of strength, patience, coordination, and dexterity.

WOODEN ACTING

Heinrich von Kleist's essay of 1810 "On the Marionette Theater," staged as a conversation in a Berlin park between himself and a famous ballet master, attempts to mark the sources of the marionette's peculiar and inhuman grace of motion. It is one of the best accounts we have of this question, even if the essay is about other things, including the stakes, the wonder, of all art, all fictional creation, all forms of knowledge. The dancer insists that the marionette's grace comes from a leap into the limitations of the puppet itself. The puppeteer knows he cannot control each limb separately, and thereby imitate in perfect detail the natural movements of human bodies. Rather, the manipulator learns to yield himself to the specific weight, the pendular motion and momentum of that thing suspended from strings. That's where the puppet's soul is found, in its merely physical center of gravity, which is the line of its spirit. The soul lies in the motion it has a material object and not a living body, and it is this to which the puppeteer must give himself up, to which he must lend his own living soul, desires, and bodily motion. This is why, the dancer insists, the puppet is a creature who has little to do with the fallen state of dying, pain-filled, self-conscious human beings. It is both more material and more spiritual at once, an Edenic creature, in fact, its stories bound to an unknown innocence and simplicity of means.

By contrast, human beings inevitably become more dead, more wooden than puppets, when they try by will to overcome their own fallen-ness, to shed the necessary disguises that puppets never even think of assuming, or when they try self-consciously, in vanity, to fix a grace that can only come through impulse or accident. Hence the narrator's story of a young man who loses all of his youthful, easy charm when he tries, at first playfully and then with obsessive will, to assume the perfect lines of a classical statue he had once achieved only be accident. Thwarted in his efforts, yet fixated on the lost image, he turns into a graceless, self-hating misanthrope, living his life staring in a mirror. Human performers, it turns out—indeed,

Kenneth Gross, from "Wooden Acting," *Puppet*, pp. 63–73. Copyright © 2011 by University of Chicago Press. Reprinted with permission.

human beings in general—do not, mysteriously enough, know where to put their souls. Thus the ballet master's remark about a famous dancer whose soul, when we see him dance, "is located (and it is a fright to perceive) in his elbow."

In speaking of the puppet's special grace, Kleist leaves to one side what is eerily, necessarily unnatural, even clumsy and grotesque in its movements. A puppet's soul might well be happy inhabiting its elbow, or displaced into some other oversize appendage. That too would be part of its peculiar, unfallen grace. What Kleist does make clear is why the passage from the inanimate to the animate is no simple thing, no one-way street. The immediacy of human feeling in a puppet's gestures can be astonishing. A small thing with an unmoving face and blocklike hands can be eloquent in registering pain, boredom, wonder, and love. You can feel the work of the puppeteer allowing his own human feeling and impulse to be drawn toward and translated through the inanimate body, finding a home for them there, making the puppet itself into an actor. "I watched their faces become like the faces of the puppets they moved. They were more amazing than the puppets. They were monsters of invention and hope. Always hope. They were ready to sacrifice themselves for the puppets." This is what the Italian puppeteer Giuseppina Volpicelli said to me, elated and nostalgic at the same moment, as she recalled the men and women who worked in the shows created by her mother, Maria Signorelli

(shows that included brilliant ballets and ambitious versions of Sophocles, Dantes, Shakespeare, Goldoni, and García Lorca, and which traveled throughout Europe from the 1950s through the 1980s). And yet it is a curious relation. The power of a particular puppet-actor, even as it mirrors a human face or gesture, will lie in the fact that the object given life inevitably retains something of its specific gravity, its thing-ness, as an object. In its form, and in its motion, it will keep its resemblance to the artifact, tool, machine, or musical instrument. In such a case, any human expressiveness makes that thing-ness all the stranger, the more penetrating, among other things by its power to show us something of the mechanical side of human life itself, and how it conditions the movements of its manipulator. Each depends on the other.

A puppet can possess a flexibility, a lightness and speed, an ability to stop and start in a moment, possible to no human body, even that of the trained dancer and acrobat. There can also be a rigidity of feature and limitation of motion that in humans might indicate sickness or a wound, a loss of function, but that in the puppet constitutes its eloquence, part of what grabs at our hearts. Even the clumsy, inhuman gait of marionettes, tedious as it often is, such a poor imitation of human movement, can become an aspect of a puppet's character. It is the walk of a spirit of wood, wood's longing, wood's patience, wood's self-absorption, its impatience and impersonal being. Here the puppet's very awkwardness, its material limitation, can be as essential as its freedom. Marionettes have a wonderful power to fly aloft, to leap and turn, and float free of gravitation; they can saunter and slink and rotate in ways no human can. The marionette ballerina barely needs to touch the ground; the marionette bird, which rises so suddenly, can stay in flight with the most leisurely, dreamlike flapping of its wings. But I can imagine a peculiar strength or truth in a marionette whose flying is like that of Kafka's Bucket Rider, a character who, during a time of terrible scarcity, goes in search of coal riding on the very empty bucket that is the sign of his need, and who floats along streets and flies up the faces of buildings with a carriage more eerily clumsy than any passage along the earth might be, borne up by what Italo Calvino calls a "weightless gravity."

Then there was the marionette of Antigone I once saw who had hung herself with the very strings that had earlier given her life. That had its own kidn of truth.

They are often very ordinary, the wonders of puppet motion. ("Motion," it's worth recalling, was the sixteenth-century English word for a puppet show, sometimes for the puppet itself.) I once saw a carved puppet hand, not yet attached to any larger body, made by Frank Soehnle. It had long, slightly knotted fingers, evoking sculptures by Giacometti or Rodin. The hand was jointed in such a way that it opened and closed, extended all of its fingers or just a few, merely depending on

how one tilted or rotated the hand in space, allowing simple gravity to tug in a different way on one or another of its joints. You could, with practice, learn to control the movements of the fingers with some precision, and rapidly move between one posture of the hand and another. But the indirectness of the control, the dependence on collaborating with gravity through small shifts of position, meant that each new gesture seemed to spring from the wooden hand itself. The wooden hand had a life and unpredictable will of its own, making each gesture a heart breaking surprise. Puppeteers I have met indeed often speak of waiting for some impulse from the puppet they hold, a gesture or form of motion that they can then develop, often being shocked by what emerges. In some shows I have seen, the most fascinating life resides in a puppet left untouched, laid on the ground or just hanging, swaying only as motion is communicated to it by the vibrations of the air or the shakings of the stage, while other, more agile colleagues are put through their paces by the puppeteer. A puppet in its very stillness and abandonment may be charged with potential motion, becoming an object of reverie, patiently awaiting some further life.

Voice is another matter. Puppet actors are often mute. They can seem most persuasive in wordless dances, where unspeaking figures are moved by music, or in dumb shows and pantomimes. Or when they assume the forms of voiceless animals, real or invented. Silence and speechlessness indeed seem natural to the puppet. This is partly because puppets are more like words themselves—abstract yet object-like things with an intractable life of their own—and so do not need words. It is also because a puppet's words can never come from inside it. While a puppet's movements will seem to belong to the physical thing it is—even if moved by the hand of the puppeteer—the puppet's voice always comes from the outside. Its voice is always alien, never its own. Or rather, it only becomes the puppet's own in finding a way to embrace that strangeness, or in becoming puppet-like in its own right (as happens in certain forms of ventriloquism, whether the voice speaks from a wooden head, or from within a box, or from some other part of the ventriloquist's own body, something about which Steven Connor has written probingly). I have heard puppets speak Shakespearean texts as subtly as any human actor. But this never really worked unless the speaking voice was also, at the same moment, a voice peculiar to its status as puppet, which in turn might suggest an element of puppetlike being latent in the dramatic character it spoke for.

This need to link the alien voice to the voiceless figure is one reason that puppets' voices are so frequently stylized, distanced, half-comprehensible. There is something in them of the voices of animals and children, the inarticulate sounds of joy, hunger, and rage, a gestural sound that keeps close to the motions and breath of the body. At times these voices mingle their human inflections with the sounds of a musical instrument—a flute, trumpet, or drum. There can be a "grain of voice" in the puppet, but often it is fitted to the grain of wood. Here is the description by one nineteenth-century witness of what he heard at a French Guignol show: "A mysterious accompaniment of cries, of exclamations: *Oh, oh! Ah, ah!* grave and resounding like the sounds of a drum; *Crrr, brrr!* with which no chatterbox could quarrel; rapid *Hi, hi, piiiis,* sharp like the notes that reverberate on the highest string of the violin. The voice of a parakeet, whistles, shrill sighs of a clarinet, secret and strident crashes of splitting wood, a madness of interjections and intonations, the rage of battles." The voice of hand puppets like Punch is traditionally a shrill, inhuman, mysterious squeak that is likely to distort any words that Punch is given to say. It is the effect of a small metal and cloth reed—called a *pivetta* in Italian, a *sifflet-pratique* in French, and in English, a "swazzle," "call," or even "unknown tongue"—held in the puppeteer's throat, a device that has cousins in popular puppet theaters throughout Europe, Asia, and Africa. That reed, itself like a small puppet, produces a sound that mingles human voice with the noise of a tiny musical instrument, distorting it yet also lending it more volume than so tiny a wooden body could ordinarily produce (another conflict of scale). The sound of the puppet's voice in such shows, in which George Speaight hears "the authentic tones of the antique comedy," often takes the ear as sheer unsignifying noise, at once a foreign tongue requiring translation by an interlocutor (or even another puppet) and a lingua franca immediately, viscerally comprehended by the audience. The novelist Max Frisch, indeed, heard in the voices of such puppets "the word as it was in the beginning, the absolute, all-creating Word." It is the curious combination of alienation and directness, both its closeness to matter and its transfiguring of matter, that lends the puppet's voice its peculiar power. The necessity to have the voice come from the outside can, in fact, open up new spaces of intimacy and interiority within human words.

I think of the show *Peter and Wendy*, created by the New York-based Mines theater troupe, first performed in 1996. It is a show that is based on the novel of that title by J.M. Barrie, from 1911, a work more reflective, more haunted by lost childhood and adult regret than the play *Peter Pan*, from 1904. A single actress onstage moves about in a spare, abstract vision of an Edwardian nursery, with pop-up paper houses and enlarged white books. She speaks pieces of the story and acts as the child Wendy, and also performs the voices of all of the other characters. Meanwhile concrete objects—bits of clothing and furniture as well as puppets, moved by veiled but visible manipulators—give gestural form to parents, children, lost boys, pirates, a dog-nursemaid, a fairy, and a crocodile, this last being the dog-nursemaid wearing a crocodile mask. The actress's voice is drawn out and changed by the puppets that move about her, finding a different tone for each, even as it gives these puppets a new life in turn—their animations

always belonging to the domain of the nursery, though half-seen through an adult's eye. The whole is also drawn together through the actress's voicing of Barrie's narration, with its fierce, mordant, often wildly lyrical language. Through such displacements, the words of the novel gain a stranger authority, at once sustaining the book's fantasy and measuring its pathos, its weighing of the knowledge that all children grow up, and fly away.

The curious law is that the liveliness of a puppet onstage, in movement and voice, must incorporate something of the puppet's lack of life, or its belonging to a different kind of life. The very stories that the puppets are invited to tell, or the characters they imitate, must be fitted to their puppetness and yet transfigure it. This is one reason why so many puppet traditions draw on rawly simplified materials of myth, fairy tale, popular legend, or biblical story, as well as farce and satire. The puppet stage more easily than the human stage can show us the speaking dog, the handless child, the reborn corpse, the weeping statue, the enchanted ring. It is also readily pulled into use as a vehicle for moral fable and allegory. As in allegory, with its implicit surrealism, the puppet world may be composed of robotic or daemonic creatures, or of autonomous, animated parts of a living whole—a hand, ear, or eye, even a shadow cut free from the body which casts it. Remnants that would ordinarily, by themselves, be dead, can come alive and threaten the living, supplanting or disordering the rules of the world—the dilemma evoked in Nikolai Gogol's story "The Nose."

You can see this kind of implicit self-reference, this inhabiting and exploring of the puppet's puppet-ness, in the show of Punch. While some of Punch's wit, violence, shamelessness, and unkillableness comes to him through his ancestor, the commedia dell'arte clown Pulcinella, these things take on a different inflection in the puppet. His brazenness and violence, as well as his comic will to survive, reflect his existence as a thing with a head of wood, without human feelings of pain and shame. He makes his wooden head into the proper material of clowning. Punch's wild, quick, and rhythmic movements convey something of the freedom of the human hand inside that head, its flexible speed and power to grab, hit, caress, manipulate, and prod. Punch's shrill voice—a voice made to be heard over the myriad noises of the street—is, again, an incomprehensible thing. The words he speaks, when we can understand them, are full of the broken matter of language: bad puns, malapropisms, nonsense words, and jingling rhymes; what meaning they have is always tentative, always in negotiation, as one scholar notes. This disordered speech makes music along with the percussive sounds of Punch's stick, with which he both dances and kills other puppets; it accompanies the music of his wooden head itself knocked rhythmically against the stage, by which he keeps time as he dances. In this way, the voice of Punch is made to *belong* to this puppet. In the hands of a skillful manipulator,

the simple hand puppet Punch can manifest quite human glee, lust, and fear. But still this figure gains much of his peculiar strength by being a puppet who knows himself to be a puppet. That's in a way what he tries to teach the other puppets he beats and kills with his stick, and sometimes turns into sausages—a wife, a neighbor, a doctor, a policeman, a hangman, even the devil himself. These are puppets who want Punch to obey human rules, to stop being a puppet, or at least to be a puppet that, like human beings, is obedient to law and custom. If he refuses, they seek to make him pay the human price for such refusal, refusing all the time to know what they themselves are.

The working of puppets and the stories they enact also condition each other in the more sophisticated tradition of Japanese Bunraku theater, whose forms crystallized in the seventeenth century. Here, the half-life-size figures, with finely carved features and highly articulated heads and hands, all in traditional garb, are manipulated by three persons, all visible to the audience—two apprentices hooded and robed in black, one moving the feet and another the left arm, and the master puppeteer, in a simple kimono, who moves the head and right arm, his uncovered face always impassive, his eyes focused wholly on the puppet. To the right of the stage, on a separate platform, sits the *tayu*, in formal garb, master of the art of *joruri*, narration. He supplies the story and all of the voices, in a rhythmic, operatic manner, his whole body moving, wildly shifting in his voice as a character moans, laughs, laments, shouts, accuses, whispers, or cries out in pain. Beside the *tayu* sits the samisen player, who provides a stark, nervous, plucked, percussive music—often a "low gutteral snap"— to underline the narration, establish an atmosphere, or accompany a voice. The collaboration of artists in this theater is the result of a lifetime of training (traditionally, an apprentice puppeteer spent his first seven years learning to work just the puppet's feet). All remain distinct, their artifices exposed, and yet they aim to create a single spirit that converges from multiple directions. The puppeteers "create for each puppet not only a distinct personality but also a complex and visible nervous system," as Barbara Adachi says, even as, in Donald Keene's words, these visible manipulators "seem like witnesses to the actions rather than the cause." Though both voice and movement are often stylized, dance-like, the realism and the emotional immediacy, the sense of human feelings at once exposed and withheld, can be astonishing. The puppets breathe. It comes through in the smallest gestures, as a puppet bangs at a door, picks up or sets down a fan, stumbles on a path, draws a sword, throws down coins in anger, or heaves his chest in grief. A hidden youth draws his lover's foot across his throat, unseen by her companions, to signify to her his willingness to commit suicide. A father blindfolds himself, speechlessly embracing his son, a fugitive, so he does not have to report to the authorities that he has seen or heard him, or knows where he goes.

These human gestures are animated, given their starkest meaning, by being made visible in the puppets.

The dramatic texts in the Bunraku canon, mostly secular in subject, many composed by Chikamatsu Monzaemon (1653–1725), ask the puppets to represent human beings caught between conflicting demands, passions, and fates, caught by compulsions that always exceed their individual mastery, moved and blocked by forces over which they have lost control, that emerge at once from outside and inside them. Love is thwarted by jealousy or family honor, by poverty or prior claims of marriage or legal contract (especially those of courtesans). Inward shame and public scorn, private game or criminal extortion compel the characters, while the forms of freedom they might seek, such as exile or suicide, become themselves a trap, a madness (a mad translation of love and honor), a desperate gamble. These compelling, overmastering forces at once humanize the characters, lend them a kind of self-possessed strength, and set them at risk, shame them, make them helpless. These conflicting forces are made themselves to seem— somewhat as in Shakespeare—at once arbitrary or merely conventional and fatally binding, at once contingent and inescapable, mirrors of the movements of the puppets by their manipulators. "I am an autumn leaf careening madly of itself, too unsettled to alight; for me there is no waking and no sleeping; only tears of waiting wet my sleeve"—thus the fleeing lover in Chikamatsu's *The Uprooted Pine*, caught between the need to escape an unjust accusation and the shame of letting others bear the risk for him. To see a puppet made angry, or driven to despair, or just made to adjust a veil, by the aid of manipulators at once visible and invisible, doubles of fate and instinct, is an astonishment, and a truth. Writing in "Prose of Departure" about a Bunraku performance in which he has watched a puppet commit suicide, James Merrill notes: "Seldom do we the living ... feel more 'ourselves' than when spoken through, or motivated, by 'invisible' forces such as these. It is especially true if, like a puppet overcome by woe, we also appear to be struggling free of them." The world evoked is one that the puppets are most skilled at showing to us, a world into which humans are invited to enter, in which they can recognize themselves more truly and more strange.

The making and remaking of puppets itself can suggest something of this strange intimacy of relation. I once had the chance to watch the theater artist Julie Archer dismember and repair a puppet she had made years before, and that had come through many shows—Nana from *Peter and Wendy*. What struck me was the combination of ruthlessness and steady care in the process, and the presence of life that stayed in the divided pieces of the puppet as the repair went on. It seemed to me that she was remaking a part of herself.

The Representational Actor

Acting training in the representational tradition has altered greatly since the late nineteenth and early twentieth centuries. One aspect that has remained constant, however, is that acting in this tradition involves interpreting a dramatic text. Actor training prior to the late 1800s created actors who now seem somewhat overdramatic and exaggerated. Acting technique stressed exaggeration in vocal and physical technique. Because most actors were training for stage acting in large houses, they employed a generalization of emotion and character type. Actors would sometimes learn particular lines of business—certain types of characters—which they would then perfect and perform throughout their careers. Before the twentieth century, representational acting was learned through apprenticeship. An individual would decide to become an actor, would make an effort to become part of an acting company, and would then learn how to act by watching the professionals. The aspiring actor would travel with an acting company, doing whatever jobs were required. He would eventually acquire a non-speaking role on stage, which might then lead to one line, then to a small part, with the hope of one day becoming skilled enough to take on a major role. Acting technique would also be passed down from parent to child as it was, in some ways, the family business. To this day, there is some evidence of this as parents, children, brothers, and sisters continue to pass on their expertise and artistry.

At the start of the twentieth century, the types of plays that were being written—psychological realism—demanded a different type of acting, and acting training became more formal. Constantin Stanislavski (1863–1938) and his Moscow Art Theatre set out to develop a systematic approach to acting. This approach was greatly influenced by the newly-developed science of psychology. The company, and especially Stanislavski, worked to discern what made great actors great. He took a very scientific approach to the task, hypothesizing, experimenting, observing, and making conclusions. The company devised a system and took their performances around the world to demonstrate this new technique. Stanislavski recorded his observations and findings in a journal, which was then translated into English and many other languages.

The technique has been adopted as the foundation for most representational—and especially realistic—acting training programs. These programs began as informal studios, then moved into more formal theatre training academies, and in the 1970s, began to be seen in college and university training programs. "The System," as it has become known, focuses on given circumstances, the super objective, the objective, the magic "if," emotional/affective memory, and psychophysical action. Stanislavski notes the importance of physical and vocal training for the actor but does not include these elements in his system. He states the importance of training the body and mind in such a way that it releases the actor's natural energy. This left the field open for others to develop various types of training methodologies in these areas. They include Vsevolod Meyerhold (biomechanics), Jacques Copeau, Michel Saint Denis, Kristen Linklater, Arthur Lessac, Cecily Berry, and many others. In the 1960s and 1970s, explorations into Asian philosophy and religion by theatre artists brought many influences and techniques of training the body and mind into representational acting training. Some of these influences include meditation, yoga, centering, energy work, Reiki, and relaxation techniques.

What may be noted is that a career in acting, no matter which style an actor trains in, requires hard work and endless training. An actor's life is not easy. There are endless disappointments and physical and emotional challenges. An actor must have a strong ego and a strong sense of self. He does his work in public and leaves himself open to public criticism and ridicule, as well as the stress of public admiration. In some countries, the unemployment rate for actors stays at a constant rate of 95% or higher. There can be long periods between engagements and, in some cases, long periods of no-paying work or very low-paying work. But many chose a life as an actor for the sheer joy of creation and contact and connection—with an audience and with his fellow actors.

PART
Three
ENHANCEMENTS TO THEATRE THROUGHOUT HISTORY— BEHIND THE SCENES

CHAPTER SIX

Design: General

WHERE THEATRE IS DONE—TYPES OF SPACES

> *In its essence, a theatre is only an arrangement of seats so grouped and spaced that the*
> *actor—the leader—can reach out and touch and hold each member of his audience.*
> *Architects of later days have learned how to add conveniences and comforts to the idea.*
> *But that is all. The idea itself never changes.*

—Robert Edmund Jones [1]

Theatre can be done just about anywhere. For much of its history,
theatre has not been performed inside theatre buildings at all. Prior to the invention of
gaslight, theatre was most often performed outdoors during the day. Throughout its history,
theatre has been performed in what are called found or created spaces. These spaces may be
town squares, parks, basements, prisons, subway stations, churches, gymnasiums—anywhere
a crowd can gather.

However, when theatre is performed indoors, there are some standard types of theatres in
which plays are performed and audiences gather. Each type of performance creates a different
type of environment and a unique experience for the audience and the performers.

---

1 Jones, Robert Edmunds. *The Dramatic Imagination: Reflections and Speculations on the Art of the Theatre.*
Taylor and Francis. 2004. p. 11.

There are four common types of theatre spaces today—the arena, the thrust, the proscenium arch, and the black box.

Arena Stage

This type of theatre space is often referred to as *theatre in the round*. With an arena stage, the stage area is in the center, surrounded by audience on all sides. The arena stage, although less common today than the other three types of theatre spaces mentioned above, is probably the oldest type of theatre environment. When large crowds gather to witness a ritual or performance, a circle is often the natural form of gathering as it allows the largest number of people to witness—and be a part of—the proceedings.

Contemporary arena stages resemble sports stadiums. The stage is level with and below the audience members who are seated on all sides of the stage. Underneath the raised seats are usually four vomitories—*voms*—that allow actors quick access to the stage. These voms often consist of tunnels and passageways that run into and under the audience, similar to the stadium tunnels through which athletes enter and leave a playing field.

One of the many advantages to the arena stage is that the audience is usually in close proximity to it, creating an intimate theatrical experience. The arena stage production brings primary focus to the actor. Sets are simple, and elaborate scenery is not possible because doors, walls, and large furniture pieces would only serve to block the audience's view.

One of the main challenges of working on an arena stage is keeping the audience's sight lines clear and open. Because the audience is on all sides, there are few places the actor can stand or sit without blocking the view of some of the audience members. If the arena stage does contain vomitories, actors will try to keep their backs to the vom, which will open up their faces and the fronts of their bodies to the majority of the audience.

Actors and directors working in this type of theatre can turn the challenges of the space into an advantage as well. Because the audience is all around, many directors coach actors to keep moving. Sometimes directors may ask actors to move, shift, or turn continually—every 30 seconds or so—to ensure that no member of the audience loses sight of their faces for too long. This type of continual movement affects the tempo of a production and can help to create a very dynamic and exciting environment.

Thrust Stage

The thrust stage usually consists of a platform that juts out into the audience, allowing the audience to sit on three sides of the stage. This type of configuration reduces the distance between the actors and the audience. Even from the back rows, the distance between the audience and the performers is small.

The thrust stage will have a permanent wall upstage. As in the arena environment, thrust stages also have voms running underneath the audience. These vomitories—usually two—allow the actors to enter and exit the stage from downstage left and right. As with the arena stage, large set pieces, doorways, walls are limited or non-existent in the thrust area of the stage. However, these scenic design elements often appear in the upstage area.

Figure 6.1 Pasant Theatre thrust stage from stage.(Copyright © 2007 by Wharton Center, (CC BY-SA 3.0) at https://commons.wikimedia.org/wiki/File:Pasant_Theatre_from_stage.JPG.)

The thrust stage creates similar, although not as extensive, sight line challenges. Actors move, shift, and turn often, and when they are on the section of the stage that thrusts into the audience, they keep their backs either to the upstage area or to the voms so as to open themselves to the audience.

This type of theatre is ideal for an intimate play as the close proximity between actor and audience allows for a more intimate style of acting. Audience members in this type of environment are exposed to a production in which the actor is in more direct contact with them than they would be experiencing in a production in a proscenium stage with a recessed stage.

Proscenium Arch Stage

Currently, the most common and familiar stage space is the proscenium arch theatre. This type of theatre probably originated in Italy in mid-1500 or early 1600s. This variety of theatre is similar to a movie theatre where the audience sits in the dark looking through a picture frame at the actors on the other side. These theatres often include an ornamental facade that frames the stage like a picture frame. For this reason, proscenium arch theatres are sometimes referred to as picture frame theatres. The audience is separated from the actors by distance, which creates a more formal atmosphere. The architectural design of this sort of theatre space frames the actors so that the audience can feel as if it is observing them in their setting, creating a greater sense of aesthetic distance. At times, the physical distance between actors and audience is made even greater through the addition of an orchestra pit. In addition, the playing area of the stage is usually hidden by a curtain until it is time for the play's world to be "discovered" by the audience, which creates an even greater feeling of separation between the world of the audience and the world of the play.

The traditional proscenium arch theatre will have a great deal of space above the stage in which a fly system—an elaborate system of pulleys, riggings, and counterweights—is hidden. This system is used to change scenery by raising and lowering

Figure 6.2 Proscenium Arch Theater: Capital Theater, Broadway, NY. (Gottscho-Schleisner, Inc. / Library of Congress.)

scenic pieces. There are also areas on the sides of the proscenium arch stage that are hidden from the audience's sight. These are called wings. Actors make entrances and exits from these areas, and scenic pieces can be stored and/or moved onto the stage from this area as well.

The development of the proscenium arch theatre created an environment for the growth of innovative scenic and painting techniques. Scenic designers worked within this picture frame concept to create a more realistic illusion, such as that of a detailed realistic painting. Theatrical designers explored the use of perspective scenery and moveable scenic pieces to achieve the pictorial illusion of recognizable worlds. The configuration of the proscenium arch stage—and the ability to hide set pieces from the audience—also led to the development of new systems for changing scenery. Productions created in proscenium arch environments combine staging, scenery, lighting, sound, and production style to indicate that what is happening inside the proscenium arch is a self-contained world. For this reason, the proscenium arch theatre is ideal for realistic plays.

In some modern proscenium arch theatres, actors may get closer to the audience by coming out on the lip, or apron, of the stage. The apron is a part of the stage that extends into the audience's side of the picture frame arch. Some aprons are on hydraulic or manual elevators and can be raised or lowered. When the apron is raised, it becomes part of the stage. The extension allows the actors to be in closer proximity to the audience. When the apron is lowered, it becomes the orchestra pit, which creates a partition between the audience and the players.

Black Box Stage

Black box theatres are small and intimate. These theatres usually seat fewer than 100 people, allowing the audience to be in very close proximity to the action of the play. Black box theatres are ideal venues for intimate plays with small casts.

These venues are called black box because the walls are usually painted black to make them unnoticeable, and the space is often a square or rectangle. Black box theatres do not have permanent seating arrangements and are usually equipped with moveable risers and chairs. This means that seats may be arranged differently for every production. This type of venue gives the director and scenic designer a great deal of flexibility in determining the actor/audience relationship. These theatres do not have fly systems. If the director and designer require voms, wings, or a backstage area, these elements must be created as part of the overall scenic design.

TRANSFORMATION—DESIGN

When a play is read or a story is told, the reader or listener uses his imagination to create the sights, sounds, smells, and textures of the environment. He transforms words into visual and aural images. When theatre is performed, it is the designers' job to transform all visual and aural elements of the story into the world of the performance. The designers do this work in collaboration with the director to create a cohesive vision for the production.

Theatrical design exists in all cultures throughout history. It may be simple or complex. The design may be created by one artist or a group of artists, working in collaboration. The intricacy and complexity of the design depends on a number of factors—the resources available, the style of the production, the vision for the production, the capabilities and experience of the designers, and the space (or spaces) in which the production will take place. Design elements that have existed throughout time are scenic or set design, costume design, and sound design. Lighting design is a more recent addition and has developed exponentially since the invention of electrical lighting.

What Do Designers Do?

Theatrical designers visualize and create what the audience sees and much of what it hears in a performance. These artists create an environment in which the actors can "live" their parts and an atmosphere in which the audience can absorb the meaning and metaphor of the production. They make an impression on the audience by choosing visual and aural elements to be included in the production. In a good design, all of these details will carry meaning and will enhance the spectators' involvement and appreciation of a theatrical event.

GOALS OF THEATRICAL DESIGN

Design–Telling the Story

Guys and Dolls *is a fantastic opportunity for storytelling. … The writer created an amazing cast of characters in his stories. In the opening sequence of the piece … there is no dialogue yet, there are no characters established, but THE WORLD IS ESTABLISHED (emphasis mine) … and it is just of characters and people crossing the street, … That's where my job as storyteller is essential. Some of them are characterized by age—we have "bobby soxers." Some of them are characterized by what they do—we have cops and streetwalkers. Some are characterized by their economic station, of course, where they are from—we have Texans … And all of that needs to be almost instantaneous. And we like to work with the company and cast them well too, so that they'll become storytellers, and they'll work WITH the costumes as they go.*

—Shaw Festival, *Guys and Dolls* Costume Designer, Sue LaPage

As designer Sue LaPage indicates, a production's design assists in telling the story by giving the audience visual and aural information. In performance traditions in which there is no or little dialogue, design plays a very large role in storytelling. The audience is made aware of a character's state in life by clothing and environs. Design will apprise the audience of changes that occur in time, place, status, health, mood, etc.

Creating a Visual Metaphor for the Director's Concept or Vision (Establishing the Director's Point of View)

Production meetings allow the designers and director an opportunity to discuss the director's concept or vision for a production. Theatre is an art form that encourages the collaboration of many creative individuals. One of the designer's tasks is to find a way to create visual and aural symbols that will evoke the audience's mind and imagination to absorb the play's meaning as influenced by the director's interpretation.

Creating a sense of time, place, and social and cultural milieu—The world is filled with visual and aural clues that communicate where we are in space and time. A person's clothing, physical surroundings (including solid objects and light), and aural surroundings may convey cultural heritage, geographical location, social status, time of day, time of year, education, status, and life circumstance.

Creating mood—Details of our surroundings that we often take for granted have a profound impact on our emotions. Line, color, texture, mass, rhythm/movement, space, harmony, balance, proportion, contrast, unity, emphasis, intensity and focus, and the pitch, rhythm, and tempo of sound are all elements of design that make the audience feel a particular way. Artists attempt to capture and express moods and emotions through the use of color, light, line, texture, and the like. Some choices the artist makes to create mood are very obvious; others are more subtle and nuanced. There is no guarantee that the choices the artist makes will create the intended mood as each individual may have a different impression of the mood or emotional state that is being created. However, if elements of design are working together, the collaboration of all artists in a production can succeed in creating a distinct mood in a production.

Providing a world that embodies the character's lives—The designer takes the descriptive words of the playwright or storyteller and director and uses these clues and his imagination to make the description visually and aurally graphic to create a seemingly real world out of those words.

Defining the style of the production—The style of a production is the combination of distinctive features of expression, execution, and performance that characterize a specific school, person, group, era, or set of rules. Some examples of style would include: abstract, realism, symbolism, expressionism, and others. The designers use the tools of their trade (line, color, texture, etc.) to define the style of the production. The style of the production will be based on the director's vision, and it will affect the look and sound of the design as well as the approach to acting and movement.

Practical considerations—Theatre is done by people, live, in front of other people. There are many practical considerations that theatrical designers must keep in mind because they are collaborating with others to create a living art form. The designer must consider the practical needs of the physical action and production in all elements of design. If the design inhibits what must practically be done, the design must be discarded or adjusted. The living aspect of theatre must always remain paramount in all design.

Establishing the director's point of view—After many readings of a script, much research, and great use of her imagination, a director will approach a production of a play with a specific point of view. The director will communicate this point of view to her design team. As designers develop the visual and aural manifestation of the world of the play, they must always keep the director's point of view and collaborate to fulfill that one vision or point of view.

Visual Elements of Theatrical Design

Color—provokes a direct physical response. It can excite, agitate, or calm an audience. The impact that color has is interpreted through cultural conventions. For example, in one culture, the color white may symbolize innocence and purity; in another, white may suggest evil. The intensity of a color modifies the impact it has. The more intense a color is, the stronger impact it will have. An object's color will combine with or stand out from different backgrounds, allowing that object to blend or be separate.

Texture—the visual and especially the tactile quality of a surface. Theatrical design also makes great use of the illusion of texture—roughness or smoothness. Thick textures absorb light, and smooth textures reflect it. Texture also influences movement; thick texture limits movement, and thin is more fluid. Texture can also signify social status and emotional and physical states.

Mass—refers to the shape, size, and weight of objects on stage. Heavy objects create dense, oppressive space; light objects can create open space. Ornamentation and detail in design affect the perceived mass of objects on stage. The quantity of objects on the stage will also influence the perception of mass in the design of a production. More objects will give a sense of greater mass; fewer objects will give a sense of less mass.

Line—The world is constructed of lines. Line is the element of design used to define shape, contours, and outline. Line may also suggest mass and volume. It can function independently to suggest forms that can be recognized even when the lines are limited. A great deal of information can be conveyed with very limited line. Lines can be combined with other lines to create pattern and texture. The use of line in combination results in the development of form and value, which are other elements of design. Lines give definition and evoke feelings. The psychological impact of a line will be created by its direction, weight, and the variations thereof. For example: straight lines impart a feeling of rigidity and entrapment; curved lines impart a more organic, soft, and calm feeling; horizontal lines suggest a feeling of rest and repose; vertical lines communicate a feeling of loftiness and spirituality; diagonal lines imply a feeling of movement; horizontal and vertical lines that are synthesized suggest stability; deep, drastic curves suggest confusion, unrest, even frenzy.

Balance—the concept of visual equilibrium relating to our physical sense of stability or instability. A designer may create a sense of symmetry, which implies balance; or asymmetry, which implies imbalance or disorientation; or excessive symmetry, which implies rigidity, control, artificiality.

Proportion/Scale—refers to how the size of the design elements relate to each other and to the actors. The main issue to be grappled with is the issue of the relationship between objects and individuals on the stage and on the whole. Proportion/scale may reflect reality or may distort the world for stylistic or metaphorical purposes. The audience's eyes are drawn to large objects on stage. If most objects and people are large on the stage, the eye will be drawn to the small object or person.

Rhythm—the principle of design that brings order to a pattern and controls movement. Visual statements on stage can repeat or shift abruptly. Repetition may impart a sense of calm and order; constant shifting may imply frenzy and chaos. The designer may also use rhythm to bring emphasis to a particular element of the overall design. There are three major properties of rhythm—regular, flowing, and progressive—and each of these evoke different emotions in the viewer. When the elements of design—lines, shape, color—are similar in length, size, and interval, the rhythm is considered to be regular. Each element is viewed individually in an ordered manner. A flowing or linear rhythm is created when the viewer's eye is carried smoothly from one element to the next through the use of line, shape, and color. This rhythm allows the designer to lead the audience through the entire design smoothly so that the entire design is appreciated and is absorbed without any sense of division between the parts that make up the whole. Progressive rhythm incorporates a sequence of elements that are repeated in a series of steps—becoming larger and larger; wider and wider; smaller and smaller; etc. The designer is able to lead the audience through a journey without an obvious sense of order, and the movement becomes barely discernible.

Unity—in design, it means harmony, when all of the elements agree with each other. Unity is what provides cohesiveness to the design, pulling all of the elements together. Unharmonious or conflicting elements will always carry meaning—they must be included deliberately. In a production, the characters see their world as a whole; the design must reflect this world as a whole. Elements that are jarring or at odds with that world will assuredly pull the audience's focus and become significant.

Focus—in theatrical design, it refers to the designer's ability to direct the audience's vision. The director decides where she wants the audience to look at any given moment. The designer helps the director to do this by using line, color, texture, and scale to influence where the audience should focus. Theatrical design must also orient the audience within the space—it enables the audience to know where they are in relation to the performance/action. The design elements of a production also control the audience's line of sight and determine what can be seen, and what cannot be seen, by the audience.

The Designers' Process and Tools

Close analysis of the text—For the written tradition, designers begin their process with a close analysis of the text. The first step each designer takes is to read the text a number of times and focus on both the story as a whole and those references to their particular area of design (e.g., lighting, sound, set, costuming). References to the aspects of design can be found in both dialogue and stage directions. As the designer reads, he will absorb not only the literal meaning of the words but will also focus on the visual and aural images the work brings to mind. He will focus on the feelings that the text evokes, the visual and aural images that seem most important, and how the design can support and enhance the dramatic action.

Production meetings—Once a collaborative team has been selected, it will meet to discuss the production and exchange ideas about the look and sound of the world that will be created to support the director's vision. Most productions utilize a series of production meetings at which designers confer and collaborate about the creation and evolution of what will become a concrete design. Designers will bring examples of visual and aural research to early meetings. They will also discuss ways in which they might make these visual/aural ideas and expressions a practical, concrete, and living reality. Informal exchanges—between director and designers or among designers—may also take place outside of these meetings throughout the production process. However, it is important that a series of meetings be planned at which all designers are present because all elements of design need to complement each other and work together. Competent and consistent communication is vital to the coordination of practical and creative needs when developing a show's design.

The first production meeting usually involves a discussion of the text, the director's concept, and how particular problems that the play presents will be solved. The designers will ask a lot of questions about the concept and leave the meeting with a clear understanding of the director's vision for the production.

Visual/aural research—After the first production meeting, the designers will continue to use the text as the primary resource but will now be informed by the director's concept as well. With continued readings, each designer will find that the words will create images in his mind. He will begin to research photos, songs, drawings, sculptures, etc., that reflect the time, place, or directorial concept. There are usually three levels of research: objective—historical research that reflects the historic moment of the play, discovering elements of society and culture and period style; subjective—reflects the history, sociology, culture, and style of the director's concept; inspirational—images that may not be specifically related to the play or the director's concept but spur the designer's imagination and creative impulses. He will begin to illustrate the world of the play in his mind, using references accessible to him from his life experience.

Creating sketches and renderings—Eventually, designers will settle on a specific look or sound that they believe supports the production concept. Designers who are working with visual aspects of design will then create basic sketches to present at subsequent design meetings. These sketches will be shown and discussed, changes and alterations may be made, or collaborative discussions may bring designers to move in a whole new direction. Once all designers have come to a consensus with the director on the look of the show, they will create more complete, fleshed-out renderings, (see Figures 8.17, 8.18, 10.11, 10.13, 10.15, 10.24–26, 10.34–35) and often models of the design. (See Figure 8.21.) These renderings are presented at subsequent production meetings and are approved by the director and the entire design team.

From idea/image to reality—Once the designs have been rendered, drafted, and approved, the designers pass the designs on to the individuals who will make the images come to life. How this occurs depends on many factors, some of which include budget, staffing levels, timeline, and space for building and/or storage. Most of the larger repertory theatres have staff and shops in which they build design elements. If they have storage for sets, props, costumes, etc., they may also pull some items from their stock and modify them to match the design concept. Anything that cannot be pulled from stock will be built, bought, or rented. Many theatres have stock that they will rent or loan to other companies. Borrowing often works, and it has the advantage of keeping budgets down. One disadvantage is that pieces that are borrowed or rented cannot be altered to match the design concept. The set is constructed in the shop, usually in many pieces, that need to be assembled later on the stage itself. About a week before the show opens, all technical elements of the production are loaded into the theatre and assembled. At this time, the designers will be on hand to work closely with the technical director. Design elements will be completed over the following days when the stage is not being used for rehearsals. During this week, the designers will also participate in technical rehearsals with the crew, stage manager, TD (technical director), and director (dry tech) and later with all of those members of the production team plus the cast (wet tech). These technical rehearsals are often stop-and-go and can be very time consuming—sometimes lasting 12 hours or more. After each technical rehearsal, all members of the crew (and sometimes the cast) work on technical elements of the production that need adjustments before the next technical rehearsal. The night before the show opens is a full dress rehearsal, and every attempt is made to run the show with all technical elements in place, without stopping.

CHAPTER SEVEN

Specific Elements of Scenic Design

GOALS SPECIFIC TO SCENIC DESIGN

Determining the relationship between the audience and the dramatic action; orienting the audience within the space—the scenic designer, along with the director, will design where the action will take place in the performance space. Depending upon the architectural limitations of the performance space being used, this decision may be easy or more complicated. With a proscenium or thrust theatre with fixed seats, there are fewer options as the seats cannot be moved. A black box theatre, outdoor theatre, or unconventional space will give the production team many more options for audience/action relationships. Questions any team will ask itself include:

- Where do we want the audience to be looking at any given time?
- Do we want the audience and performance space to create a sense of separation or unity?
- Do we want the audience to feel as if it is in the production?
- Do we want audience members to be able to see and interact with each other and the performers?
- Do we want the audience to be able to interact with the performance environment (set pieces, costuming, etc.)?

Controlling the audience's line of sight—The audience's line of sight is what the audience is able to see without making much effort. If a production is well crafted, things will flow from one moment to the next, and the audience will most often observe those areas that the production team WANTS it to observe. However, the audience is rarely told where to look at any specific time. The audience's line of sight is controlled by the production team in various ways. Flats, scrims, draperies, and placement of audience members are used by set designers to conceal areas in the space. Lighting designers also assist in controlling the audience's line of sight by intensifying light in areas that are to be viewed and dimming light or eliminating illumination in areas that are meant to be obscured from the audience's view.

PROCESS SPECIFIC TO SCENIC DESIGN

Once the scenic design has been agreed upon by all members of the production team, the set designer translates his ideas into a concrete visual image. As was mentioned previously, the designer will begin with sketches for discussion that can be altered before the final design decisions are made. If there are set changes, the designer will create a storyboard. A storyboard is a series of sketches that show how the set changes to tell the story and denote changes in time and location. Use of the storyboard is an efficient and inexpensive way to easily solve practical problems. The designer will then create a detailed rendering of the set and/or a three-dimensional scale model. A scaled human figure is always placed in the model to help everyone envision the actor in the space (see Figure 8.21). This three-dimensional model will also show how the design will look and work in the space. The model has moveable furniture and scenery that allow directors and designers to toy with the placement of set pieces for greatest effect. These design devices can uncover where ideas that looked good on paper may not work in reality. This allows for changes to be made before the set is built. These detailed design elements are shown and agreed upon at the final design meetings and then are usually revealed to the cast at the first read-through. Directors often continue to use the scale model in rehearsal to give themselves and the actors a better perception of the environment. The scale model can also help the director adjust movement patterns. Once rehearsals have gotten underway, the set designer will want to visit some rehearsals to get a sense of how the stage is being used in action.

The scenic designer will then draft the ground plan (see Figure 8.19A) and elevations (see Figure 8.19B) of each element of the set, which will, in turn, be given to the shop where the set will be built. The ground plan gives a view of the dimensions of the stage and the placement of the set pieces. The scenic designer must, therefore, have drafting skills and experience transferring visual concepts to builders via accurately scaled drawings. Drawings must be extremely precise and contain as much information as possible about the size, shape, function, and look for every piece of the set. A copy of the ground plan is also distributed to the stage manager so that she can tape out a facsimile of the ground plan of the set in the rehearsal space. The actual set is not available to the actors until a few days before the production opens. It is important that they can get a feel for the size, shape, and dimensions of the set while they are rehearsing to make the transition from rehearsal room to stage as seamless as possible.

The scenic designer also supplies the shop with in-scale color renderings of each scenic element, which show the application of color and texture to all stage surfaces. The set designer will also provide sample colors to the paint shop.

The scenic designer continues to collaborate with the director, the rest of the design team, and the technical director—whoever is in charge of building the set—throughout the build process. She must remain flexible and open to minor changes that may be needed to accommodate artistic discoveries that occur during the rehearsal process.

Either before rehearsals begin or early on in the rehearsal process, the scenic designer works with either the stage manager or the assistant stage manager and director to create a list of objects that are necessary for any stage action; these are known as props. This list of props may fluctuate throughout the rehearsal period. The scenic designer selects or at least approves of—in conjunction with the director—any items that are on the stage that must conform to the design concept.

Once the set is built and loaded into the theatre, the set designer will want to see what the set looks like and how it functions. She may make some minor adjustments that improve visual quality, functionality, or safety. She may also oversee or do some scenic painting, which will be primarily detail work to create specific textures and finishes. Finally, the set designer will "dress the set." This entails final touches, upholstery, small objects for tables and shelves, pillows, curtains, wall hangings, etc.

TOOLS SPECIFIC TO SET DESIGN

Set elements do not need to meet the same building codes as units that are built for use in the real world. Sets are not built to last or to be lived in the way a house or office building are. There are, however, standards of safety that must be met for set design. Sets, quite often, must be readily assembled and readily disassembled (struck). They need to be made of material that looks heavy and solid but is actually quite lightweight. This is because set pieces need to be moved and changed quite often and quite rapidly. These are some of the tools that set designers use to create sets that give the illusion of permanence and stability.

Flats (see Figure 7.1) are single-unit pieces made of a frame covered in either canvas or a very lightweight wood called luan. They can be painted and repainted any color or texture. They are light enough to be carried by one person but are strong enough to last for the run of a show.

Platforms (see Figure 7.2) are frames covered in wood and then legged to create various levels, heights, and dimensions on the stage. They are light enough to be carried by two people but sturdy enough to carry the weight of a number of adults.

Drapes (see Figures 8.11, 12.13–14, and 12.17) are used in many different ways in the theatre. Most stages are dressed with drapes that serve the purpose of isolating areas, masking backstage areas or stage lighting, or hiding what is happening on the stage from the audience before, after, and during set changes of a performance. Drapes may also be used as decoration on the stage.

Drops are large pieces of canvas that are painted to give the impression of particular locales. Drops are often hung in the back of the stage, but they may be dropped or flown in anywhere on stage to create the sense of a change in locale.

A **scrim** (see Figures 8.24–8.26) is a drape that is made of a particular type of cloth that lets light pass through it. If light shines on this cloth from the front, it looks opaque like any drape. If light shines on it from the back, it becomes transparent and reveals scenic elements and/or actors behind it. A painted scrim can unveil different scenic locations or settings with a change in lighting.

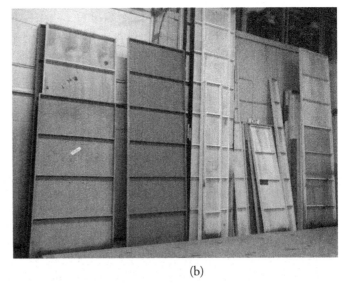

(a)   (b)

Figure 7.1 (a) Traditional luan theatrical flat—from rear. (b) Theatrical luan flats of various sizes and shapes—from rear. (Copyright © by Anthony Phelps. Reprinted with permission.)

(a)   (b)

Figure 7.2 (a) Open frame six inch platform—topside
(b) Open frame six inch platform—underside.
(Copyright © by Richard Gray/BeNT Productions. Reprinted with permission.)

Furniture and set dressing make a space specific. They can also be used to relate the scale of the actor to the set. Furniture may be used symbolically, practically, or realistically. A symbolic set would have minimal furniture or, perhaps, only a single set piece that would carry great meaning. (See Figures 8.2–8.4) A realistic set would have a plethora of set pieces, some without any meaning at all, but all present to create a more authentic-looking location. (See Figures 12.13–12.15)

Technology—Theatre has always embraced new technology. High-tech equipment is an integral part of many current theatrical designs from using computer programs to conceptualize, visualize, and communicate the design to the construction of the set pieces, and control and management of their movement on the stage. Designers also use technical tools for scenic effects—turntables, holograms, screen projectors (see Figures 8.5, 8.6, and 8.25), videography, interactive computer imagery, etc. Designers must develop the ability to incorporate technical tools into design and stay current in the advances in technology that have an impact on their craft.

Other Materials (natural elements: water, dirt, sand, fire; metal work, steel, wire, etc.)—Great set designers look beyond wood and fabric when considering what the best material will be for a design. Sets may be composed of anything in the world. Some elements are very exciting to explore because in addition to visual qualities, they may add a new dimension to the sound, smell, and reflection, or they may allow us to reconnect with the simpler elements of existence. A set designer will keep her creative energies open to all that is around her and use the material that will best evoke the essence of the director's concept.

CHAPTER EIGHT

The Work of Scenic Designer Janie Howland

Janie E. Howland has designed scenery for over 200 productions, received three IRNE (The Independent Reviewers of New England) awards and three Elliot Norton awards (named for the eminent Boston theatre critic) for best scenic design. She received her MFA from Brandeis University in Scene Design and Painting and is a member of USA Local 829. Recently, her work was included in an art exhibition, *Consenses,* conceived by Sally Taylor, at Wellesley College, Davis Square, and Martha's Vineyard with hopes of a future tour. She has taught design, drafting, and computer rendering at Wellesley College, Emerson College, and Northeastern University. Theatre credits include: Weston Playhouse, New Jersey Shakespeare Festival, Lyric Stage Company of Boston, New Rep, Speakeasy Stage Company, Actor's Shakespeare Project, Central Square Theatre, Nora Theatre Company, Boston Conservatory of Music, Opera on the James, Barter Theatre, Huntington Theatre Studio 210, North Shore Music Theatre, Stoneham Theatre, Boston Children's Theatre, Wheelock Family Theatre, Merrimack Repertory Theatre, Company One, and A.R.T. Institute. In 1996, she was a co-founder of CYCO Scenic, Design and Production Company, a design/build company that created scenery for the Macy's Christmas windows, Domain Furniture stores, Motorola trade shows, and other theatres and trade shows. Janie is a Boston native.

Figure 8.1 Janie Howland, scenic designer. (Copyright © by Skylar Shankman Photography. Reprinted with permission.)

Eurydice

This production is a poetic version of the Greek tragedy *Eurydice,* with a modern feel. The play is set in a watery and ephemeral world. The scenic effects include: a trough of water with a working pump; rain showers upstage; and an elevator that rains inside when the doors open. The set is abstract and evocative, using color and texture to create fluidity and a poetic watery quality.

This production created many challenges for the scenic designer and the TD as they were dealing with complicated practical elements of scenic design: water, electricity, and live actors who must move on the stage in this watery world. It was imperative that scenic designer Janie Howland and the TD work very closely together on these challenges. Howland said that once the design was created, she and the TD had an ongoing conversation throughout the build period. Having water on the set affects the materials used and the paint treatment. Designing the special effects was a joint effort between the designer and the TD. Howland said it was exciting to collaborate with the TD as they figured out the mechanics of the design. Ultimately, most of the engineering, including the mechanics of the pump, fell to the expertise of the TD. The TD was also responsible for pricing out all of the elements required to make the engineering work continuously and consistently throughout the run of the show. Howland determined the location of the water, the catch system, and the aesthetics of the design.

On a purely aesthetic level, the set design also reflects the manner in which the script is written. The text is a poem, and the scenic design reflects the lyrical sound and images created by the words. The globes are abstract and imply a universal image of raindrops, tears, planets, or, perhaps, some other concept in the viewer's conscious or subconscious mind. The color and texture of the set comes from a painting that struck the scenic designer as she conducted research to find a look that would support the imagistic world of the play.

The rods that are seen in Figure 8.2 serve multiple purposes. They suggest a familiar image of the solar system. These rods also support the action of the play. In the play, Eurydice's father must create a house out of one piece of string. These rods serve as attachment points for the string, which enable the father to complete the action.

Figure 8.2 Eurydice by Sarah Ruehl, New Repertory Theatre, 2008. Director: Rick Lombardo, Scenic: Janie Howland, Lighting: Deb Sullivan, Costumes: Frances Nelson McSherry. (Copyright © 2008 by Janie Howland. Reprinted with permission.)

Henry VIII

Using simple forms and a unit set, scenic designer Janie Howland created a space where *Henry VIII*—an episodic play that includes numerous locations—could take place. In Figure 8.4, the platforms and symbols on stage are arranged in hierarchical order; the church is the most powerful (the cross appears at the highest elevation on stage), followed by the King (the padded stools that represent the thrones of the King and Queen are slightly elevated), and finally, the knights (the round table appears at ground level). The symbol on the floor is a realistic reproduction of the top of King Henry's round table where he gathered with his knights. The design was at once very simple and powerful and effective.

Henry VIII tells the story of the King's struggle with the Catholic Church. The scenic design is intentionally altar-like. Each of the levels are symbolic, but they are also large enough to be playing areas, which enables the director to have many actors clearly seen while on stage at the same time.

> **Mass**—When looking at Figures 8.3 and 8.4, it is easy to see that the most powerful force is revealed through the scenic design, assisting in telling the story and reinforcing the meaning and metaphor of the play. The mighty Catholic Church, with which Henry must battle, is represented by a large cross, a structure that has more mass than any other piece on the stage. This strong scenic design statement draws the eye to this area, creating a visual sense of dominance. The King and Queen's chairs have less mass. The knight's round table has no mass at all: it is a one-dimensional painting.

> **Balance**—Figures 8.3 and 8.4 demonstrate that, despite the fact that the cross has the most mass, the balance of the set design communicates that there will be a struggle for dominance. The Church is dominant; it is represented by the massive cross that occupies the highest point on stage. But the area governed by the royals is a larger playing area, creating a sense of balance. The

Figure 8.3 Henry VIII by William Shakespeare, Actors' Shakespeare Project, 2014. Director: Tina Packer, Scenic: Janie Howland, Lighting: Dan Jensen, Costumes: Tyler Kinney; Photo by Janie Howland. (Copyright © 2014 by Janie Howland. Reprinted with permission.)

area controlled by the knights is the largest area, again creating a sense of balance on stage.

Perspective—because the cross is upstage (figures 8.3, 8.4—farther away from the audience—it is not completely dominant. If the cross were downstage, it would wholly overpower the royals and the knights. The farther upstage an element is placed, the smaller it becomes. The cross does dominate because of its mass and placement, but it is not absolute in its power due to perspective (and balance).

CREATING MULTIPLE LOCATIONS WITH SIMPLE, INEXPENSIVE DESIGN ELEMENTS.

In Figures 8.3 and 8.4, the floor is painted in a marble pattern using a dark gray palette. These images demonstrate how excellent scenic painting can create the illusion of a much more expensive—and monetarily impractical material—like marble.

The stage right area is more open, and the stair unit is cut out. This design component was created for aesthetic as well as practical reasons; larger set pieces were brought onto the stage to create a specific location outside of the castle, and the design accommodates a fluid set change that could be done quickly and would not interrupt the flow of the production.

The two stools that are used as thrones in Figure 8.4 are seen as a bed in Figure 8.3, creating yet another locale: a bedroom. This was achieved by pushing the stools together and covering them with a large piece of cloth, a very simple, yet effective, contrivance.

Figure 8.4 Henry VIII by William Shakespeare, Actors' Shakespeare Project, 2014. Director: Tina Packer, Scenic: Janie Howland, Lighting: Dan Jensen, Costumes: Tyler Kinney, Actor: Robert Walsh, Photo by Janie Howland. (Copyright © 2014 by Janie Howland. Reprinted with permission.)

Big River

The scenic design of *Big River* at the Lyric Stage of Boston—an intimate thrust theatre without a fly space—tested Janie Howland's ability to create an abstraction of the world of Tom Sawyer, Huck Finn, and Jim. The scenery had to be stationery due to the limitations of the space. However, the characters are seen in many different locales, including moving on a boat down the Mississippi River.

Figure 8.5 is an example of using projections on a non-traditional surface. The wall is made of whitewashed, rough-cut boards. Still images and video are projected from the front throughout the show to create a sense that the audience is moving with the characters from place

Figure 8.5 Big River by Lyric Stage Company, 2011. Director: Spiro Veloudos, Scenic: Janie Howland, Lighting: Scott Clyve, Costumes and Projection Design: Seaghan McKay, Photo by Janie Howland.(Copyright © 2011 by Janie Howland. Reprinted with permission.)

to place. This photo (Figure 8.5) of the pre-show image gives the audience a sense of the journey on which they are about to embark. The trees on the side of the platform are inspired by American folk art. They create a sense of simplicity and a connection to the natural elements—important aspects of this timeless American coming-of-age story by Mark Twain. This design component also served a practical purpose: a pole from the tree is pulled out and used to ferry the raft down river.

The main platform became the raft through the use of hinged platform pieces, light, and projections. When you look closely at Figure 8.6 and compare it to Figure 8.5, you can see that a section of the platform just behind Jim is now open. This piece was hinged and flipped onto the larger platform, which became the dock upstage. Tom and Jim would flip up this hinged platform to "cast off" the raft. At times, characters were on the "shore," which was divided from Tom and Jim—on the raft—by this small open space. The actors' own belief in the conceit, along with the scenic design,

Figure 8.6 Big River by Lyric Stage Company, 2011. Director: Spiro Veloudos, Scenic: Janie Howland, Lighting: Scott Clyve, Costumes and Projection Design: Seaghan McKay, Actors (bottom to top): Jordan Ahnquist and De'Lon Grant, Photo by Janie Howland. (Copyright © 2011 by Janie Howland. Reprinted with permission.)

helped the audience to suspend disbelief so that the story of a journey down a

Figure 8.7 Big River by Lyric Stage Company, 2011. Director: Spiro Veloudos, Scenic: Janie Howland, Lighting: Scott Clyve, Costumes and Projection Design: Seaghan McKay, Actors (right to left): Jordan Ahnquist and Paul Parwell, Photo by Janie Howland. (Copyright © 2011 by Janie Howland. Reprinted with permission.)

Figure 8.8 Big River by Lyric Stage Company, 2011. Director: Spiro Veloudos, Scenic: Janie Howland, Lighting: Scott Clyve, Costumes and Projection Design: Seaghan McKay, Actors (clockwise from top): De'Lon Grant, Leigh Barrett, Jordan Ahnquist, and Maureen Keiler, Photo by Janie Howland. (Copyright © 2011 by Janie Howland. Reprinted with permission.)

massive river could be told in a small theater space. Lights were placed under the center platform and were cued to create a sense of moving water under the raft. Video of a moving river was projected onto the upstage wall when traveling on the river, creating a sense of movement. When the river video looked as if the raft was turning, the actors' movements would reflect this. The lights, projection, and acting created a sense of movement that transported the action to the Mississippi River and made the audience feel as if it was floating on the Mississippi along with the characters in the play.

The upstage white clapboard wall was also hinged and became huge barn doors that opened and revealed a wood wagon on which set pieces were brought downstage to set up for new locales. In Figure 8.7, a bench has been brought on, and that, along with a projection, creates the interior of Tom's bedroom. One barn door remains open, revealing a cool, damp, misty moonlit night on the exterior of Tom's room.

In Figure 8.8, a dining set has been brought in through the large barn doors, which have been left fully open to reveal a hot, red, southern sunset.

Breaking the Code

Central Square Theatre is a black box with flexible seating. In this case (Figure 8.9), scenic designer Howland created an octagon of seating. The play, *Breaking the Code* is about connections. The set is environmental in that strings are used to make connections all around and across the space. The platforming reflects the Fibonacci series[1] and the golden mean[2], two mathematical concepts that are integral to the story of the play. The red seats in the audience also represent a mathematical equation. Equations are painted on the walls of the theatre.

Actors used playing spaces throughout the theatre, and different actors had different "stations," which served as their home bases. This design device assisted the flow of the performance, helped to tell the story, and created specific areas of focus throughout.

Figure 8.9 *Breaking the Code* by Hugh Whitemore, Central Square Theatre. Director: Adam Zahler, Scenic: Janie Howland, Lighting: Frank Meissner, Photo by Janie Howland. (Copyright © by Janie Howland. Reprinted with permission.)

---

1   a simple numerical sequence that is the foundation for the mathematical relationship behind pi
2   In mathematics, two quantities are in the golden mean if their ratio is the same as the ratio of their sum to the larger of the two quantities

Figure 8.10 Romeo and Juliet by William Shakespeare, Actors Shakespeare Project, 2013. Directors: Bobbie Steinbeck and Allyn Burrows, Scenic: Janie Howland, Lighting: Jen Rock, Photo by Janie Howland. (Copyright © 2013 by Janie Howland. Reprinted with permission.)

Figure 8.11 Romeo and Juliet by William Shakespeare, Actors Shakespeare Project, 2013. Directors: Bobbie Steinbeck and Allyn Burrows, Scenic: Janie Howland, Lighting: Jen Rock, Photo by Janie Howland. (Copyright © 2013 by Janie Howland. Reprinted with permission.)

Romeo and Juliet

Actors Shakespeare Project produced Shakespeare's *Romeo and Juliet* in the Strand Theatre, a 1,400-seat proscenium stage in Boston. The director wanted to create a more intimate space, so scenic designer Janie Howland reconfigured the space to create an arena stage. She did this without changing the existing architecture of this historic movie and vaudeville palace. All of the permanent seating remained in the theatre, but she created an arena stage by placing seating risers on the proscenium stage and using these on stage seats and the permanent orchestra seats in the house for the audience. She designed a surround of banners (drops) around all the seating, on stage, and in the house orchestra section (Figure 8.10). These drops are inspired by tarot cards and tagging. The banners reflected the journey of the play through tarot card images of family, love, fighting, death, grief, sun, moon, etc. They were done in the style of tagging. Tagging is signing your name or any other representation of yourself on public places like walls, bus stops, alleyways, etc., in one or two colors with a spray paint or thick marker. These graphic images are often used by gangs to claim ownership of a location or person.

This design reflected the message and metaphor in the production, and although the Strand is a huge proscenium theatre with a fly space, the new configuration demonstrated the designer's ability to create a new relationship between the audience and the playing area to enhance the theatre-going experience.

This photo of the tomb (Figure 8.11) where the lovers meet their demise is made of a simple column of white chiffon that descends from the sky and encompasses the final resting place of the star-crossed lovers. This image is present as the audience enters during the pre-show and is then repeated at the end of the show. It is a hauntingly beautiful image that captures the mournful essence of the story as well as the innocence of the young lovers who are destroyed by the hatred that surrounds them.

Photograph 51

A play about ambition, isolation, and the race for greatness, *Photograph 51* is set in London in 1953. The term Photograph 51 is the nickname given to an X-ray diffraction image of DNA taken by a PhD student under the supervision of Rosalind Franklin, which was critical evidence in identifying the structure of DNA. Franklin provided the key to the double helix, considered one of the major scientific breakthroughs of the twentieth century. Then what kept Franklin out of the history books? James Watson was shown the photo by Franklin's student without her approval or knowledge. Along with Francis Crick, Watson used characteristics and features of Photograph 51 to develop the chemical model of the DNA molecule. In 1962, the Nobel Prize in Physiology or Medicine was awarded to the student, along with Crick and Watson, with no recognition for Franklin.

Research—The scenic design in Figure 8.13 is influenced by the Photograph 51 itself as well as this image (Figure 8.12) of the scientists Watson and Crick with their model of DNA.

How does the research inform the final design? Referencing the shapes of atoms and the double helix, the scenic designer used pentagons and hexagons to shape the set (see Figure 8.13).

Figure 8.12 Research photo for scenic design: Photograph 51. (Copyright © 1953 by A. Barrington Brown.)

Figure 8.13 Photograph 51 by Anna Zieglar, Central Square Theater 2012. Director: Daniel Gidron, Scenic: Janie Howland, Lighting: John Malinowski, Costumes: Gail Astrid Buckley, Photo by Janie Howland. (Copyright © 2012 by Janie Howland. Reprinted with permission.)

The Imaginary Invalid

Figure 8.14 Imaginary Invalid by Moliere, Concord Academy. Director: Megan Gleeson, Scenic: Janie Howland, Photo by Janie Howland. (Copyright © by Janie Howland. Reprinted with permission.)

PERSPECTIVE, CREATING A SPACE, FOCUS, AND TELLING THE STORY

The director for this production of *The Imaginary Invalid* asked that the scenic design reflect the themes in the play and create a space that was "somewhere between a jewelry box and a puppet theatre." The set is skewed and warped (see Figure 8.14) like the play. The perspective is forced and angled. The doors get smaller as they go upstage and the walls are angled to push the illusion of depth. The checkerboard floor serves two purposes: it follows the false perspective, and it creates the sense of a game, such as a chess board, which accentuates one of the themes of the play.

The play is an absurd, over-the-top piece about enemas and medical procedures. Designer Howland's research included viewing drawings of medical procedures and instruments from seventeenth century France—the period to which Moliere's play belongs. She then pieced these images together to create a painted banner and side flats filled with resemblances of her research. These design components both bring the focus to the action and reinforce the themes of the play. Howland also outlined areas of the set with rubber tubing, reflecting a piece of the medical device used for enemas.

The Miracle Worker

The set for *The Miracle Worker* (see figure 8.15) was designed from the point of view of Helen Keller herself. The production team decided to keep the upstage dark and not use a cyclorama because Helen's blindness and deafness leave her, literally, in darkness. The platforms are slightly disconnected, seemingly difficult to navigate.

Janie's research included examining photos of the actual Keller home. The set references realism in that it reflects the actual Keller house, but the home, like the family, is somewhat being broken apart. The house is also unkempt and becoming overgrown with vines and shrubs. This design element reflects the way in which the family was overwhelmed by its situation. There was a working pump on stage, as required by the script.

> **Defining the space:** The space is quite open; there are no solid walls. The differentiation between the exterior and interior spaces is defined by the shutters and beams. The exterior of Annie Sullivan's cottage was visible throughout. When scenes took place in the interior of her cottage, this set piece was rolled on to the stage on a wagon and rotated to reveal an interior side.

Figure 8.15 Miracle Worker by William Gibson, Wheelock Family Theatre 2012. Director: Susan Kosoff, Scenic: Janie Howland, Lighting: Scott Clyve, Costumes: Lisa Simpson, Photo by Janie Howland. (Copyright © 2012 by Janie Howland. Reprinted with permission.)

Nicholas Nickelby

This production of *Nicholas Nickelby* (see Figure 8.16) was all about storytelling. The painted murals on the second level were taken from engravings of Victorian London. The furniture and cast members were under the second level for much of the play, watching and waiting for their scenes.

Designer Howland used a platform to create a second level across the space as well as a boxing ring on the stage floor. Different locations were defined by individual pieces of furniture. The garden scene was created by opening a small trap door in the lower platform to reveal dirt in which the actor could dig. Parts of the proscenium walls were dressed with fake brick (sections made out of lightweight material and painted to look like real brick), and a false theatrical back wall was created with this same material.

Figure 8.16 The Life and Adventures of Nicholas Nickleby by Charles Dickens, Lyric Stage Company, 2010. Director: Spiro Veloudos, Scenic: Janie Howland, Lighting: Scott Clyve, Costumes: Rafael Jaen. (Copyright © 2010 by Janie Howland. Reprinted with permission.)

Other Desert Cities

Elements of the scenic designer's process—from idea to reality.

Figure 8.17 depicts the final pencil sketch—pencil on tracing paper—of the scenic design for Speakeasy Stage's production of *Other Desert Cities.*

Figure 8.17 Other Desert Cities by Jon Robin Baitz, Speakeasy Stage Company. Director: Scott Edmiston, Scenic: Janie Howland, Lighting: Karen Perlow, Costumes: Charles Schoonmaker. (Copyright © 2012 by Janie Howland. Reprinted with permission.)

Figure 8.18 shows the Final Sketch up rendering of the scenic design for the same production.

Figure 8.18 Other Desert Cities by Jon Robin Baitz, Speakeasy Stage Company. Director: Scott Edmiston, Scenic: Janie Howland, Lighting: Karen Perlow, Costumes: Charles Schoonmaker. (Copyright © 2012 by Janie Howland. Reprinted with permission.)

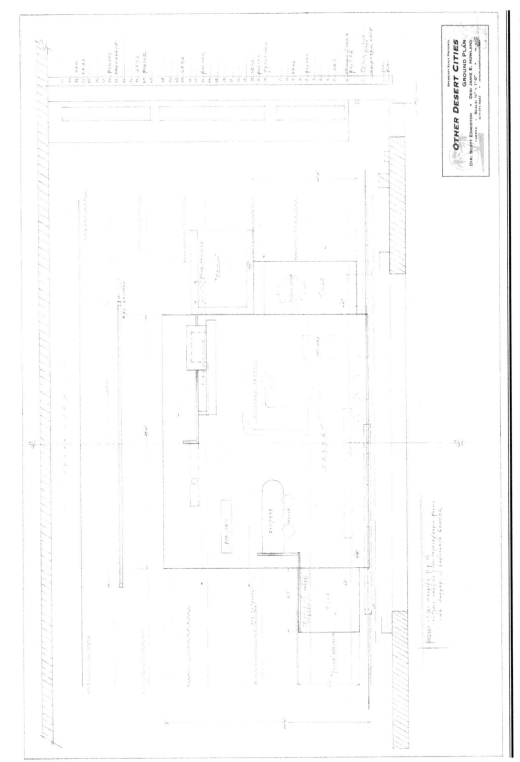

Figure 8.19a Other Desert Cities by Jon Robin Baitz, Speakeasy Stage Company. Director: Scott Edmiston, Scenic: Janie Howland, Lighting: Karen Perlow, Costumes: Charles Schoonmaker. (Copyright © 2012 by Janie Howland. Reprinted with permission.

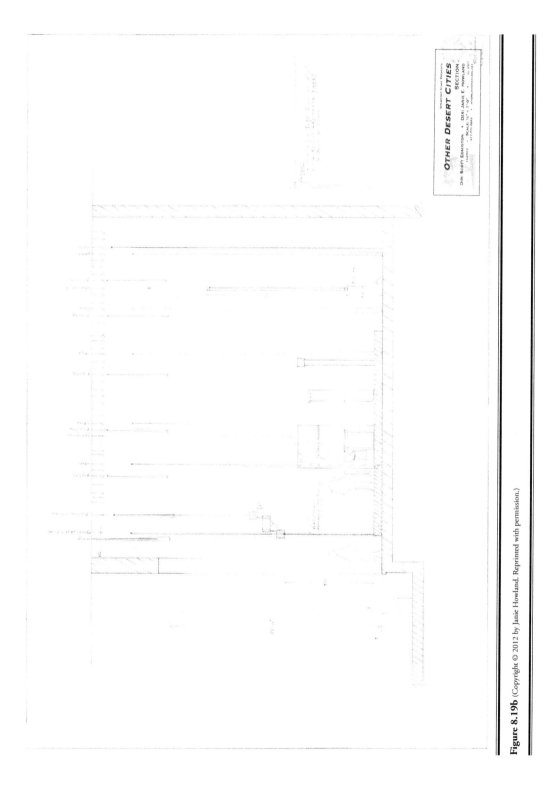

OTHER DESERT CITIES
SECTION

DIR: SCOTT EDMISTON • DES: JANIE E. HOWLAND
SCALE: ½" = 1'-0"

Figure 8.19b (Copyright © 2012 by Janie Howland. Reprinted with permission.)

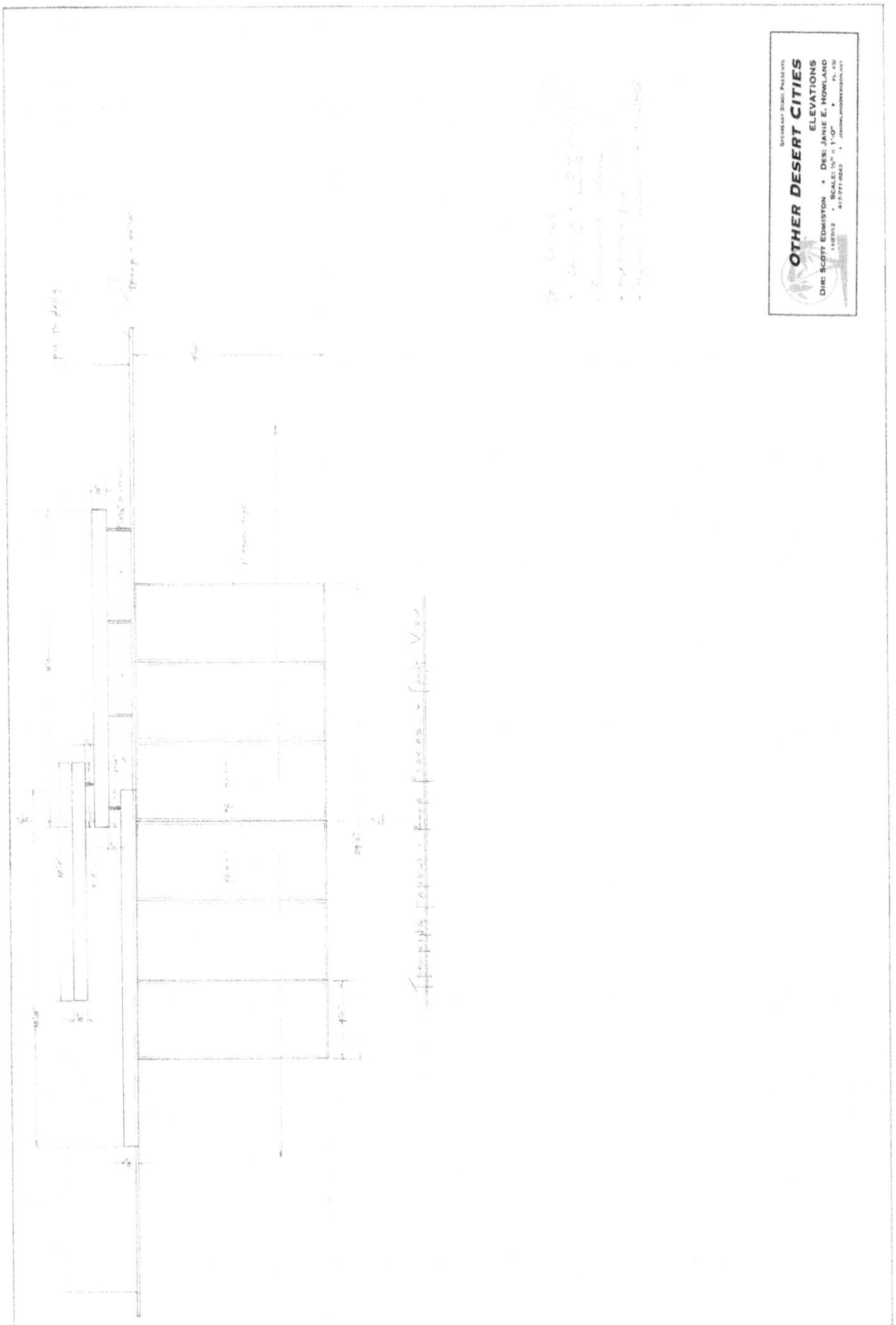

Figure 8.19c (Copyright © 2012 by Janie Howland. Reprinted with permission.)

Drafting—plan section and elevations of the scenic design for Speakeasy Stage's production of *Other Desert Cities*. This ground plan (Figure 8.19A), section (Figure 8.19B), and elevation, (Figure 8.19C), along with the sketches and renderings in Figures 8.18 and 8.17, would be given to the TD and shop for purposes of scenic construction.

Figure 8.20 shows how the design for Speakeasy Stage's production of *Other Desert Cities* looked in production once it was completed.

Figure 8.20 Other Desert Cities by Jon Robin Baitz, Speakeasy Stage Company. Director: Scott Edmiston, Scenic: Janie Howland, Lighting: Karen Perlow, Costumes: Charles Schoonmaker. (Copyright © by Janie Howland. Reprinted with permission.)

Into the Woods

Figure 8.21 Into the Woods by James Lapine and Stephen Sondheim, Emerson Stage, Emerson College 2010. Director: Scott LaFeber, Scenic: Janie Howland, Costumes: Tyler Kinney. (Copyright © 2010 by Janie Howland. Reprinted with permission.)

Figure 8.21 is a white model of the scenic design for *Into the Woods*. A white model is not painted; it is more of a sketch model. It is a three-dimensional representation that demonstrates what the set will look like. The model shows how all of the scenic design elements fit together. It is a tool used by a scenic designer in the design process for sculptural purposes and is easy to adjust if the design team needs to make changes. It would be given to the technical director along with paint elevations.

> **Show photo**—Figure 8.22 shows the actual set for *Into the Woods* in production. It is structurally the same as the white model, and the paint elevations have been applied. It shows the set with the lights on it. One element of the design that stands out with the lights that is not obvious in the model is the cut-out leaves. Janie Howland added this detail to her design to make the forest look denser and to create shadows on the cyclorama to give a fuller feeling to the space.

Howland used a scrim (see Figure 8.23) as a show curtain in this production, conveying the magical fairy tale environment of the show from the moment the audience enters the space. What looks like a traditional proscenium stage curtain, is actually an image painted on to the scrim, stage right and left, to give the illusion of a large proscenium stage. (See Figure 8.23.)

Figure 8.22 Into the Woods by James Lapine and Stephen Sondheim, Emerson Stage, Emerson College 2010. Director: Scott LaFeber, Scenic: Janie Howland, Costumes: Tyler Kinney. (Copyright © 2010 by Janie Howland. Reprinted with permission.)

Figure 8.23 Into the Woods by James Lapine and Stephen Sondheim, Emerson Stage, Emerson College 2010. Director: Scott LaFeber, Scenic: Janie Howland, Costumes: Tyler Kinney. (Copyright © 2010 by Janie Howland. Reprinted with permission.)

Figure 8.24 The Other Place by Sharr White, Central Square Theater, 2013. Director: Bridget Kathleen O'Leary, Scenic: Janie Howland, Lighting: Chris Brusberg, Costume: Leslie Held, Actor: Debra Wise. (Copyright © 2013 by Janie Howland. Reprinted with permission.)

Figure 8.25 The Other Place by Sharr White, Central Square Theater, 2013. Director: Bridget Kathleen O'Leary, Scenic: Janie Howland, Lighting: Chris Brusberg, Costume: Leslie Held (Copyright © 2013 by Janie Howland. Reprinted with permission.)

The Other Place

In this production of *The Other Place*, the design team used a scrim to differentiate between the past and the present. The past was hidden behind the scrim. A doorway was cut into the scrim to allow the actors to move between the past and present. When scenes were played in the past, characters interacted with each other from both sides of the scrim. The scrim was also used as a projection surface. Using a scrim on stage is highly dependent on lighting. The set, lighting, and projection designer must work very closely together. Projections make the design process more complicated. The scenic designer must consider how to create a suitable surface on which to project. Working together, the production team must decide where the projections are going to be on the set, and on what they will be projected. The projections must be integrated into the scenic design. Just hanging a projection screen separates the projections from the overall design of the show and pulls the audience's focus away from the play as a whole. It is helpful for the scenic and projection designer to set locations for projections before rehearsals begin so that the movement and flow of the action can be integrated with the design, making the production cohesive.

Figure 8.24 shows the scrim being used to create past and present. The present is the space where the actor is sitting, and the past is the area that is visible behind the scrim.

Figure 8.25 shows the projections used in the show and what Howland refers to as a "happy accident." Originally, only one image of the little girl was supposed to be projected, but in the tech rehearsal, there was a technical malfunction with the projector and numerous images appeared on the scrim. In this case, a mistake became a better idea; the production team liked this collection of images better than the single image that was planned and felt that it created a stronger impact. They kept it as part of the design.

Miss Witherspoon

Miss Witherspoon is a fantastical black comedy that references India, reincarnation, and that place where souls of the past and future hang out in the ether. Howland used a scrim to create a surround. The shape of the scrim references an Indian design.(see Figure 8.26) At times, the scrim physically separates the souls yet to be born (indicated by bookcases full of wig heads and hats) from the environment of Miss Witherspoon. The hats and heads help to tell the story. The heads are the different souls that Miss Witherspoon can be, and when she takes a hat off the bookshelf and places it on her head, she becomes another person.

The scrim confined a certain space, but the action happens behind and in front of the scrim. By using a scrim, the beings behind the scrim are omnipresent—creating a sense that "they are there and yet they are not"—throughout the entire production. These souls are also represented by the dolls that are suspended from the rafters.

Howland used circles to enhance the ethereal, never-ending sense of time and place in the design, which reflects one of the main concepts in the play. The scrim is curved, and the floor is painted in a circular pattern: a universal heavenly pattern that suggests an unearthly space.

Figure 8.26 Miss Witherspoon by Christopher Durang, Lyric Stage Company. Director: Scott Edmiston, Lighting: Karen Perlow, Costume: Gail Astrid Buckley. (Copyright © by Janie Howland. Reprinted with permission.)

CHAPTER NINE

Specific Elements Costume/ Makeup/Mask Design

GOALS SPECIFIC TO COSTUME DESIGN

Shape identity and essence of character—The way that a person covers and adorns her body influences how she moves, how she feels about herself, and the image of herself that she wants to project in the world. An actor uses costume pieces—their texture, fit, and shape—to feel the character in her body. The actor's costume is like a second skin. It must move with the body and enable her to reveal the character's habits and personality. Costume also helps the audience to define the character. The costume designer—at times, with some collaboration from the actor—will choose details to express character through costume. Consideration is given to the cut of the garment, the material used, accessories, and the newness/wear of the clothing.

   Dealing with actors' personal body image issues—Performers must be able to act with ease and confidence. The costume designer must always keep this in mind. The costume designer works more closely with actors than any of the other members of the design team. Actors are psychological beings who have deep-rooted feelings about their bodies. Like all people, actors have preferences about what makes them feel comfortable and at ease on stage. They know what materials and cuts of clothing inhibit or liberate their bodies. Some actors come to costume designers having devised very strong opinions about their character and what he/she would wear. A costume designer, more than any other designer on the team, must be able to handle the strong opinions of actors. She must be able to balance the director's concept and the design team's plans with the actor's feelings about her body. By the time the actor is seeing the costume designs, decisions about the overall design of the show are in the final stages.

The costume designer is looking at how each piece fits into the whole design. The actor is focused solely on her character. The costume designer needs to be a skilled communicator who can breach this divide if it occurs.

Demonstrate relationships among characters and specify characters' social and professional roles—Costume colors and patterns can be used to visually unite or divide couples, families, teams, citizens, classes, etc. Certain cuts, colors, and uniformity in design can signify a character's profession or social status. A medical worker from a certain era will wear scrubs and a white coat, and a chef might wear a tall white hat, a white jacket, and checked pants; a baseball player will wear a cap and uniform signifying the team he is on. These uniforms or easily recognizable symbolic clothing may be realistic or over the top.

Directing audience's attention to particular parts of the body—At times, a director or designer will want the audience to focus on a particular part of the character's body. The costume designer can help to do this through the cut and ornamentation on a costume. For example, a low-cut top on a woman will bring the audience's focus to that character's cleavage; extra material or padding in the shoulders of a man's costume will give the impression of a broad shoulder and chest area; ruffles at the neck of a costume will bring focus to the head whereas ruffles at the wrists will bring the focus to the hands.

Bring audience's focus to central characters—The clothing that characters wear can either make them stand out or recede from view. Designers use color and ornamentation in the designs of central characters to make them stand out to the audience.

Changing audience's impression of the body's natural proportions—The design of clothing throughout history and in different cultures has, at times, brought focus and accentuation to those areas of the body that were considered beautiful in a particular time period. At other times, the design of clothing has meant to hide parts of the body that were seen as undignified for or unbefitting public viewing. Some examples of this practice are bustles, which created the impression of an arched spine and protruding buttocks; sixteenth-century men wearing puffy sleeves and stockings on the legs, which gave the impression of bulk in the torso and trimness of legs; stays and hoop skirts, which make a woman's waist look tiny and push the bosoms up to look full and voluptuous.

Line—The line, silhouette, and overall shape of a costume will draw the audience's eyes in a particular direction. Social ideas of various historical periods and cultures are expressed in the clothing people wear. The line of a garment, like the proportion, will draw eyes in a particular direction. This is especially true in women's clothing. For example, the line and silhouette of clothing in the Victorian era in England and the 1950s in the United States demonstrate the sexual repression that was dominant in those eras. The line and silhouette of women's clothing in the U.S. in the 1920s and 1960s indicate a sense of sexual liberation.

PROCESS SPECIFIC TO COSTUME DESIGN

Sketches and Swatches—The costume designer will begin with thumbnail sketches of characters' costumes. These sketches are simple and not very detailed. They serve to assist the designer in finding a direction for the evolving costume designs. Final sketches show each costume in great detail, presenting all clothing and accessories that the character will wear. These sketches give a clear idea of how actors will look together on stage and how the clothing will help to clarify their relationship. Fabric swatches are usually attached to these sketches for the director's approval. (See Figures 10.11, 10.13, 10.15, 10.24–26, 10.34, and 10.35) These swatches convey the exact color, texture, and pattern of the material the designer intends to use. They also allow the design team to see how the materials' texture and color will look under the lights and how they will fit together with the set design and the director's vision.

Costume plot—The designer will create a costume plot (see Figure 9.1) that will indicate all of the items that each character will wear in each scene. This plot may be made with visual images or with words.

Attending rehearsals and fittings—As was noted before, the costume designer must work closely with the actors. The costume designer will attend rehearsals and note what physical actions and types of movement the actor is required to achieve in his costume. If there are any aspects of the costume that may impede the actor's ability to achieve the necessary physical demands of the role, adjustments must be made to the costume design. The costume crew, along with the designer, will take an actor's measurements for the costume. The designer will see the actor's body and how the costume falls on it in fittings as the garment is being constructed. She will adjust costumes to the actor's body type so as to make the costumes look faithful to the design on this unique actor's body. If an actor is particularly uncomfortable with a particular piece of a costume, the designer may try to alter the costume to accommodate the actor's needs while still remaining true to the design concept.

Dress parade and dress rehearsal—As the costumes are being built, the actors attend a series of fittings. At that time, any necessary adjustments are made. Once the costumes are nearly finished, the actors will do a dress parade on the set with lighting. This allows the director and designers to see all of the costumes for each scene under the stage lights. This also allows the actors and designers an opportunity to make sure costumes fit well, move well, and look appropriate together. At the dress rehearsal, the costumes are put into action, and the actor has an opportunity to live and work in the costume. The director and designers take notes and make any necessary final adjustments to costumes at this time.

The Importance of Being Earnest
Costume Plot

Character	Actor	Act One- London flat-July-5-6 pm	Act Two- Garden at Manor House	Act Three- Morning room- moments later
Algernon Moncrieff	Joe Smith	x- plate 1 navy velvet robe white shirt black striped trousers gold paisley vest velvet slippers	x- plate 2 white shirt tan tweed suit teal floral vest rust cravat brown boots straw boater	x- same
Lane	Dan Browning	X-plate 3 gray morning coat white pique vest black striped trousers white bow tie white formal shirt black shoes		
Jack Worthing	Roy Jones	x-plate 4 dark gray morning coat burgundy vest white dress shirt black striped trousers gray dotted cravat gray gloves black top hat black boots	x- plate 5 black frock coat black vest white dress shirt black trousers black boots black crepe sash black gloves black top hat	x-plate 6 cream plaid suit white dress shirt burgundy vest brown paisley cravat brown boots brown bowler
Lady Bracknell	Sally Smith	x-plate 7 silver jacket with trim black blouse purple vest silver gored skirt with trim black petticoat with striped ruffle beaded purse black hat with feathers black heeled shoes	x- plate 7 silver jacket with trim black blouse purple vest purple gored skirt with trim beaded purse black hat with purple ribbons black heeled shoes	x-same

Character	Actor			
Gwendolen Fairfax	Judy Jones	x- plate 8 cream plaid jacket matching cream plaid skirt peach vest white blouse lavender petticoat white boots white hat with peach flowers	x- plate 8 pink and cream jacket cream skirt peach vest white blouse lavender petticoat white boots white hat with white flowers lorgnette cream parasol	x-same
Miss Prism	Eve Taylor		x- plate 9 lavender plaid blouse tan linen skirt cream petticoat brown leather belt brown boots straw hat eyeglasses	x-same
Cecily Cardew	Ruth Morgan		x-plate 10 white and yellow floral blouse yellow skirt green sash white petticoat brown boots straw hat with green band	x-same
Dr Chasuble	Dave Regan		x- plate 11 black cassock long black vest black dickey with white collar white shirt black trousers black boots black parson's hat eyeglasses	x-same
Merriman	John Jones		x- plate 3 black and gray livery jacket white formal shirt black tail coat black tie black trousers black shoes white gloves	x-same add white apron

Figure 9.1 Costume Plot (Copyright © by Frances Nelson McSherry. Reprinted with permission.)

TOOLS SPECIFIC TO COSTUME DESIGN

Fabric—the costume designer's most basic tool. Costume designers must understand how color, texture, movement, and flexibility of materials influence how an actor can move in a particular material and feel on stage. She must also understand how materials will affect the way in which the audience understands the character and the world of the play. The costume designer must also be familiar with how other materials—metal, plastic, wood, bone, etc.—can be used with fabric to alter the shape and disguise or to reveal certain aspects of the human body.

Ornament and Accessories—Ornament is added to clothing to give it more detail and style. Ornamentation on a costume can indicate style, period, social class, or the personality of a character. Some common ornamentation includes tassels, sequins, buttons, badges, lace, and ribbons. Accessories are the details that add the finishing touches to a costume. Some common accessories are scarves, hats, glasses, jewelry, fans, canes, shoes, purses, and watches. These elements of costume can help actors to create a character's mannerisms and gestures.

Hairstyles and Wigs—The costume designer will decide what an actor's hair should look like. Hairstyle and facial hair reflect the accepted norms of certain historical periods, a person's social class, and personality. Actors may be asked by the costume designer to alter their own hair—shave, grow facial hair, grow or cut their hair, dye their hair. Or, if there is a sufficient budget and the actor does not want to alter his appearance—for personal or professional reasons—the costume designer will provide the actor with wigs, hair pieces, hair extensions, bald caps, or facial hair that can be applied with spirit gum.

Makeup—Costumes designers are often—but not always—responsible for an actor's makeup design. Makeup can help an actor get into a character's skin. There are three major categories of stage makeup. *Straight makeup* enhances the actor's facial features—especially the eyes, cheeks, and mouth—to keep them from disappearing and losing definition under the stage lights. This makeup is meant to make the actor look natural but allows facial expression to be read from a distance. *Character makeup* can make an actor look older or younger, may accentuate certain features on an actor's face to point out certain character traits, or may completely reshape an actor's face. Character makeup tools include mustaches and beards; prosthetic noses, cheeks, eyebrows, and chins; and contact lenses. These tools, used skillfully, allow actors to make huge facial transformations. *Special effects makeup* may be used to give the impression of injury to the character—scars; bruises; cuts; blackened, stained, or missing teeth, etc. This type of makeup may also be highly-stylized and may be created to transform the actor into the character of an animal, a spirit, a demon, a zombie, an alien being, and so forth.

Masks—When masks are used in costume design, they immediately set a presentational style to the performance rendered by these characters. The use of masks requires heightened theatricality because the actor cannot use his face to make expressions and must use his body and movement to convey much of what would be conveyed through the face in a realistic production. Actors who wear masks must know how to enlarge movement and make it specific to communicate the action and emotion that is otherwise communicated through the face. Masks can also serve to create a similarity between groups of characters. Characters who all wear similar masks become a chorus and are bound together due to this similarity.

CHAPTER TEN

The Work of Costume Designer Frances Nelson McSherry

Frances Nelson McSherry is a professional costume designer who has worked in theaters from Boston to California. Her favorite projects include new works and world premieres, as well as old favorites told in a new way. She has designed at San Jose Repertory Theatre, New York City Opera, Opera Theatre of Saint Louis, Glimmerglass Opera, Merrimack Repertory Theatre, New Repertory Theatre, Lyric Stage Company, Gloucester Stage Company, and Stoneham Theatre Company. Her designs for a new rock musical called *The Snow Queen*, a featured new work at the New York Musical Theatre Festival (NYMF), received rave reviews and the NYMF Overall Best Design Award for 2014. Frances currently teaches theatre design and fashion history at Northeastern University in Boston, MA. She received her MFA in Theater Design at NYU's Tisch School of the Arts and is a member of United Scenic Artists, Local 829. Production photographs from her favorite shows can be found on her website at www.francesnelsonmcsherry.com.

Figure 10.1 Frances Nelson McSherry, costume designer. Photo: Headshots by SkylarShankman. (Copyright © by Skylar Shankman Photography. Reprinted with permission.)

Figure 10.2 The Three Penny Opera by Bertolt Brecht and Kurt Weil, New Repertory Theatre 2004. Director: Rick Lombardo, Scenic: Peter Colao, Costume: Frances Nelson McSherry, Lighting: John Ambrosone, Actors: (L to R) Nancy E. Carroll, Susan Malloy, and Paul D. Farwell, Photo by Richard Feldman. (Copyright © 2004 by Richard Feldman. Reprinted with permission.)

Figure 10.3 The Three Penny Opera by Bertolt Brecht and Kurt Weil, New Repertory Theatre 2004. Director: Rick Lombardo, Scenic: Peter Colao, Costume: Frances Nelson McSherry, Lighting: John Ambrosone, Actors: (L to R) Todd Alan Johnson and Susan Malloy, Photo by Richard Feldman. (Copyright © 2004 by Richard Feldman. Reprinted with permission.)

The Three Penny Opera

The concept for this production was apocalyptic; it is moments before the end of the world, and these people come into a vaudeville theatre because they MUST perform before they die. The costume design creates a visual metaphor for the director's concept by fabricating a macabre world through expressionistic hair and makeup design and clothing pieces that distort the bodies of the actors. Costume designer Frances McSherry redefines the shapes of the actor's bodies using padding and corsets. The visual mass of certain costume elements also creates a warped world. The blending of Victorian attire with modern elements signals to the audience that this is an off-kilter world. Many of the actors are not completely clothed, revealing lots of flesh and body parts of both the men and women and reflecting the depravity and debauchery of this apocalyptic world. Brechtian theatre utilizes the alienation effect; the audience is meant to be aware of the fact that they are in a theatre watching a play at all times. In order to reinforce this style of production, McSherry had costume pieces, mirrors, and makeup available on the stage. The actors dressed and put on makeup as they entered the stage, creating this alienation effect and reinforcing the concept that the characters were creating the production in a "found" theatre space with "found" theatre props and costumes. All design elements made the audience very aware that it was watching theatre. For example, harsh stage lighting (saturated greens, reds, and purples) were utilized. When the lights changed, they drastically changed the color of actors' faces and costumes, creating a visceral sense of theatricality.

Figure 10.2 shows an example of the distortion of the body—the big belly on the actor at right—which was accomplished through the use of padding. The actress at left has a hugely distorted protruding backside and a frilly skirt that is too short and does not match the seemingly Victorian jacket that she wears on the top of her body. The frilly skirt seems to end even before it comes around to the front of her body. This photo also displays the theatrical makeup and hair design.

Figure 10.3 is a photo of the character Polly. She is seemingly the most pure and naive character in the play. She is dressed in white, as white is a typical symbolic color for a pure and naive character. However, in the world created for this production, her dress—which is a hybrid of a Victorian cut with modern elements—is filthy, caked with dirt, mold, and dust.

Romeo and Juliet

The design concept for this production of Shakespeare's classic is modern clothing with a Renaissance feel, which is established through the line of the costumes. The idea of division—among families and classes—is also accentuated in the color and style of the costumes. The Montagues and Capulets are members of the ruling class. They are in more opulent and formal attire but are in starkly different colors. The Montagues are in a cool blue, and the Capulets are in a hot red. Members of the non-ruling class or non-elite are not in formal attire; their clothing is more rustic. They do not really seem to be clothed in the same period, but elements of their costumes put them in the same world as the ruling class. Because the play is so physical—including numerous fight scenes, the ascent of a balcony, and other physical activities—the costume designer had to pay special attention to movement and choreography. The costumes needed to look formal but could not be physically restrictive or cumbersome.

Figure 10.4 displays Romeo and Juliet's first meeting at the ball. The texture and line of their clothing supports the concept of modernity with a Renaissance feel. The reflective texture of their costumes implies wealth. The color of their costumes—black and white—in a room filled with color brings the audience's focus to the central characters.

Figure 10.5 is a photo of Mercutio (left) at the ball. His mask is that of a peacock, a beautiful proud bird, which symbolizes immortality. This mask reflects elements of Mercutio's personality and brings focus to his character, endearing him to the audience at this early point in the play. His mask is also larger and more opulent than those of his comrades, which indicates his very important role in the play; his murder is the catalyst for all of the ensuing tragedy in the play. He is costumed in a pink shirt, which is often associated with femininity, tenderness, intuition, and insightfulness, all elements of Mercutio's

Figure 10.4 Romeo and Juliet by William Shakespeare, New Repertory Theatre 2005. Director and Scenic Design: John Howell Hood, Costume Design: Frances Nelson McSherry, Lighting: Franklin Meissner, Jr., Actors (L to R) Jennifer LaFleur and Lucas Hall, Photo by Richard Feldman. (Copyright © 2005 by Richard Feldman. Reprinted with permission.)

Figure 10.5 Romeo and Juliet by William Shakespeare, New Repertory Theatre 2005. Director and Scenic Design: John Howell Hood, Costume Design: Frances Nelson McSherry, Lighting: Franklin Meissner, Jr., Actors (L to R): Joseph Plummer, Dan Cozzens, Will Keary, and Mason Sand, Photo by Richard Feldman. (Copyright © 2005 by Richard Feldman. Reprinted with permission.)

Figure 10.6 Romeo and Juliet by William Shakespeare, New Repertory Theatre 2005. Director and Scenic Design: John Howell Hood, Costume Design: Frances Nelson McSherry, Lighting: Franklin Meissner, Jr., Actor: Adam Zahler, Photo by Richard Feldman. (Copyright © 2005 by Richard Feldman. Reprinted with permission.)

Figure 10.7 Romeo and Juliet by William Shakespeare, New Repertory Theatre 2005. Director and Scenic Design: John Howell Hood, Costume Design: Frances Nelson McSherry, Lighting: Franklin Meissner, Jr., Actors: Jennifer LaFleur and BobbieSteinbach, Photo by Richard Feldman. (Copyright © 2005 by Richard Feldman. Reprinted with permission.)

Figure 10.8 Romeo and Juliet by William Shakespeare, New Repertory Theatre 2005. Director and Scenic Design: John Howell Hood, Costume Design: Frances Nelson McSherry, Lighting: Franklin Meissner, Jr., Actors (L to R) Joseph Plummer and Ted Hewlett. (Copyright © 2005 by Richard Feldman. Reprinted with permission.)

character; they symbolize his struggle for acceptance as a gay man in an unaccepting society.

Figures 10.6 and 10.7 show the difference in costuming between the elite and the commoners in the play. Peter and Juliet's Nurse are both servants. Their clothing is more rustic and rumpled looking. They are dressed in numerous bulky layers and each has costume pieces—Peter's aviator goggles and the Nurse's rope—that add a sense of whimsy and humor to their appearance. The texture of their clothing has little sheen, indicating that they are lower class.

Figure 10.8 exhibits the way in which the costumes moved with the actors as they incorporated broad and very athletic movement into their performances. This photo also shows that the costumes help the audience to know who is on which side in a fight; the red cape of the actor on the right is a sign that he is of the house of Capulet. In this way, the costumes help to tell the story; we visually know who is winning or losing a fight as we watch the action unfold.

Quills

Set in the 1800s, *Quills* is a macabre play about the Marquis de Sade. The marquis was a French aristocrat, revolutionary politician, philosopher, and writer famous for his libertine sexuality. The words "sadism" and "sadistic" are derived from his last name. *Quills* is filled with many strange characters who are bold and ugly. There are also common characters—a priest and a maid—who appear in the play, creating a visual and moral contrast to the marquis and his lascivious cohorts. The production design is based on the Grand Guignol, a melodramatic theatrical event with gory special effects and stylized acting. The costume design was accurate to the period in which the play was set and, along with makeup and wig design, accentuated the shocking elements of the play. Designer McSherry used a limited color palate and incorporated fashions from 1800–1815, the time period in which the play was set, into the costume design.

Figure 10.9 shows the marquis in the first act of the play. Here he is dressed in smooth and silky attire in light pink, salmon, white, and baby blue colors. These light colors are appropriate for the period in which the play is set, but they also give the audience an unsettled feeling as they experience the idea of such a lewd character who is dressed in colors we often associate with children and innocence. His wig is suitable for the time, but it is not set correctly on his head. That, and his makeup design, create the essence of a character who is a bit weird and off.

In Figure 10.10, we see the priest and the maid, the two characters in the play who are most unlike the marquis. By putting the marquis in a light-colored, silky costume and the priest and maid in costumes with black and earth tone colors and flat textures that create a homespun appearance, McSherry created a great deal of visual distance between the priest and maid and the marquis.

Figure 10.9 Quills by Doug Wright, New Repertory Theatre 2005. Director: Rick Lombardo, Scenic: Richard Chambers, Costume: Frances Nelson McSherry, Lighting: John Malinowski, Actor: Austin Pendleton, Photo by Richard Feldman. (Copyright © 2005 by Richard Feldman. Reprinted with permission.)

Figure 10.10 Quills by Doug Wright, New Repertory Theatre 2005. Director: Rick Lombardo, Scenic: Richard Chambers, Costume: Frances Nelson McSherry, Lighting: John Malinowski, Actors: (L to R) Marianna Bassham and Benjamin Evett, Photo by Richard Feldman. (Copyright © 2005 by Richard Feldman. Reprinted with permission.)

Figure 10.12 Quills by Doug Wright, New Repertory Theatre 2005. Director: Rick Lombardo, Scenic: Richard Chambers, Costume: Frances Nelson McSherry, Lighting: John Malinowski, Actor: Rachel Harker, Photo by Richard Feldman. (Copyright © 2005 by Richard Feldman. Reprinted with permission.)

Figure 10.11 Quills by Doug Wright. Costume sketch/rendering for Renee Pelagie created by Frances Nelson McSherry. (Copyright © by Frances Nelson McSherry. Reprinted with permission.)

In Figure 10.11, you see designer McSherry's rendering for the character Renee Pelagie. In Figure 10.12, you see the costume in its final form, creating a living image—through clothing, accessories, hair, makeup, posture and movement—of a middle class woman from 1800s France.

Wild Party

Wild Party is a 1920s Jazz opera with no spoken dialogue and almost continuous dancing. The characters in this play are eccentric, eclectic, bold, and diverse personalities whom designer Frances McSherry calls a "motley and flamboyant group of people." The clothing is colorful and flashy. Since characters are seen on stage in their undergarments, she started by designing period-appropriate lingerie and then designed up from there. In her research, she looked back at 1920s cartoons from *The New Yorker* and then translated and adapted that information to inform her overall design and renderings for the show.

Figure 10.13 is the costume rendering with material swatches for the character of Madelaine True; Figure 10.14 is the finished costume on the actress who plays Madelaine. The line and the flow of the costume establish that her character is a masculine woman living a bohemian lifestyle in the 1920s.

Figure 10.14 Wild Party by Andrew Lippa, New Repertory Theatre 2007. Director: Rick Lombardo, Scenic: Janie Howland, Costume: Frances Nelson McSherry, Lighting: Franklin Meissner, Jr., Actor: Leigh Barrett, Photo by Andrew Brilliant. (Copyright © by Frances Nelson McSherry. Reprinted with permission.)

Figure 10.13 Wild Party by Andrew Lippa. Costume sketch/rendering with fabric swatches for Madelaine True created by Frances Nelson McSherry. (Copyright © 2007 by Andrew Brilliant.)

Figure 10.15 Wild Party by Andrew Lippa. Costume sketch/rendering with fabric swatches for Kate and Dolores created by Frances Nelson McSherry. (Copyright © by Frances Nelson McSherry. Reprinted with permission.)

Figure 10.15 is the costume rendering with material swatches for Kate and Delores. These two women are the bad girls as displayed in Figures 10.16 and 10.17. The actors do a lot to convey the roles that they play, but the costumes communicate quite a bit on their own. Their costumes are low-cut on top and reveal a lot of flesh. Kate is in a seductive red color, and Delores has an orange and black silky velvet top, which barely covers her breasts.

Figure 10.18 demonstrates how a simple costume piece can specify a character's social and professional role. If you attach a red ball to the end of someone's nose, the audience then considers him to be a clown.

Figure 10.16 Wild Party by Andrew Lippa, New Repertory Theatre 2007. Director: Rick Lombardo, Scenic: Janie Howland, Costume: Frances Nelson McSherry, Lighting: Franklin Meissner, Jr., Actors: (L to R) Jake Mosser and Michele A. DeLuca, Photo by Andrew Brilliant. (Copyright © 2007 by Andrew Brilliant.)

Figure 10.18 Wild Party by Andrew Lippa, New Repertory Theatre 2007. Director: Rick Lombardo, Scenic: Janie Howland, Costume: Frances Nelson McSherry, Lighting: Franklin Meissner, Jr., Actor: Todd Alan Johnson, Photo by Andrew Brilliant. (Copyright © 2007 by Andrew Brilliant.)

Figure 10.17 Wild Party by Andrew Lippa, New Repertory Theatre 2007. Director: Rick Lombardo, Scenic: Janie Howland, Costume: Frances Nelson McSherry, Lighting: Franklin Meissner, Jr., Actor: Sarah Covey, Photo by Andrew Brilliant. (Copyright © 2007 by Andrew Brilliant.)

A Streetcar Named Desire

Figure 10.19 A Streetcar Named Desire by Tennessee Williams, New Repertory Theatre 2007. Director: Rick Lombardo, Scenic: Janie Howland, Costume: Frances Nelson McSherry, Lighting: John Malinowski, Actors: (L to R) Marianna Bassham and Rachel Harker, Photo by Andrew Brilliant. (Copyright © 2007 by Andrew Brilliant.)

Figure 10.20 A Streetcar Named Desire by Tennessee Williams, New Repertory Theatre 2007. Director: Rick Lombardo, Scenic: Janie Howland, Costume: Frances Nelson McSherry, Lighting: John Malinowski, Actors: (L to R) Rachel Harker and Marianna Basham, Photo by Andrew Brilliant. (Copyright © 2007 by Andrew Brilliant.)

Family, sex, relationships between men and women, and social class are all important themes in *A Streetcar Named Desire*. The costumes in this production create a visual reminder of these themes. They also help to tell the story and create a strong sense of time, place, and social/cultural milieu.

Figure 10.19 demonstrates how costuming can clearly define character. Stella and Blanche are sisters who have taken very different paths in life. This is an important aspect of Williams' play. Some of their differences are indicated in the clothes they wear. In this scene, Stella is wearing a simple, soft cotton dress. She looks very homey and lower middle class. Blanche, by contrast, is wearing more stylish clothing. Her outfit is more put together and she looks quite chic and upper class.

In Figure 10.20, Stella and Blanche are dressed up for a night on the town. Blanche's dress is lower-cut and more revealing. Her dress and hat look like they are made of fine, expensive materials. The ensemble looks as if it was designed for her. She

Figure 10.21 A Streetcar Named Desire by Tennessee Williams, New Repertory Theatre 2007. Director: Rick Lombardo, Scenic: Janie Howland, Costume: Frances Nelson McSherry, Lighting: John Malinowski, Actors: (Clockwise) Bates Wilder (standing), Todd Alan Johnson, Paul D. Farwell, and Luis Negron, Photo by Andrew Brilliant. (Copyright © 2007 by Andrew Brilliant.)

Figure 10.22 A Streetcar Named Desire by Tennessee Williams, New Repertory Theatre 2007. Director: Rick Lombardo, Scenic: Janie Howland, Costume: Frances Nelson McSherry, Lighting: John Malinowski, Actors: (L to R) Todd Alan Johnson, Marianna Basham, and Rachel Harker, Photo by Andrew Brilliant. (Copyright © 2007 by Andrew Brilliant.)

looks elegant, like the true Southern belle she claims to be. Stella's dress is straightforward and buttoned up, literally and figuratively. Her garb is not revealing and looks as if it was bought off a rack in a department store. The material looks like a cheap polyester, and the cut of the dress is not stylish or becoming. She does not really look like Blanche's younger sister but more like her mother—a role she sometimes seems to take on in the play.

The clothing—and how it is worn—in Figure 10.21 helps to establish setting and mood. It is a scorchingly hot evening in New Orleans in a building with no air conditioning. The men in this photo look hot. They are sitting under the hot lights in a hot room in the city. The way that they wear the clothing—unbuttoned, wrinkled, untidy—makes them look like they are sweating. The acting and the clothing work together to create the environment and heat of the play.

Figure 10.22 demonstrates the way in which clothing can help tell the story and indicate passage of time. Stella is pregnant and her belly has swelled enough to indicate that months have passed. The actress works with this element of her costume to communicate her feelings: as a future mother, toward her unborn child's father, and toward her sister.

The costume in Figure 10.23 conveys a great deal about Blanche. In this one dress we see who Blanche was, who she has become, and the demise of her psyche. McSherry and Rachel Harker—the actress playing Blanche—had a long conversation about Blanche and what might be in her trunk. From that conversation, research into the time period, discussions with the director and design team, and close examination of the script, McSherry developed the design for this important costume, which reveals so much about the real Blanche who has been hiding throughout the play. The style of the dress is taken from the period when Blanche would have been a young teen "coming out" as a Southern belle, long before the era in which the play is set. However, this is how Blanche still sees herself; this is who she is in her mind: the beautiful, young, vibrant flirtatious girl of years gone by. But the costume also conveys to the audience who Blanche really is. It seems to be made of old lace and is almost ghost-like in its silver and white tones. To enhance the sense of age and the demise of her youth—and her mind—the material is painted with greens and grays to give a moldiness to its appearance. The accessories that accompany the dress symbolize aspects of Blanche as well. She wear a series of pearls and chains around her neck that are hooked together but do not really belong together. The small tiara on her head is something that a child would wear and adds to the sense that Blanche is no longer in her present reality as an adult woman. The actress thanked McSherry for this costume, telling the designer that she used the costume to "get where she needed to go" in this very challenging moment in the show. This costume design and implementation demonstrates how an actor and designer, working in collaboration, can create a more powerful impact than either could by working in isolation.

Figure 10.23 A Streetcar Named Desire by Tennessee Williams, New Repertory Theatre 2007. Director: Rick Lombardo, Scenic: Janie Howland, Costume: Frances Nelson McSherry, Lighting: John Malinowski, Actor: Rachel Harker, Photo by Andrew Brilliant. (Copyright © 2007 by Andrew Brilliant.)

Dessa Rose

Dessa Rose is a play set in the American antebellum South of the 1840s. The costume design requires period clothing as well as a clear distinction between the landowners and the slaves. Cast members play multiple roles and have numerous fast changes, a practical consideration which adds a layer of complexity to designing costumes for the theatre—how to design clothing so that quick costume changes may be successfully executed.

Figure 10.24 is a costume rendering for the four characters that one actor plays. The trousers remain the same for three of the four characters, and the shirt is consistent over all four characters. By changing hats, coats, vests and ties/cravats, the actor is able to appear in quick succession as four men whose clothing visually reinforces their distinct stations in life and personalities.

Figures 10.25 through 10.27 show renderings and final versions of the period clothing worn by the female characters in the play. The difference in the line, texture, fabric, and ornamentation of the dresses creates a clear class distinction. The costumes of the slave women are rough and loose. The dresses are constructed of cotton that is printed with a small pattern. The width of the dresses and the corsets designed for the

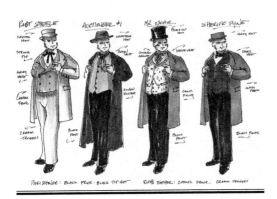

Figure 10.24 Dessa Rose by Lynn Ahrens and Stephen Flaherty, based on the book by Sherley Anne Williams. Costume sketch/rendering for Steele/Auctioneer/Mr. Oscar/Pyne created by Frances Nelson McSherry. (Copyright © by Frances Nelson McSherry. Reprinted with permission.)

Figure 10.25 Dessa Rose by Lynn Ahrens and Stephen Flaherty, based on the book by Sherley Anne Williams. Costume sketch/rendering for Ruth created by Frances Nelson McSherry. (Copyright © by Frances Nelson McSherry. Reprinted with permission.)

Figure 10.26 Dessa Rose by Lynn Ahrens and Stephen Flaherty, based on the book by Sherley Anne Williams. Costume sketch/rendering for Dessa Rose created by Frances Nelson McSherry. (Copyright © by Frances Nelson McSherry. Reprinted with permission.)

women who are part of the landowning class is appropriate to the period, and create a more controlled and refined look. However, in creating the costumes, the costume designer made alterations in the construction process. The corsets are made of a more flexible material than would have been used in authentic corsets of the 1840s, which make breathing and movement very difficult. The width of the dresses has been reduced (i.e., they are less bell-shaped) to accommodate the limited space on the stage. The texture of their costumes is more reflective, seemingly made of a rich silk fabric with larger, more ornate patterns.

Figure 10.27 Dessa Rose by Lynn Ahrens and Stephen Flaherty, based on the book by Sherley Anne Williams. Director: Rick Lombardo, Scenic: Peter Colao, Costumes: Frances Nelson McSherry, Lighting: Franklin Meissner, Jr., Actors: (clockwise from center) Peter A. Carey, Michael Kreutz, Todd Alan Johnson, A'Lisa D. Miles, Uzo Aduba, Leigh Barrett, Dee Crawford, De'Lon Grant, Kami Rushell Smith, and Joshua W. Heggie, Photo by Andrew Brilliant. (Copyright © 2007 by Andrew Brilliant.)

Eurydice

The costume designer's mission in this production is linked to that of the scenic designer as referred to in the scenic design montage of this book. However, costume designer McSherry was required to differentiate between the world above ground and the eerie watery wonderland of the underground—which is the world that scenic designer Janie Howland created (as previously discussed in Chapter Eight)—through the costumes worn by the actors. Clothing and props define the people in this world. The costume design is a fusion of modern and 1960s fashion, with highly theatrical pieces designed for the spirits of the underworld. As there was water on the set floor, and actors did lie on the floor, this was a practical consideration that was kept in mind as McSherry chose fabrics for costumes.

Figure 10.28 Eurydice by Sarah Ruehl, New Repertory Theatre, 2008. Director: Rick Lombardo, Scenic: Janie Howland, Lighting: Deb Sullivan, Costumes: Frances Nelson McSherry, Actor: Zilah Glory, Photo by Andrew Brilliant. (Copyright © 2008 by Andrew Brilliant.)

Figure 10.28 shows the way in which costume design and movement can work together to create action and meaning. In this scene in the play, the bride (in red) is supposed to be falling down stairs. However, as the action of the play is so fluid, it was not appropriate for the scenic designer to create actual stairs on the set; it did not serve the rest of the play. McSherry worked closely with the director, actress, and other designers to create a costume that could, through its movement, create the image of someone falling down stairs. She created a vibrant red ball gown with a full billowing skirt and attached an extremely long veil to the actress's head. Movement and costume created a very lyrical and abstract moment that allowed the audience to suspend disbelief and use its imagination to see the

Figure 10.29 Eurydice by Sarah Ruehl, New Repertory Theatre, 2008. Director: Rick Lombardo, Scenic: Janie Howland, Lighting: Deb Sullivan, Costumes: Frances Nelson McSherry, Actors: (L to R) Brain Quint, Rebecca Stevens, Whitney Stanford, Abby Spare, Zilah Glory, and Ken Baltan, Photo by Andrew Brilliant. (Copyright © 2008 by Andrew Brilliant.)

woman falling.

In Figures 10.29 and 10.30, we get a look at the fantastical characters of the underworld. The underworld in this production is colorful and bizarre. The Lord of the Underworld is dressed as private schoolboy, with his beanie, extra-long tie, and stilts. The chorus of "stones" is often seen as Victorian females in black and white. These characters speak in rhyme, and their lines are very singsong. The director wanted to cast tween girls in these roles; the dialogue impressed him as the language that girls of this age might use. Frances McSherry found her inspiration for these costumes in Japanese anime, which has a youthful, theatrical, and ethereal quality, as the characters in anime often possess super-human or other-worldly characteristics. Figure 10.29 also shows the actress (in pink) on the floor getting wet. The costume was made out of a material that would not become too cumbersome when wet and would dry quickly so as not to limit the actress's ability to move.

Figure 10.30 Eurydice by Sarah Ruehl, New Repertory Theatre, 2008. Director: Rick Lombardo, Scenic: Janie Howland, Lighting: Deb Sullivan, Costumes: Frances Nelson McSherry, Actors: (L to R) Whitney Stanford, Abby Spare, and Rebecca Stevens, Photo by Andrew Brilliant. (Copyright © 2008 by Andrew Brilliant.)

Figure 10.31 displays the lead character's costume, which was inspired by the high-couture fashions worn by Jacqueline Kennedy in the 1960s. The umbrella is an appropriate costume design concept for that period, and it is also a practical choice: the clear fabric allows stage lighting to hit the actor's face as the umbrella protects her from the "rain" that is falling on stage.

Figure 10.31 Eurydice by Sarah Ruehl, New Repertory Theatre, 2008. Director: Rick Lombardo, Scenic: Janie Howland, Lighting: Deb Sullivan, Costumes: Frances Nelson McSherry, Actor: Zilah Glory, Photo by Andrew Brilliant. (Copyright © 2008 by Andrew Brilliant.)

Cabaret

Figure 10.32 Cabaret by John Kander and Fred Ebb based on the novel by Christopher Isherwood, New Repertory Theatre 2009. Director: Rick Lombardo, Scenic: Peter Colao, Costume: Frances Nelson McSherry, Lighting: Franklin Meissner, Jr., Photo bu Andrew Brilliant. (Copyright © 2009 by Andrew Brilliant.)

Cabaret is set in the Weimar Republic in the 1930s. The concept for this production was inspired by the artwork of German painter George Grosz. Act I of the play is polished and precise. However, in Act II, the world of the characters devolves into desperation. The play revolves around a character who performs at the unsavory, sleezy nightclub in Berlin called the Kit Kat Club. There are numerous scenes set in the club where actors who play the nightclub entertainers appear in costumes that are very revealing. One challenge for costume designer McSherry was making the actors feel comfortable in the costumes (in which they spend a lot of time on stage) as seen in images Figures 10.32 and 10.33.

The costumes were based on actual dance costumes worn by German nightclub workers during this time period. The cut of the costumes—particularly where the stockings meet the garters—made several of the female dancers highly aware of their thighs, which the costumes accentuated as a prominent part of their bodies. When dealing with this issue, the designer said: "A lot of what I do in the fitting room feels like I am a therapist. I need to make sure that the actors can learn to be comfortable in what they are wearing. If they are not, it will affect the way in which they perform. We must all strive to create the best possible production."

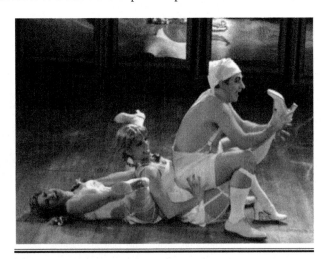

Figure 10.33 Cabaret by John Kander and Fred Ebb based on the novel by Christopher Isherwood, New Repertory Theatre 2009. Director: Rick Lombardo, Scenic: Peter Colao, Costume: Frances Nelson McSherry, Lighting: Franklin Meissner, Jr., Actors (L to R): Annie Kerins, Michele A. DeLuca, and John Kuntz. (Copyright © 2009 by Andrew Brilliant.)

Picasso at the Lapine Agile

This play is a set in a bohemian bar at the turn of the twentieth century. It is filled with eccentric and eclectic characters, many of whom are recognizable historical figures.

In Figures 10.34 and 10.35, we see designer Frances McSherry's renderings, which include actual photos of Einstein and Picasso: real historical figures who appear in the play. Frances took this research—real pictures of famous individuals—and molded aspects of the research into her design. The identities of the characters in a play like this are presented clearly through both acting and design.

Figure 10.36 is a photo of the cast in costume in the production. Although the actors do not look exactly like the historical figures, the costumes, hair, makeup, and gestures that they use communicate the essence of these famous people who are brought together in this comedy through the imagination of playwright and comedian Steve Martin and the expertise of the artists who collaborated to create this production.

Figure 10.34 Picasso at the Lapine Agile by Steve Martin, Costume sketch/rendering for Einstein created by Frances Nelson McSherry (Copyright © by Frances Nelson McSherry. Reprinted with permission.)

Figure 10.36 Picasso at the Lapine Agile by Steve Martin, New Repertory Theatre 2009. Director: Daniel Gidron, Scenic: Cristina Todesco, Costumes: Frances Nelson McSherry, Lighting: John R. Malinowsk, Actors (Clockwise from UC): Owen Doyle, Scott Sweatt, Paul D. Farwell, Dennis Trainor, Stacey Fischer, Neil A. Casey, and Marianna Bassham. (Copyright © 2009 by Andrew Brilliant. Reprinted with permission.)

Figure 10.35 Picasso at the Lapine Agile by Steve Martin. Costume sketch/rendering for Picasso created by Frances Nelson McSherry. (Copyright © by Frances Nelson McSherry. Reprinted with permission.)

Figure 10.37 Black Pearl Sings by Frank Higgins, San Jose Repertory Theatre 2011. Director: Rick Lombardo, Scenic: John Iacovelli, Costumes: Frances Nelson McSherry, Lighting: Daniel Meeker, Actors (L to R): Jessica Wortham and Jannie Jones, Photo by Kevin Berne. (Copyright © 2011 by Kevin Berne. Reprinted with permission.)

Black Pearl Sings

This play is a two-woman a cappella musical. Act I is set in a 1930s Texas prison, and Act II is set in 1935 Greenwich Village in the heart of a vibrant jazz scene.

Figure 10.38 Black Pearl Sings by Frank Higgins, San Jose Repertory Theatre 2011. Director: Rick Lombardo, Scenic: John Iacovelli, Costumes: Frances Nelson McSherry, Lighting: Daniel Meeker, Actors (L to R): Jessica Wortham and Jannie Jones, Photo by Kevin Berne. (Copyright © 2011 by Kevin Berne. Reprinted with permission.)

The costume design in this show helps to reinforce that these two characters are very different women who work together over the years in two very contrasting environments. The play follows the journey of a faculty member (Susannah), who is looking to make her mark in the academia by finding and recording slave songs, and a woman (Pearl), who has been imprisoned for murder and who knows and can perform those songs. This production of the play moves from a bare, hot, and spare existence in a Texas prison to an explosion of lush life in jazzy Greenwich Village. This concept is supported by the costume design.

In Figure 10.37, we see Susannah and Pearl as they appear in Act I, dressed in monochromatic costumes, devoid of any signs of real life.

Figure 10.38 reveals these women as they appear in Act II. Pearl is dressed in an explosion of vibrant colors. The cut of her clothing is free flowing, allowing her to embrace the colorful, rich, and resonant life she is experiencing. Susannah's clothes are more richly colorful than in the first act, but the cut of her clothes suggests that she is still somewhat restrained, academic, and controlled.

Amadeus

For this production of Peter Schaffer's classic tale of Mozart and Salieri set in Austria circa 1793, the costumes, footwear, wigs, makeup, and undergarments are accurate to the period. During this period, the image of beauty (for both men and women) was very different than it is today. Clothing for men was more elaborate and colorful. Men's lower legs were revealed, covered only by stockings. Just as in nature, the males were more ornate and often more vibrant

Figure 10.40 Amadeus by Peter Shaffer, New Repertory Theatre 2013. Director: Jim Petosa, Scenic: Cristina Todesco, Costume: Frances Nelson McSherry, Lighting: Mary Ellen Stebbins, Actors: Esme Allen and Benjamin Evett, Photo by Andrew Brilliant. (Copyright © 2013 by Andrew Brilliant.)

than the females in their appearance. Both men and women wore numerous layers, jewelry, ornate foot coverings, and high wigs. In fact, men's shoes were sometimes more radiant (as in the king's red shoes in Figure 10.39) than women's because they were more visible. High fashion during this period distorted women's bodies. The

Figure 10.39 Amadeus by Peter Shaffer, New Repertory Theatre 2013. Director: Jim Petosa, Scenic: Cristina Todesco, Costume: Frances Nelson McSherry, Lighting: Mary Ellen Stebbins, Ensemble, Photo by Andrew Brilliant. (Copyright © 2013 by Andrew Brilliant.)

Figure 10.41 Amadeus by Peter Shaffer, New Repertory Theatre 2013. Director: Jim Petosa, Scenic: Cristina Todesco, Costume: Frances Nelson McSherry, Lighting: Mary Ellen Stebbins, Actors: (L to R) Tim Spears and Russell Garrett, Photo by Andrew Brilliant. (Copyright © 2013 by Andrew Brilliant.)

Figure 10.42 Amadeus by Peter Shaffer, New Repertory Theatre 2013. Director: Jim Petosa, Scenic: Cristina Todesco, Costume: Frances Nelson McSherry, Lighting: Mary Ellen Stebbins, Actors (L to R): Benjamin Evett, McCaela Donovan, and Tim Spears, Photo by Andrew Brilliant. (Copyright © 2013 by Andrew Brilliant.)

impression of the natural proportions of a woman's body were changed through the use of corsets and hoop skirts.

The corsets—as seen on the women in Figures 10.39 and 10.40—cinched in the waist and pushed up the bosoms. The hoop skirts, also seen in these two photos, create a silhouette of sideways width at the hips. The legs are hidden beneath the many layers of fabric that make up the skirts of the dresses. Figures 10.41 and 10.42 demonstrate the way in which costume helps to tell the story. Both pictures are of Mozart at different points in his life.

In Figure 10.41, Mozart is seen as a musical genius at the height of his popularity. His clothes reveal a man who is eccentric, wealthy, well-respected, and the toast of the town. His costume is made of a colorful smooth silk-like material, embellished with numerous layers of ornamentation and rich texture. It is well-fitted to his body. His wig, costume, and physicality show a man who is light, vibrant, and energetic.

By contrast, Figure 10.42 reveals Mozart's demise later in the play. He has lost his money and is losing his mind. The texture of his costume is rough, and the color is of dirt. He no longer wears a wig, which puts him out of sync with the wealthy ruling class in this place and time. His cloak drowns him, and he looks unkempt, wrinkled, and disheveled.

CHAPTER ELEVEN

Specific Elements of Lighting Design

PROCESS SPECIFIC TO LIGHTING DESIGN

Attending rehearsals—The lighting designer will attend an early run-through of the play to make sure that the light design and light plot will fulfill the director's vision. Lighting design is greatly affected by the blocking of the actors. Blocking refers to the section of the stage where actors are at a given point. A lighting designer needs to attend rehearsals to understand the flow and rhythm of the show as well for this will determine the speed of light cue changes and the number of light cues that the designer will create. Light changes can help to enhance emotional changes, changes in circumstance of characters, and many other elements that affect the flow and meaning of a production. A lighting designer needs to be in the rehearsal room as the production comes together to feel, see, and hear the rhythm of the show.

Light plot, lighting section, channel hook-up, and instrumental schedule—A Light Plot (Figure 11.1) is a bird's eye view of the theater. The theater architecture is on the initial layer, the set/scenic elements, are on the 2nd layer (ground plan), and the lighting designer (LD) drafts the light plot over it (or on a subsequent layer). It is, at its most basic level, a "map" for the Master Electrician & her team. It informs them where the lighting units are placed (hung) and the channel number, the locations at which the beams of light will be focused, the colors that will be emitted from these instruments—using gels, and the shapes that will be emitted from the instruments—using gobos. (See definition of terms below.) It includes a legend or key explaining the unique symbols. The creation of the light plot requires that

109

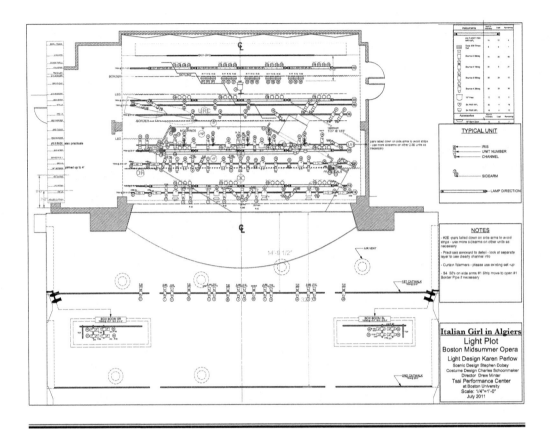

Figure 11.1 Light Plot for An Italian Girl in Algiers at Boston Midsummer Opera, drafted by Karen Perlow. (Copyright © 2011 by Karen Perlow. Reprinted with permission.)

the lighting designer have some drafting skills. The light plot should have some standard information, including:

- Scale; most often ½" = 1'-0" or ¼" = 1'0"
- Lighting instrument information and definitions—focus, position, color, and circuiting;
- A title block and legend containing show information and details of how to identify the symbols on the plot; and
- The relationship between the lighting instruments and the architecture of the space, scenic elements, and the lighting positions.

Figure 11.1 is the Light Plot for An Italian Girl in Algiers, by Gioachinno Rossini, Boston Midsummer Opera 2011, (see also Figure a 12.16) Notice the instrument information in the top right corner of Figure 11.1, and the scenic layer

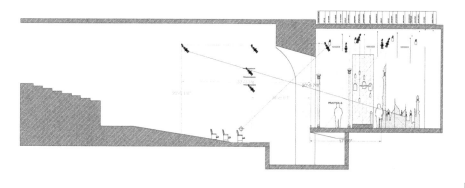

Figure 11.2 Lighting Section for An Italian Girl in Algiers at Boston Midsummer Opera, drafted by Karen Perlow. (Copyright © 2011 by Karen Perlow. Reprinted with permission.)

underneath. There are 13 different lighting positions on this plot. Can you find them all?

A Lighting Section is a working drawing the LD uses in order to determine the possible angles of light from different positions in the theater (both over the stage, and over the audience/house), as well as what scenic elements might interfere with certain positions. It is based on the section drawn by the scenic designer and shows the stage cut down the center-line. The scenic designer must provide both a ground plan and a section so that the lighting designer has all the necessary information to create a light plot. Figure 11.2 is a lighting section for An Italian Girl in Algiers, by Gioachinno Rossini, Boston Midsummer Opera 2011, (see also Figure a 12.16). This lighting section (Figure 11.2) uses different colored angles to show which lighting positions could be used to light different areas of the stage. It indicates both front and back light options, and shows the different heights of the scenic elements as well as the practicals (small pendant lights).

The channel hook-up organizes all of the lighting information by the channel number associated with that instrument. Channel numbers are often assigned to instruments based on the location they illuminate and/or their purpose—frontlight, sidelight, practicals, specials, etc. This is the document most useful to the designer as it's grouped by systems.

The instrument schedule lists all of the lighting instruments and information about how they are used in a production. The instruments are organized by their positions on stage. The schedule includes all information about every instrument, including hanging location, instrument number, instrument type, wattage, color, focus area, circuit, dimmer, and templates. This document is used by the ME to quickly locate units and turn on lighting units, as it's arranged by position.

TOOLS SPECIFIC TO LIGHTING

Instruments—floodlights, strips, spots, Fresnels, ellipsoidals, intelligent lights—these are some of the varieties of lighting instruments used for various types of design effects.

Pars—are used to cover a large amount of space on the stage. The lighting is flat and the beam spread of the unit is not adjustable. There is often a hot ellipse of light that can be rotated.

Strip lights—also known as cyclorama or cyc lights—are long metal housings usually containing a number of lamps along the length of the instrument. They emit light perpendicular to the length of the instrument and are often used to light a cyclorama or curtain at the back of the stage.

Fresnels— are small instruments that give a soft-edged pool of light. You can adjust the size of the light, but not the shape.

Ellipsodials—are more sophisticated units and their beam can be manipulated in different ways. They can provide either a hard-edged or soft beam. Internal shutters can shape the light and be used to "cut off" light from unwanted areas. They also have a gate at their focal point, which allows for the insertion of gobos to add pattern to the beam of light (example a window, or leaves) Larger versions of this type of light, which must be operated by a single technician and are often seen in musicals and popular music concerts, are referred to as "follow spots."

Intelligent lights—also known as moving lights came into widespread use at concerts in the 1980s. Over time, they have become less expensive and are increasingly used in theatrical productions. The output beams, focus, and panning and tilting of these instruments can be controlled remotely. Often, these instruments also contain controls that can change the texture and color and shape of light through the use of a gobo or dichroic wheels. This allows one light to perform many functions and cover many areas of the stage. The instruments can also move while they are illuminated, creating moving light effects.

Practicals—lights that are fully seen on the stage that often appear to be controlled by the characters on the stage. These would include things like lamps, overhead lights, fireplaces, and candles.

Gobos—metal or glass inserts that are cut into patterns. They are then placed in ellipsoidal lights to create patterns on the stage.

Gels—sheets of colored plastic that may be cut and placed over a beam of light to change the color.

CHAPTER TWELVE

The Work of Lighting Designer Karen Perlow

Karen Perlow is a freelance lighting designer and educator based in Boston, MA. She has been on the faculty at MIT and Northeastern University. She enjoys melding her professional and her teaching worlds by bringing her students to professional rehearsals and with discussions of her works-in-progress in the classroom. She recently designed *Far From Heaven* at Speakeasy Stage Company, *Reconsidering Hanna(h)* at Boston Playwrights' Theatre, *Dear Elizabeth* at Lyric Stage Company, and *The Little Prince* at New Repertory Theater. Additionally, Karen's work has been seen at Actor's Shakespeare Project, Central Square Theater, ART Zero Arrow, Boston Midsummer Opera, and Shakespeare & Company. Karen has been a guest designer at Boston Conservatory, Boston College, Brandeis University, and Emerson College. She is proud to serve as the treasurer of the Theater Community Benevolent Fund, an organization that helps theater artists in need. She is the recipient of the 2002, 2006, and 2008 IRNE (The Independent Reviewers of New England) Award for Best Lighting Design, and the NYC SOLO Fest Best LD in 2013. You'll find her work at karenperlowlightdesign.com.

Figure 12.1 Karen Perlow, Lighting Designer. Photo: Headshots Skylar Shankman. (Copyright © by Skylar Shankman Photography. Reprinted with permission.)

Figure 12.2 Henry V by William Shakespeare, Shakespare and Company 2002. Director: Jonathan Epstein, Scenic: Kiki Smith, Lighting: Karen Perlow, Costume: Govane Lohbauer, Actor: Allyn Burrows, Photo by Kevin Sprague. (Copyright © 2002 by Kevin Sprague. Reprinted with permission.)

Henry V

Figure 12.2 shows a scene outdoors in the evening. The challenge faced by the lighting designer is that it must seem like night, but the audience needs to see the actors clearly. The audience must suspend disbelief, and the lighting designer must assist them through a cue (look) that creates an illusion of nighttime. The designer accomplishes this by using directional lighting, colored gels, and motivated light from below. A romanticized version of night is created by using blue light on stage to create a semblance of moonlight and by creating the appearance of firelight. The stage has a trap. The piece of the stage that covers the trap is removed during this scene. Lighting instruments have been placed in this area below the stage and have been focused to hit the actor on his chest and face. These lights could be moving fixtures but are actually a much less sophisticated trio of static lights that have been programmed to "chase." Static lights that "chase" illuminate at various intensities and times to create the illusion of actual firelight, producing a sense of movement.

Reckless

Reckless is a play of poignant scenes filled with dark humor. The structure of the play requires multiple quick transitions. The design concept—and its execution—are integral to the storytelling and the transformation that happens to the characters in the course of the play. The lighting design helps to "pull" the main character from one scene to the next.

Above and behind the actor are set pieces—doorways and scrim, balls, and Christmas trees. These set pieces will change in appearance throughout the course of the play—becoming invisible, changing color, seemingly changing dimension—with the use of skilled lighting design. As you look at these three photos (Figures 12.3, 12.4, 12.5) of the same production, you will notice that there are no set changes—all of the changes in location and mood are done through lighting to help tell the story. Aiding these "sleights of hand" is the scrim—the black drop dividing the space stage right to stage left. It's a loose-weave fabric that when lit from the front, appears opaque, but when figures or scenery are illuminated behind it, becomes translucent. This simple, yet effective device can be used to create stage magic—things appearing and disappearing fluidly.

In Figure 12.3, we see a gauzy translucent fabric draped over the main character through which light can travel to illuminate the actor below. This fabric—and the light on it—create movement and may symbolize many things to the audience (protection, a dreamlike state, snow, etc). The doorways are visually dominant, the orbs hanging in the air could be Christmas ornaments or an illusion of celestial orbs. The Christmas trees that are hung behind the scrim are barely—if at all—visible. By not lighting the trees at all—they

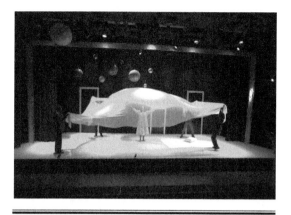

Figure 12.3 Reckless, by Craig Lucas, Speakeasy Stage 2009. Director: Scott Edmiston, Scenic: Christina Tedesco, Lighting: Karen Perlow, Costume: Charles Schoonmaker, Actors: Marianna Bassham (C) and Ensemble, Photo by Craig Bailey/Perspective Photo. (Copyright © 2009 by Karen Perlow. Reprinted with permission.)

Figure 12.4 Reckless, by Craig Lucas, Speakeasy Stage 2009. Director: Scott Edmiston, Scenic: Christina Tedesco, Lighting: Karen Perlow, Costume: Charles Schoonmaker, Actors (L to R): Marianna Bassham and Paula Plum, Photo: Craig Bailey/Perspective Photo. (Copyright © 2009 by Karen Perlow. Reprinted with permission.)

practically disappear. The scrim acts as more of an opaque drop when nothing upstage of it is lit.

In Figure 12.4, there are a number of changes in lighting that reflect what is happening in the play. This scene is a moment of clarity for the main character. The trees behind the scrim are lit by sidelight, which makes them all appear to be the same. There is a uniform visual picture created by the lights, which helps to create a mood of stability—reflecting the feelings of the character and movement of the action of the play.

Figure 12.5 is a photo of a game show scene that occurs in the play. The lights are very colorful—especially on the trees—which makes them "pop," or draw the viewer's attention. The lavish color and high intensity of light creates excitement and high energy—like that experienced on a TV game show. Additional stimulation is created in this scene by cuing the lights to "move"—the intensity of the light changes continually, and lights are turned on and off quickly in a repetitive pattern—which gives the sense of activity and moving light.

Figure 12.5 Reckless, by Craig Lucas, Speakeasy Stage 2009. Director: Scott Edmiston, Scenic: Christina Tedesco, Lighting: Karen Perlow, Costume: Charles Schoonmaker, Actors (L to R): Karl Baker Olsen, Will McGarrahan, Marianna Bassham, and Kerry Dowling, Photo by Craig Bailey/Perspective Photo. (Copyright © 2009 by Karen Perlow. Reprinted with permission.)

Cherry Docs

The design concept for this show is that nothing is hidden, everything is exposed. As in Brecht's work, the audience members are always aware that they are watching a play because they can see the theatre building all around them—nothing is masked by curtains or flats. This design concept sprang from the director's desire to present an exposed world—a world in which nothing is hidden. The set and lights also give a sense of forced perspective—everything in this world is askew. Practicals are hung at angles to keep the illusion of forced perspective. There are no scene changes in the play; therefore, much of the job of storytelling, setting mood, and representing passage of time falls on the lighting designer.

Figure 12.6 Cherry Docs by David Gow, New Repertory Theater 2010. Director: David R Gammons, Scenic: Jenna McFarland Lord, Lighting: Karen Perlow, Costume: Gail Astrid Buckley, Photo by David R. Gammons. (Copyright © 2010 by David R. Gammons. Reprinted with permission.)

In Figure 12.6, there are a variety of sources of light. There are large glass panels with lights behind. These do not practically provide a great deal of illumination on the stage but create a meaningful visual impact, leaving the audience wondering what is on the other side of these panels—is it one-way glass? Is someone behind these glass panels watching an interrogation? Is it a frosted window with daylight on the other side? Outside of the scenery (i.e., off stage) are special lights called mercury vapor lights. Mercury vapor lights are very large non-theatrical fixtures, such as those that are found in a parking lot or warehouse. In this photo, one can be seen glowing just off stage, upstage right. The green oozes onto the stage in this pre-show look because the plastic covers on the fluorescent lights are translucent. The fixtures, which provide the light in this shot, are structured so as to accommodate both fluorescent tubes and stage lights above. The fluorescent light does illuminate the stage but cannot be controlled like the theatrical light. The combination of these two types of lights "tricks" the audience into believing that the space is lit by florescent light. In truth, the stage lights are doing the lighting job that is necessary in the theatre, with instruments that can be adjusted for timing, intensity, and color. The florescent lights, which are practicals, draw the audience's focus and can give the illusion that they are the only lights on the stage.

The light cue in Figure 12.7 reveals many important aspects of designing with light. A practical is lit—hanging from the ceiling. It would appear that the light in the room is coming exclusively from this source. However, both the practical and fluorescent (which is top light) are lighting the standing actor with "support" from invisible front of house lights. Downstage, the young man is lit almost

Figure 12.7 Cherry Docs by David Gow, New Repertory Theater 2010. Director: David R Gammons, Scenic: Jenna McFarland Lord, Lighting: Karen Perlow, Costume: Gail Astrid Buckley, Actors (L to R): Benjamin Evett and Tim Eliot, Photo by David R. Gammons. (Copyright © 2010 by David R. Gammons. Reprinted with permission.)

exclusively by a theatrical effect. He is lit by a little disk halogen light—the type that is used used primarily under cabinets. The depth between the grate and the floor was only about four inches, so a theatrical light would not fit in this space. Designer Perlow had to create a fixture that would create the effect desired by the director within the structural limitations of the theatrical space.

Look at the difference in the color and intensity of the two light sources and how they reflect on the actors, costumes, and set. Look at the shadows and patterns created by the light. This light cue is meant to create a sense that the characters are separated emotionally, physically, and spiritually. Imagine taking the lighting design away. Would it be possible to create the same mood and relationship between the characters so quickly? The lighting designer has used color, pattern, shadow, and warm and cool colors to help tell the story, set the mood, and enhance the action in the scene.

Lighting designer Karen Perlow refers to the light cue in Figure 12.8 as the "come to Jesus moment" of the play. This light cue produces a warm set, the implication being that it is sunrise. This cue is created with a single source of light, a brilliant light that comes through the glass window. You can tell that there is a single source of light by looking at the shadows. Noticing where shadows fall on stage can inform the viewer as to where the light source originates.

Figure 12.9 also shows a single source of light, coming from a low boom. Ms. Perlow was asked to create "another space" for this character's monologue. This was the only moment in the production when the light came exclusively from this side of the stage. The light is also very warm and direct, and the angle at which the light is focused creates unique patterns through shadow and a softer look than we usually see. Although it cannot be seen in this picture, it is important to note that the older actor's shadow fell on the young man who was sitting against the wall—blocking him from view—creating a visual metaphor for one of the messages in the play.

Figure 12.8 Cherry Docs by David Gow, New Repertory Theater 2010. Director: David R Gammons, Scenic: Jenna McFarland Lord, Lighting: Karen Perlow, Costume: Gail Astrid Buckley, Actors (L to R): Tim Eliot and Benjamin Evett, Photo by David R. Gammons. (Copyright © 2010 by David R. Gammons. Reprinted with permission.)

Figure 12.9 Cherry Docs by David Gow, New Repertory Theater 2010. Director: David R Gammons, Scenic: Jenna McFarland Lord, Lighting: Karen Perlow, Costume: Gail Astrid Buckley, Actors: Benjamin Evett, Photo by David R. Gammons. (Copyright © 2010 by David R. Gammons. Reprinted with permission.)

The Farm

This play required a very realistic set with realistic lighting over the main playing area, with a separate other-worldly playing area. The stage was long and thin, which presented the designers with a challenge—how to create two distinct "worlds" in such a small space and on a limited scale. Another challenge faced by the designers was that the two worlds become more and more enmeshed as the play progresses.

Figure 12.10 The Farm by Walt McGough, Boston Playwrights' Theater 2011. Director: David R Gammons, Scenic: Jon Savage, Lighting: Karen Perlow, Costume: Gail Astrid Buckley, Actors (L to R): Nael Nacer, Lindsey McWhorter, and Dale Place, Photo by David R. Gammons. (Copyright © 2011 by David R. Gammons. Reprinted with permission.)

Figure 12.10 illustrates that the set was a cluttered, run down, skeevy basement office/interrogation area. Lighting designer Perlow used numerous florescent lights above the stage to create a realistic, unpleasant office lighting effect over the stage. She then created a "ghost path" area where a mysterious character lurks in the shadows. It was lit only by a repulsive green sidelight, leaving portions of the actor's face and body in shadow at all times. By lighting the stage in this way, using only color and focus of lights, a distinct contrast was created between the realistic world of the office and the "other" world.

Figure 12.11 The Farm by Walt McGough, Boston Playwrights' Theater 2011. Director: David R Gammons, Scenic: Jon Savage, Lighting: Karen Perlow, Costume: Gail Astrid Buckley, Actors (L to R): Nael Nacer, Dale Place, and Lindsey McWhorter, Photo by David R. Gammons. (Copyright © 2011 by David R. Gammons. Reprinted with permission.)

Figure 12.11 highlights the way in which the lighting changed as the mysterious character—and his world—began to engage with the realistic world. As this creepy character entered the interrogation area, the lighting in the main playing area became increasingly strange and non-realistic. This change in lighting signaled the effect the strange ghostly character's presence had on the environment and the other characters in the play. The change in light, which was coordinated with the actor's movement, enhanced the character's power and influence. The change in environment that was created by changing the color, intensity, and direction of the light as the ghostly character entered the realistic playing area communicated a very strong visual message to the audience.

Betrayal

The production concept for The Nora Theater's *Betrayal* is that the play is like a game of chess or a game of supremacy. The characters are in their own worlds, but their lives also intersect. The doors allow the characters to do a lot of eavesdropping and enable them to listen in on each other's conversations. The set and lighting (see Figure 12.12) highlight these themes. Additionally, the costume palette was extremely controlled—almost exclusively blacks and whites, with splashes of color for emphasis. All of these design elements reinforced the metaphor of a chess game and the characters in the play as the chess pieces. Pools of light are created using sharp top light specials, which allow each character's domain to be clearly defined while it also "spills" into their partners' playing area. All of the light comes from these three overhead specials, which are set at 100% intensity. The white set allows enough light to bounce up to light the actors' faces to give fill so that the actors' faces do not seem flat. The photos on the wall are also symbolic, as the photo stage right is an expanded close up of the photo center stage, which is an expanded closeup of the photo stage left. These design details create a sense of flow and rhythm to the set, as well as having a part in visually telling the story.

Figure 12.12 Betrayal by Harold Pinter, Nora Theater Company 2003, Elliott Norton Award Winner. Director: Scott Edmiston, Scenic: Janie Howland, Lighting: Karen Perlow, Costume: Gail Astrid Buckley, Actors (L to R): Joe Pacheco, Anne Gottlieb, and Jason Asprey, Photo by Karen Perlow. (Copyright © 2003 by Karen Perlow. Reprinted with permission.)

Cat on a Hot Tin Roof

Cat on a Hot Tin Roof takes place in the deep South of the United States during the summer on one of the longest days of the year. The events of the play occur over the course of one afternoon and evening. Director Scott Edmiston wanted his designers to create a strong sense of HEAT; lighting designer Karen Perlow claimed it was "over the top hot!" In this production, the stage never went to black. Lights were on from pre-show until the final moment of the play. The set was primarily white in color—which allowed Perlow to completely change the color of the set with light cues. White sets are also a challenge, however, as they create a lot of bounce, and particular attention must be played to lighting intensity. The upstage walls were made of a translucent chiffon material, framed by a solid cornice, and fixed with solid door frames, which indicated the delineation between the interior and exterior. Hanging from the columns on the exterior is gypsy moss—a vegetation that is common in the southern United States. The use of the semi-transparent chiffon by scenic designer Janie Howland enhanced Perlow's ability to create gorgeous light cues that intensify mood and the themes of the play while also creating a sense of passage of time and change in temperature inside and out.

Figure 12.13 Cat on a Hot Tin Roof, by Tennessee Williams, The Lyric Stage Company 2009. Director: Scott Edmiston, Scenic: Janie Howland, Lighting: Karen Perlow, Costume: Gail Astrid Buckley, Photo by Janie Howland. (Copyright © 2009 by Janie Howland. Reprinted with permission.)

Figure 12.13 is the pre-show light cue, which gives the audience a sense of the ambience of the play. The lighting creates a feeling of romanticized time of day. The exterior is summer daylight. Warm-to-burning hot tones fill the interior, and beautiful cool tones are projected on the cyclorama upstage, fashioning a strong delineation between the two atmospheres. The gypsy moss is lit from the side, which generates a sense of graceful elegance on the exterior porch upstage and creates a sense of depth on a stage that actually had very little depth.

Time passes, and the light cue in Figure 12.14 reveals a very hot sunset pouring into the room. The action of the play is very fiery at this point as well. The cyclorama upstage is lit with an orange light, and the chiffon is not lit at all, enabling the chiffon material to lose much of its translucency, creating a more "solid-wall"

Figure 12.14 Cat on a Hot Tin Roof, by Tennessee Williams, The Lyric Stage Company 2009. Director: Scott Edmiston, Scenic: Janie Howland, Lighting: Karen Perlow, Costume: Gail Astrid Buckley, Actors: Kelby Akin and Georgia Lyman, Photo by Janie Howland. (Copyright © 2009 by Janie Howland. Reprinted with permission.)

effect. The cool exterior has disappeared, just as the cool exteriors Maggie and Brick maintain at the start of the play have melted.

When Figure 12.15 is compared to Figures 12.13 and 12.14, it is clear how much the lights change the color of the set. This cue, which occurs late in the play, is moonlight. The colors are cool-to-cold inside and out. All of the warmth is gone from the environment—just as any warmth that existed in the family has also disappeared at this point in the play. For the first time, the lamp (a practical) is illuminated next to the bed, indicating that the room is lit by this device and not by the natural light coming in through the windows. The cyclorama is lit in a beautiful blue, and there is a device called a moon box that is hung against the cyclorama upstage left that looks like an actual full moon.

Figure 12.15 Cat on a Hot Tin Roof, by Tennessee Williams, The Lyric Stage Company 2009. Director: Scott Edmiston, Scenic: Janie Howland, Lighting: Karen Perlow, Costume: Gail Astrid Buckley, Photo by Janie Howland. (Copyright © 2009 by Janie Howland. Reprinted with permission.)

Italian Girl in Algiers

Figure 12.16 demonstrates how the silhouette of a set can be revealed through a light cue. A silhouette allows the audience to see the outline and form of the set piece, leaving the set piece's details in shadow. In this picture, the cyclorama is lit by a blue light, which produces most of the light in the cue—and because the set is lit from the upstage cyclorama without front light, a silhouette is created. Another element of note in this cue are the practicals on the walls of the buildings, which seem to provide illumination and pattern on the floor—but in actuality do not. The pattern on the floor looks like it is being created by the hanging lanterns. It is, in fact, coming from a gobo in a lighting instrument that is hanging above the stage and focused on the floor, which gives the illusion of casting a shadow.

Figure 12.16 Italian Girl in Algiers by Gioachinno Rossini, Boston Midsummer Opera 2011. Director: Drew Minter, Music Director and Conductor: Susan Davenny Wyner, Scenic: Stephen Dobay, Lighting: Karen Perlow, Costumes: Charles Schoonmaker, Photo by Stephen Dobay. (Copyright © 2011 by Stephen Dobay. Reprinted with permission.)

MacBeth

Figure 12.17 from *MacBeth* represents the scene in which a large army is discovered hiding in a forest. With a small cast and stage, the designers were called upon to help create an image that would imply an army hiding in a forest. This concept was created using a few actors holding branches behind a translucent piece of fabric. In this picture, the wall behind the actors was lit, and they were downstage of it in silhouette. The gauze was downstage of the actors, and the light that was focused on the wall illuminated a clean outline of the actors but no color or details.

Figure 12.17 MacBeth by William Shakespeare, Actors' Shakespeare Project 2012. Director: Paula Plum, Scenic: Jenna MacFarland Lord, Lighting: Karen Perlow, Costumes: Anna-Alisa Belous. (Copyright © 2012 by J. Stratton McCrady. Reprinted with permission.)

MIT Dramashop

Figure 12.18 is another example of actors behind a drop. In this photo, however, the actors are back lit at approximately chest height. This allows their shadows to be projected on the muslin drop DS of them. What's so wonderful about this simple effect is that the further the actors are from the material, the larger their shadows appear. When they get very close to the drop, their shadows are life-sized. Hamlet is SR, close to the drop, and the crowd carrying his dead father is approximately two feet away.

Figure 12.18 MIT Dramashop 2003. Director: Janet Sondenberg, Lighting: Karen Perlow. (Copyright © 2003 by Eric Levenson. Reprinted with permission.)

CHAPTER THIRTEEN

Specific Elements of Sound and/or Music Design

PROCESS SPECIFIC TO SOUND DESIGN

Unlike the other design elements, which are primarily visual, sound and music design is completely aural. The sound designer will do his research using recordings and experimenting with the sounds that instruments and objects make. The sound designer will then make recordings of possible music and sound cues for the design team and director to listen to. Together with the director, the sound designer will select the sound cues and music, and the sound designer will do what is necessary to create the sound track for the production. Sometimes sounds will be created live; other times they will be recorded.

TOOLS SPECIFIC TO SOUND

Live sound effects—still used on many low-budget/low-tech productions.

Live music—used in many productions. The musicians may perform on stage, off stage, or in an orchestra pit. Although it is more expensive to employ live musicians for the run of a performance, many directors prefer the sound and flexibility of live music.

Sound Reinforcement System (SRS)—This system is composed of microphones that are connected to an audio signal processor, which connects to an audio power amplifier, which is, in turn, linked to a loudspeaker system.

- **Microphones** ("mics," pronounced "mikes")—A microphone is a sensor that converts sound (acoustics) into an electrical signal. In theatre, microphones are most often used to amplify actors' voices. Actors with trained voices who are in a space with decent acoustics and not competing against an orchestra will often forgo microphones. The use of microphones for stage acting is a relatively new phenomenon. Before the invention of this technology, actors relied on their well-trained voices and wisely-constructed venues with superior acoustics to enable the members of the audience in the last row to hear and understand every utterance in a live show. However, more and more productions—especially musicals, performances in very large venues, and those with very loud sound effects that play over dialogue—have come to rely on using wireless body microphones for main characters and area mics to amplify other voices on the stage. Advances in technology have brought about smaller, less expensive wireless microphones. Because of this fact, many theatres and actors have come to rely on this amplification. Many theatre patrons object to actors using mics on stage for non-musical productions because they do not like the "canned" sound. Theatre practitioners are divided on this subject.
- **Audio power amplifier (amp)**—This is an electronic amplifier that amplifies low-power audio signals to a level suitable for driving loudspeakers.
- **Loudspeaker (speaker)**—This is an electroacoustic transducer (converts one form of energy to another) that produces sound in response to an electrical audio signal input.
- **Audio signal processor/audio effects unit**—This device, sometimes referred to as an "audio processor," is used to intentionally alter auditory signals or sound. The sound effects or audio effects unit alters sound to create effects. This unit allows the designer to create effects within prerecorded or live sound. Effects include echo, pitch shift, time stretching, chorus, robotic voice effects, or filtering.
- **Recordings—sound effects and music**. Sound designers often create and record their own music and sound effects for a production. Many sound designers are also musicians and consider the sound design to be their score of the production. There are also prerecorded stock sound effects and recordings of music through which they may score a show. Permission must be obtained if a sound designer chooses music that is under a copyright.

PART

Four

ENHANCEMENTS TO THEATRE THROUGHOUT HISTORY— DIRECTING, TECHNICAL SUPPORT, AND THE CRITIC

CHAPTER FOURTEEN

The Director ‖

WHAT IS A THEATRE DIRECTOR?

The director in the theatre is the person who is at the center of the creative process. She is the person who takes all of the various pieces of the production and molds them into a cohesive work of art.

SKILLS AND TRAINING NEEDED

A director must have knowledge of the various creative arts that make up a theatrical production. She must have a vocabulary with which to speak with artists, technicians, and administrators.

A director needs to be curious about life and work hard to educate herself about humankind throughout history.

Many directors begin their work in theatre as actors, writers, stage managers, or designers. At some point, they decide they are passionate about bringing their vision of a play to an audience. They like to analyze a play and work out how to bring their concept of that play to the artists with whom they will work, and then work with them to bring that concept to an audience. They look at that play and they imagine all aspects of it: the acting, the set, the costumes, the music, the sounds, the relationship to the audience. Many directors feel as if they see the play in their imagination as they are reading it. If they are actors, they may move from focusing primarily on one character to focusing on all of the characters, where they are, what they are wearing. If they are costume designers, their focus may move from concentrating solely on what the characters are wearing to what they are saying and doing and to finding the play's rhythm.

Most directors, like most theatre artists, are first exposed to theatre in school, in community performing-arts programs, or by attending a production (professional, community, or educational). Educational programs and youth theatre programs usually have adults who serve as teachers/directors. It is unusual for young people to have the opportunity to direct productions. However, the early training they acquire in school and in community groups can give them strong foundations, which will serve them well as directors in the future.

From these playful beginnings, many directors are bitten by the theatre bug, and they continue to study, practice, and work in theatre to hone their craft.

In contemporary Western society, much of the advanced training available for directors has moved into the university setting. Most directors who work professionally have at least a bachelor's degree (BS, BA, or BFA) and many have a master's of fine arts (MFA) in directing. Some directors who have worked in the theatre for a long time may not have a degree and learned their craft through apprenticeship programs. However, this has become increasingly rare since training has moved more extensively into higher education.

WHAT DOES THE DIRECTOR DO?

The director has a vision for her particular production, and all elements of the production are meant to support and enhance that vision.

HOW A DIRECTOR WORKS: PROCESS

Directors are artists, and as artists, each director will work a bit differently. What you will find is that many directors work in the way described in the following example because it is a proven method. However, as in all aspects of theatre, along with the traditional methods of working and performance, new ways of creating are constantly being explored.

Working with a Written Script: Vision and Design
If a director is working with a published written script, she would most likely work in a manner similar to that described in the following journal recording of the director's process.

Journal entry that might appear at the beginning of the director's process—interpretation and creation of a cohesive creative vision for the production:

Tennessee Williams' Cat on a Hot Tin Roof is a beautifully written piece that is filled with abundant opportunities for all artists involved. As I read the play and imagine the world, the characters, the movement, the rhythm, and the beautiful sounds of the text, I want to explore bringing that vision to life. Perhaps I can convince one of my artistic director friends that it is a show that belongs in their season? In order to make the pitch to someone to produce the show in his season, I will need to have a solid idea of what I want to do with the show. I better get to work!

(Alternate scenarios might be that you are a student director, you have the monetary means to produce a production yourself or with a group of colleagues, an artistic director or producer who knows your work asks you to direct a production, or you are the artistic director of a theatre company and want to include this production as part of your season and want to direct it yourself.)

Journal entry that might appear nine months to many years before the production is seen by an audience:

I feel as if I have read this script about a hundred times. I have seen at least ten productions of the play. What is it that keeps drawing me back to this play? What is it about the story that speaks to me? What is it that I want an audience to take away from a production that I direct? I think it is the theme of denial of reality. I want to play with this idea of fantasy and reality. Why do we continue to deny the elephant in the room? What is it about human nature that pushes some of us to hold on to a life of fantasy in an attempt to survive? Is it the way that we survive pain and heartbreak? Is it the way we attempt to cheat death, to control a life that we have no control over? The forces of nature are so much stronger than we tiny humans are. These are reflected in the power of the storm, the power of terminal illness, the power of the sexuality we are born with, the power of the feelings that rage inside of us (love, fear, anger, jealousy, greed, etc.). This is how I want to approach this play—as a struggle between fantasy and reality; of power and powerlessness. I need to go back and look at the script again with this vision in mind. The text, the acting, the design must all support this vision. Things to research:

- *Reality and fantasy in art and music,*
- *The time and location in which the play is set,*
- *Views toward homosexuals during this time period,*
- *High school sports heroes during this time period,*
- *Suicide,*
- *Tennessee Williams's bio, and*
- *Alcoholism.*

At Least Six Months Before the Production is Seen by an Audience, Production Meetings Begin

Production meetings are those in which the director and her team meet to make the director's vision a reality. The director's vision is often enhanced and more fully developed by the other professionals with whom she works at this stage in the process. Production meetings bring designers (costume, set, lighting, and sound), administrators (the people with the budgets and timelines), director, technical director, and stage manager together to make what is in the director's imagination a reality. Many directors have designers with whom they work continually. There are good and bad aspects to this. Communication is often easier if you have worked with someone a good deal, and this can be advantageous to the process. However, working with someone new can open your eyes to looking at the world in a different way.

Production meeting #1—This is a critical meeting for the director. The director must explain in words, pictures, sounds—whatever means available and necessary—what is in her imagination. She must explain how she "sees" the production, what feeling or mood she wants the show to have, and the major and minor themes of the production that she wants to communicate to an audience. At this meeting, designers will listen, watch, and ask a lot of questions. This meeting can be very challenging for a director and it will test her communication skills. When was the last time you tried to explain what was in your imagination with words, pictures, and sounds? The director is also communicating the feeling of the show. This is a very challenging aspect to communicate and requires a good grasp of many different aspects of life, including, perhaps, art, history, psychology, music, nature, literature, science—basically any aspect of life may be expressed in a play. We know this because theatre is a reflection of life.

Designers will go away from this meeting with a clear idea of the director's vision and will begin their research.

Production meetings #2 and beyond—The team (designers, director, stage manager, technical director, administrators) has a number of meetings at which they talk about and present drawings, models, and audio clips that will create the world of the production and fulfill and enhance the director's vision. The director must be able to work collaboratively and lead the team. The director must be aware of budgetary constraints and must sometimes help designers find ways to create something while staying within budget. The team will decide on a design, and the technical director will create a schedule that will afford enough time to complete all elements of the design in time for technical rehearsals.

Working with a Written Script: Casting the Performers

The playwright often offers a physical description of the characters in the written script. As the director reads the script numerous times in preparation for work on the production, she may have a visual sense of what the characters look like. This is called character *type*. Oftentimes, actors are cast by physical type. This is referred to as type casting. Many directors also have a strong sense of a character's essence. In casting a production, the way in which a talented actor's quality or essence matches that of the director's vision of the character can be as important, if not more so, in the casting decision than an actor's type. Directors may find the quality of a character in an actor of a different gender, race, or age than the playwright has written. Many directors choose to keep an open mind when they go into auditions. The best directors will look beyond an actor's exterior shape, size, age, gender, and skin color to find the actor who can best portray the role. Experienced directors who have confidence in their vision and abilities may even take what some consider risks in their casting because they believe these risks will serve their overall vision of the production more completely than more traditional choices. One very famous example of this is the role of the Leading Player in the musical *Pippin*. This role was originally written for an older white man.

> *A smaller role, the Old Man—leader of a performance troupe—proved more difficult until Fosse called in* Jesus Christ Superstar *alum Ben Vereen (decidedly not an old man [back in 1971]). In Ebony magazine, Fosse noted that the role "kept growing with Ben's ability to take anything and make it into something wonderful." The character was changed to "The Leading Player," and Schwartz expanded it to mimic the emcee in Cabaret, adding a new opening number for Vereen, "Magic to Do."*

> —Lindsay Champion, *The Magic Touch:*
> *Follow Pippin's Extraordinary Journey*
> *from Student Production to Broadway Sensation*

Vereen went on to win a Best Actor Tony Award for his performance. Years later, A.R.T. artistic director, Diane Paulus, revived the show and cast a young African American woman, Patina Miller, to play the role. She, too, won a Tony Award for Best Actress in a Musical in 2013. This was the first time in history that two actors of different genders won a Tony for playing the same role.

Many directors like to do their own casting and feel as if this is an integral aspect of a successful production. In smaller, non-commercial theatres, directors hold auditions for some or all of the roles. Some actors are called back after auditions. The callback gives the director an opportunity to work with actors and pair actors together to get a sense of their chemistry. Oftentimes, directors may choose a show knowing whom they would like to cast in a major role. Other roles are then cast to complement the skills of the pre-cast actor.

Professional directors who work a great deal may want to use a casting director to cast a show. Casting directors are professionals who are very good at what they do. They will discuss with the director what she wants and will find the people who fulfill those requirements. Sometimes, casting directors will hold large casting calls and narrow the selection down to a few actors, and the director will make the final decision.

Working with a Written Script: Rehearsals with Actors

Once the show is cast, the director begins rehearsals with the actors and the stage manager. At the first read-through of the script, the director will explain her vision for the production, and designers may show the cast what the design will look like, which will help them to visualize the world of the production their characters will inhabit. Depending on the amount of time available (this can vary from two weeks to a year or more), the director will spend her days and/or nights and weekends meeting with the cast in different configurations and working through the script. The play is usually divided into small units, and the director works on each unit with the actors a number of times before technical elements are introduced.

During rehearsals, the director must be adept at many skills:

- Coaching actors.
- Problem-solving.
- Exploring intentions and action.
- Watching from the outside, as if she is the audience, while trying to evoke creative inspiration from the actor.
- Suggesting or requiring certain physical movements from the actor to create stage pictures and blocking.

In many ways, directing a company of creative artists is similar to parenting. Very often, close relationships or bonds are formed between the ensemble members and the director. This is to be expected, as the ensemble needs to be able to trust the director to lead them and get their best work out of them, while staying true to the vision of the whole production. The director must deal with many personalities and must find the way to work best and guide the company.

Some directors, like some parents, are dictatorial or authoritarian; they bark orders and can seem distant and aloof. They have a very strong idea of what they want in their heads, and they will keep pushing the actors until they get it. These directors often are very specific in their instructions for movement, voice, tempo, blocking, etc. Some actors are drawn to this type of director and claim that this type of very specific direction during rehearsal allows for greater freedom in performance. Like a dancer who is doing a choreographed piece, the performer's body is trained to do certain things automatically, allowing the actor to focus on the creativity and emotional connection that flows from within, with no concern for what the body is doing.

Other directors are more similar to the authoritative parent who sets down guidelines, a creative framework, and an interpretation in which the artists work. This director uses rehearsal and production meetings to give artists an opportunity to explore creative ideas and work collaboratively. This director greatly values the talents and expertise of the artists with whom he is working. He expects the artists to come to rehearsals fully prepared with many ideas. He is open to the team's discovery of and finding inspiration in each other's work in the design and rehearsal process. He also expects the artist to contribute to the decision-making, but it is understood that he has the final say on the direction that the production takes. This type of director tends to establish strong bonds with his collaborative artists—bonds based on trust and mutual respect. This type of environment allows the artists a freedom to take risks, make mistakes, and discover new things.

All successful directors, no matter what their directing style, are charismatic leaders. They tend to be dynamic individuals who bring a lot of talent, knowledge, experience, and enthusiasm to the creative process. Directors are usually highly energetic and inspirational. The best directors love people. They bring out the best in artists and get a reputation for doing so. They can motivate artists to perform at a higher level.

Directors will usually break a script down into smaller sections for rehearsal and work moments. Most directors expect actors to come into rehearsals having done homework to prepare. The rehearsal process is then used to try things out and to afford the company an opportunity to create a cohesive living production through trial and error under the guidance of a trusted artistic leader. Rehearsal is a time for discovery—physical, vocal, artistic, emotional, and intellectual. A director will plan some stage pictures and some beats and moments in the production. Oftentimes, however, the most inspiring moments in a production are those that are discovered by the ensemble as they work together in rehearsal. Rehearsal is a time of collaboration between all of the artists involved a production. There is a lot of starting and stopping, and the director usually works on her feet, constantly interacting with the actors to elicit the best possible performance.

Once each small beat, bit, or section of the script has been explored, the director will begin to put the pieces back together. Toward the middle of the rehearsal period, the director will begin to run through longer sections of the script without stopping the actors. At this time, the director begins to work on the flow of the production and the timing of moments and the production as a whole. Sections of the performance that are problematic or that do not seem to be working will be rehearsed more extensively, and all members of the ensemble will be searching for ways to solve the production's problems.

Toward the end of the rehearsal period, the director will begin to run through the entire production without stopping, noting any sections that need changes and additional rehearsal time. The director is now focused on timing, flow, story, and impact of the entire production. These run-throughs are the last time that actors will have the director's undivided attention.

Working with a Written Script: Technical Rehearsals Without and With Actors

The end of the rehearsal period is dedicated to incorporating the technical elements (set, lights, props, sound, and costume) into the performance. Directors will often work with designers alone, without performers, to set technical elements with the designers and crew. Directors and designers will set each technical element in the show in order. This is called a cue-to-cue. If there is time, these members of the team will then run through all of the cues without actors in what is often called a *dry tech*. Once this is completed, actors will be called for a costume parade, which enables the director and design team to see the actors together in costume on the set and under the lights. Then, the company does *wet tech*, in which technical cues (set, light, sound, and costume) are done with actors in a cue-to-cue with sections of the script. This is a particularly critical time for any design elements that involve timing—any light, sound, costume, or set changes that occur during lines or movement. This is a very stressful period for a director, as only she knows exactly what she is looking for, and, at times, this can be accomplished only through trial and error. Very often, cues will need to repeated numerous times to get the rhythm just right. There is a lot of starting and stopping, it is exhausting, and everyone must remain focused and attentive for long periods of time.

The final chance the director has to make the production achieve her vision is during the dress rehearsals. Directors watch dress rehearsals and take notes, which are then given to members of the production team. If all has gone as planned, this is a time for fine-tuning. But because theatre is a live art form, with so many moving and temperamental parts, things don't always go as planned. Major changes sometimes need to be made for the good of the production as a whole. All must trust that the director is the person who can lead the collaborators to the realization of a beautiful and moving artistic creation.

Opening Night

The opening of a show marks the end of the director's contract. In a union house in the United States, the director cannot give notes after the show opens. All notes must come from the stage manager. The director will attend the opening performance and celebrate with the company afterwards. She will then move on to her next engagement. She may return, at times, to check up on the production and ensure that her vision is being maintained by the stage manager. If it is not, she will communicate with the stage manager and expect the production to, once again, represent the production that she created.

The following article by Michel St. Denis explores more deeply the art of directing and the collaborative art of theatre.

STYLE IN ACTING, DIRECTING, AND DESIGNING

At one end of the directing spectrum is the interpretive director like Saint-Denis, at the other the auteur director, who has become more prominent in the last fifty years. The term, borrowed from French cinema, refers to the authorial practice of the director, whose radical modifications of the text diminish the playwright's significance. The auteur director was a further development of Saint-Denis's misprised stylising director for whom powerful images or a narrowly focused interpretation were at least as important as the script. Differences between the interpretive and the auteur director can be summed up in the following ways. The interpretive director endeavors to uncover the playwright's intention; the authorial director to impose his or her own intention, using the text as a point of departure. Most contemporary directors fall somewhere in between.

The fact that Saint-Denis saw the director's role as interpretive did not mean that he found it devoid of imagination. It is the director who animates the production based on his or her understanding of it, transfiguring words on a page into a visual and auditory aesthetic experience. For Saint-Denis, the ideal director operates more as the *éminence grise* behind the production guiding the practitioners towards the desired results than as a star whose influence overpowers both the play and production.

Saint-Denis believed that theatre in the mid-twentieth century was once again in transition, theatrical modernisation on an international scale having been achieved by the first generation of reforming directors. Prognostication is always risky, but Saint-Denis was confident in predicting the dramatist's reinstatement as the theatre's central figure. When George Devine, Saint-Denis's friend, disciple, and former colleague, founded the English Stage Company in 1956, his intention was to encourage the development of playwrights whose work would represent a changed and changing England. In pursuit of that aim, in 1958 he established a Writers' Workshop. Many in the first group, which included Arnold Wesker, Anne Jellicoe, Edward Bond, John Arden, and the 1986 Nobel Laureate in literature,

Wole Soyinka—almost all under thirty—were politically engaged leftists writing about contemporary problems as seen from the working class. Saint-Denis attended some of their early meetings, which he describes here in a positive light, suppressing his concerns. On the one hand, he applauded the discovery of young dramatists; on the other, he feared that their work was too naturalistic and hearkened back to Antoine and the Théâtre Libre. When Saint-Denis gave this lecture series, few premieres of the Workshop playwrights had taken place. The coming years would see the English Stage at the Royal Court become a leader in the production of new plays.

Interestingly, Brecht, whom Saint-Denis judges too close in time to assess fully, was also a catalyst for the development of English playwriting. Almost coincident with the opening of the Royal Court in April of 1956 was the first visit of Brecht's Company, the Berliner Ensemble, four months later. (A second visit occurred in 1956.) In some ways, this first visit was akin to the arrival of the Quinze in London, some twenty-five years earlier. Once again, the younger generation of theatre practitioners was excited by a different style of drama (which, performed in a foreign language, was only partially understood), novel production techniques, and brilliant, innovative, non-psychological acting. Brecht's influence played itself out in a different way from Saint-Denis's. Saint-Denis as we know, become a major force in England as teacher and director. The Berliner Ensemble's visits

provided an inspiration for change, an opportunity to create another kind of British theatre, which sometimes called itself Brechtian. Playwrights, particularly those who were politically engaged, began experimenting with Brecht's epic style, finding it a more appropriate, imaginative, and theatrical language than traditional naturalism for the expression of their ideas.

While Saint-Denis was correct in foreseeing a burgeoning of playwriting, contrary to his opinion, the director did not lose status. The star director continued to make significant contributions, some of which built on the traditions of the 'great reformers', some of which took the theatre in different directions. Although the director as creator still raises hackles in some quarters, the idea has gained wide acceptance, in part because of a philosophical and literary shift that Saint-Denis could not have foreseen, deconstruction. In brief and very simply, deconstruction devalued language, questioning its capacity to represent truth, making the text untrustworthy.

The work of the director in the theatre is sometimes exaggerated, sometimes disparaged, but it is on the director's work that the theatre producer or manager still depends to make as sure as possible that a play is going to be a success. He also depends of course on the star actor; but he does not depend on the actor at the expense of the director. A theatrical production needs the director's talent, his personality, his imagination, his power of attraction, his authority over the actors and all the other people who collaborate in the show. It needs the confidence which he can inspire. The director is the centre of the organisation, he is the link connecting together all the elements which are involved in a modern production and which being more specialised than ever before, have a tendency to fall apart. He stands for unity, he is the guarantee of intelligence, of efficiency, of quality. I am a director myself!

During the last fifty years theatrical conditions have raised the director to an intoxicating position. Hatred, flattered, beloved in turns, he has enjoyed so many privileges that one is hesitant to speak about them.

It has been said that during the first half of the present century directors have made a more creative contribution to the theatre than the dramatists.

In dramatic literature the period was not a very productive one, and it is clear that when plays are made of the sort of literature which is antipathetic to the stage, and when dramatists are more attracted by ideas than by people, then the director, living and working as he does amidst scenic realities, has the game in his hands.

Although it may be a debatable point, it would seem that the innovations and changes which have transformed the theatre since the end of the nineteenth century have been due primarily to Antoine, Stanis-lavsky, Gordon Craig, Adolphe Appia, Granville Barker,[1] Max Rein-hardt, and Jacques Copeau, rather than to Ibsen, Strindberg, Chekhov, Shaw, Pirandello,[2] Claudel, Giraudoux, or O'Neill.[3] Those directors were 'reformers': they dealt with every aspect of the theatre: they did much to change the form of the theatre in which they worked.

During the last fifty years we had seen the contribution of the music hall, the experiments of the Russians

---

1   Harley Granville Barker (1877–1946) was a British actor, playwright, critic, and during the early years of the twentieth century considered an experimental director. Two of Granville Barker's most significant accomplishments were the launching of George Bernard Shaw as a major playwright, and his approach to Shakespeare's plays. Saint-Denis found his Prefaces to Shakespeare, which discuss the plays from a director's perspective, an invaluable reference.

2   Although Pirandello (1867–1936) was also a novelist and short story writer, he is best known as a dramatist. His most celebrated plays are metatheatrical; that is, he makes use of the theatre as a metaphor. His themes and conflicts revolve around the impossibility of discerning the difference between reality and illusion. Pirandello's plays were little known in France until Georges Pitoëff's 1923 production of Six Characters in Search of an Author, almost certainly seen by Saint-Denis, who was then working in Paris. In 1939, Pirandello became a Nobel laureate in literature.

3   Eugene O'Neill (1888–1953) was the first important American playwright and the only one to receive a Nobel Prize. He experimented with a variety of styles and forms, much as his inspiration August Strindberg had. O'Neill wrote realistic, historical, and expressionistic plays. Like his European avant-garde counterparts, he explored masks (Great God Brown). In Strange Interlude, he revived the soliloquy in order to reveal the characters' unconscious. A number of his works delve into the psychological theories of his day.

in the 1920s,[4] the discoveries of Jean-Louis Barrault in adapting the works of Faulkner, Knut Hamsun, and Cervantes,[5] and the imaginative ideas of W. B. Yeats[6] who was both a poet and dramatist; today we see the development of musical comedy, the success of Marcel Marceau,[7] and the work of Bertolt Brecht who was also a scenic reformer, though he is still too close to us for the real nature of his contribution to be clear; and above all we have the achievements of the cinema where the director has almost replaced the author: all this, in one way or another, underlines the importance of the field in which directors have shown their influence. It all belongs now to theatre history and has been recorded in books; but what has not yet been said, and what I believe to be true, is that this period of the director's supremacy is beginning to pass, anyway in Central and Western Europe.

The tendency in Europe, and very particularly in France, is now to deny that the director is what is called a creative artist. I can see the same tendency in London. The policy of an active theatrical organisation in London, the Royal Court Theatre, which shelters the English Stage Company, is resolutely to give first place to the dramatist. The Company is organised to stimulate the writing of as many contemporary plays as possible. Simple methods of staging these plays, far from spoiling them, should enhance their qualities. Meetings with young dramatists take place on Saturday afternoons. Ideas and criticisms are exchanged. Numerous people are constantly at work reading plays. I suppose you felt the same need

---

4   In the 1920s, there was a period of relative artistic freedom in Soviet Russia, which gave rise to a burst of creativity that would be stifled within a few years. During that brief moment, Russia's leading anti-realist directors Vsevolod Meyerhold (1874–1940), Alexander Tairov (1885–1950), and Evgeny Vakhtangov (1883–1929) staged some of their most innovative productions. It was also then that Meyerhold brought to fruition theatrical biomechanics, his anti-psychological movement-based acting technique. The crackdown that followed led to the sterile theatre Saint-Denis saw in the 1950s.

5   Jean-Louis Barrault, a proponent of movement theatre, gained fame in 1935 with his first production, a mime adaptation of William Faulkner's novel *As I Lay Dying*. In 1937, he incorporated dance and mask into Cervantes' sixteenth-century play *The Siege of Numancia* and in 1939 he adapted Knut Hamsun's novel *Hunger* for the stage, again integrating mime.

6   William Butler Yeats (1865–1939) was a prolific Irish poet and playwright, who won the Nobel Prize for Literature in 1923. His theatrical aesthetic shared commonalities with Saint-Denis's. His plays drew on the French symbolists and the Japanese Noh drama. One of his ambitions was to revive verse drama. He rejected psychological characterisation, scenic naturalism, and realistic acting. He was interested in the ritual aspects of theatre. It was Yeats's adaptation of Sophocles' *Oedipus* that Saint-Denis used in his celebrated 1945 production.

7   Marcel Marceau (1923–2007) did much to popularise mime through his international tours. He learned his craft with the master mime Étienne Decroux (1898–1991), who had briefly been a Copiau.

when you established the Playwrights' Company in America?[8]

What is the reason for this tendency? Is it simply a swing of the pendulum? I have already emphasised–for it is one of the themes of these lectures–that our period has a realistic character. Obviously the theatre as a form of entertainment will go on. It will always go on. But even the connotation of the word 'entertainment' has now changed considerably. People are becoming increasingly concerned with what a play means. When I look at the theatre list in the American papers I am struck by the development of the off-Broadway shows. And on Broadway itself . . . I don't say the meaning of the plays is always satisfactory, but I do say that the meaning is there, and it is on the meaning that the emphasis is put, even in musical plays. *West Side Story* is not simply entertainment. The dance part, which is the most interesting, has a meaning. Since the war, there has grown up a kind of necessity for contemporary works which deal with the position of man in modern society. This trend is equally evident in the English and French theatres.

And this need for a meaning, whether human, moral, social, or even metaphysical, is naturally connected with a liking for realism, for reality in all its aspects. And this liking for reality goes right against sheer exhibitionism, and entertainment for entertainment's sake. It goes against the spectacular director. It demands plays which have something to say.

But to say something effectively in the theatre one needs two things: substance, and the means to express it. In our transitional theatre the dramatists are like the architects, the scene designers and the directors: they are all in search of forms, of methods of transposition, of style.

If then plays are to come first, let us look at their evolution before we examine the work of the director any further.

To express modern reality in all its complexity we have to discover new forms: hence, our curiosity, our intensive study of the past, our new theories and manifestos. Painters and sculptors have done it before us–the theatre always comes last–but now, finally, we are open to all sorts of influences.

First and foremost, the influence of the Far East; of the Chinese and Japanese theatres which, for poetical purposes, invented the revolving stage and the wonderful bridges projecting into the auditorium; instruments to relate space to the passing of time, not used at all for the purposes of practical realism.

In Japan we find the Noh players and the Noh play, its stage surrounded by the public on three sides, its

---

8 The Playwrights' Company was founded in 1938 by five well-known dramatists: Maxwell Anderson, S. N. Behrman, Sidney Howard, Elmer Rice, and Robert Sherwood. The organisation's purpose was to produce the members' plays. By the time the Playwrights' Company disbanded in 1960, it had produced more than seventy plays.

costumes which are built on the actors like a piece of architecture; with its choruses of singers and musicians, with its feeling of eternity.[9]

The modern theatre, following Bertolt Brecht, likes to be called 'epic' and the word has met with considerable success in Europe. But that is only one aspect of a world-wide movement which was started under the influence of the Far Eastern theatre. Yeats was first in the field. Thornton Wilder anticipated Brecht when he wrote a play like *Our Town*.[10] And most of André Obey's plays, written for the Compagnie des Quinze, like *Bataille de la Marne* and *Loire*,[11] can be called 'epic'.

And now we must look at our own classics from the same point of view.

We do not go back to our classics simply out of respect for the past. We do not want to be congealed by our respect. By looking at the Greeks, the Spaniards, the Elizabethans, by looking at Shakespeare as well as at the Chinese and Japanese theatres, we are trying to find resources for our modern world, for our modern art, our modern theatre. We are trying to rediscover secrets of composition, of construction, of language, we are trying to rediscover what is meant by form in order that we may express substance: for modern realism needs new instruments with which to reach the heart of reality. We want to develop realism, not to kill it. There is only one theatre and it is in constant evolution as time goes by.

There is no question of acting all the classics. To put on the whole of Shakespeare from first to last, systematically, seems to me the most discouraging undertaking. In suggesting that we make a choice, let us select those classics which can be of concern to us today.

This return to the great works of the past must be achieved in a way that will attract not only scholars but a good proportion of the general public. It requires knowledge and appreciation. It should be part of a policy. It demands conviction and skill from manager and director alike.

---

9   See footnote 5 in Chapter 8 for a fuller description.

10 Wilder did not anticipate Brecht, since Brecht began writing earlier. His *Threepenny Opera*, produced in 1928, makes use of alienation effect. The strongest influence on Wilder's *Our Town* (1938) was, as he informed Saint-Denis, *Le Viol de Lucrèce*. The Quinze and Obey used techniques that paralleled Brecht's alienation effect, although their purpose was dissimilar. Wilder's *Our Town*, despite its sentimentality, is reminiscent of Brecht in its effort to make the audience conscious of the fact they were watching a play. Its non-chronological structure, use of a narrator, sparse and non-realistic scenery, short scenes, and breaking of the fourth wall can be viewed as alienation effects.

11 *Loire*, produced in 1933, is an allegorical and, in Saint-Denis's terms, poetic play, whose main character, the Loire River, is played by a woman and its main action a flood. The conflict is between the natural and the human world. Its epic quality can perhaps be found in its frank theatricality, its non-psychologically based characters, and its use of music.

Let us now consider the director and direction.

The first problem for a director is to select a play. The choice is important and should have an idea behind it. I have often seen the following extraordinary situation. A director is rung up and asked to direct a play. He reads it, he doesn't like it, or not much, and he says yes, finding in his indifference a sort of professional virtue because it's good to do what you don't like (as if the absence of love could lead to an increase in lucidity). But without initial impulse the production may be tepid and lack conviction. It seems to me that the success of a production depends first of all on the shock the play gives you when you read it through. Nothing can replace this initial impact, this first revelation. It may be confused or mysterious, but you will always have to come back to it for guidance. It works on you both as an incitement and as a brake. The difficulty is not to have ideas–the imagination of the director is generally fertile–but to check one's ideas. If you jump on your ideas, like the actor who takes hold of his character too quickly, you are in danger; you may see only one side of the play; you may simplify or systematise.

Let the play come to you. Read it again and again, and not in a fragmentary way. Try to read the play for the first time at a single sitting so as to get the feeling of the whole. Then go on reading it till the play speaks to you, until you can remember easily the sequence of events, the main movements of the text and the connecting passages, until you know clearly where

the play is weakest and strongest. Delay for as long as you can thinking about the production itself.

I won't try to make a definition of production. It can't be done. It has been attempted many times. There are as many ways of directing as there are directors. It's an empiric and a personal matter.

My purpose is to consider the production of a big classical play in a style that is remote from us, a Shakespearean or a Greek play, for instance. Here the problems of production are the broadest, the most tangible, yet the most puzzling and fascinating at the same time.

When faced with a great work of style, the director is in a complex position. He must be submissive and creative at the same time. In other words if he is to succeed in being both faithful to the work and efficient in his treatment of it, the director has to substitute himself for the dead dramatist and recreate the play.

It is very difficult to find one's way into the right sort of submission and to remain alive, inventive, and inspiring to others.

Submission should not lead to a ready-made, scholarly, or pedantic attitude.

On the other hand invention doesn't mean fantasy. To let one's imagination loose, to please oneself, to follow one's own inclinations, may not result in true invention but in an imposition, an exhibition of personal ideas and moods, however original or brilliant they may be. I believe that the time of the Hamlets in modern dress, of the Oedipus complex psychologically applied,[12] of the sensational opposition of styles, is over. Let me give you an example. A production of *A Midsummer Night's Dream* is under discussion. 'Wouldn't it be fun to do *The Dream* in nineteenth-century costume,' says the director, 'with a chorus of flying fairies and Mendelssohn's beautiful music?'

All such kinds of stylisation and fantastication are out of date. We need something deeper, closer to the dramatist's work than this flippant approach. What we want is a union between the meaning, the heart of the meaning, as it may be felt by modern man, and what I have called in a previous talk, the reality of the style which cannot be separated from the meaning.

Reality of style is composed of what elements?

- Of construction and composition. Composition in musical terms. Construction considered in all its different parts and the way in which they are connected.
- Of rhythm. Relationship between the different rhythms first taken in big chunks.
- Of the tone and colour of the language, and how the text goes from one tone to another.

There is no meaning or psychological construction in a play which can be separated from its style. The one contains the other. Style has its own meaning. It is through, not apart from, text and style that meaning and psychology should be analysed. A Freudian or a mystical Hamlet would be in danger of being prosaic or exalted, because such an interpretation would come to the director's mind apart from the reality of the play's style. An imposed motivation or interpretation, simplified or systematic, will not harmonise in the actor with the varied requirements of the text or its power of incantation. The text has its own power, it creates its own effect: it must not come into conflict in any way with psychological motivation. This is the most thrilling problem that modern actors and directors have got to solve. On its solution depend the greatness and strength of impact of the production.

It is from the director's solitary study of the text, reading and re-reading it, discovering meanings that are revealed by the play's composition, noting rhythm, colour, and tone, that he will slowly begin to realise how to cast the play: temperament of the actors, their complexion, stature, and most important for classical plays, the quality and strength of their voice, together with the essential contrasts between them—all this will gradually become clear. There is

12 In 1937, Laurence Olivier played Hamlet under Tyrone Guthrie's direction. Both Guthrie and Olivier were intrigued by the idea of incorporating Freud's Oedipal theory into the performance. To inform themselves further, they met for discussion with Ernest Jones, Freud's biographer and a psychoanalyst in his own right. In 1948, Olivier directed a film version with himself in the leading role.

a relationship between the casting of big classical plays and the casting of operas. At the Comédie-Française, following the traditions of the French classical theatre, the actors are still classified according to their types, temperament, and vocal ability. The French word is 'emploi' and these 'emplois' include fathers, juveniles, soubrettes, first and second valets, and so on, a practice which may go against 'human reality' to an excessive extent but is naturally in line with 'artistic reality'.

During the initial phase of the work, the disposition[13] of the play on the stage should also reveal itself to the director. First, the general layout: which scenes should be played where–at the back, front, side–it's a sort of geography that has to be completed early on, in the form of a plan showing the main moves of the characters, their entrances and exits: a traffic plan. This early process of adapting to the stage the broad architecture of the play should not at first be restricted by detailed, psychological motivations. The play must breathe freely. Its flow must not be interrupted on the modern stage any more than it was on the Elizabethan stage, to which it remains umbilically attached, where 'architecture was like frozen music'.[14]

The unfolding of the play, the 'geography' of the scenes, the 'traffic': from these three essentials, the layout of the set with its main changes should be evolved in collaboration with the designer. We are not designing scenery yet: we are planning how to use our space. We shall get on to the choice of shape and colour very shortly. But this choice should not be dictated by decorative so much as by dramatic, emotional, and practical considerations. Its success depends upon the balance maintained by designer and director in their vital collaboration. Complete freedom in the exchange of ideas is certainly fruitful provided that the director knows what he wants and is not gradually dominated by the designer's talent or usefulness. One does not go to a designer to get one's production smartly or appropriately furnished and dressed, nor to be presented with sensational scenery and costumes that will unbalance the production and obliterate the actors. It is a fact that many productions are indirectly directed by designers. As for scenery, its form and its colour should give a play both its background and a kind of spring-board to the action. Well-dressed actors will do the rest.

But the designing of costumes is going to face us with the most acute problems. First a general one. What do we expect from costumes? To what sort of use are they going to be put, particularly in a classical work?

---

13   Here Saint-Denis is using the French word *disposition* to mean arrangement.
14   This oft-quoted remark is attributed to the German writer Johann Wolfgang von Goethe (1749–1832).

I was very surprised on one occasion when I saw *As You Like It* with scenery and costumes in the style of Watteau.[15] Why not? 'Wouldn't it be fun to do *As You Like It* in the style of the eighteenth century', said the imaginary director I have already mentioned. But there was more to it than that. The legs of the leading actress were far from perfect. 'In Watteau style they will be hidden.'

I won't discuss the suitability of eighteenth-century style for *As You Like It*. It was fun of the most dusty sort. What seems to me dangerous in a case like this is to see a play's style subjected not only to a different period but to the individual manner o fa well-known painter of that period. The style of a period, even of a painter, may be a necessary inspiration, but the moment you begin to bring on to the stage the copy of a masterpiece, you will produce great visual effect perhaps, but almost certainly dramatic lifelessness. you copy instead of inventing. You transform the theatre into a museum. How could a costume so copied have value for a particular play? The actor is in disguise: he is not dressed. Moreover the anachronism may be striking, but it is not original. It's fun and nothing more than fun. There may be a certain

revelation in such a stunt, but how can it suit the secret style which lies at the heart of Shakespeare's play?

A costume is first of all made to be worn by an actor. It should help the actor to act physically, without trying to impose a character upon him. Otherwise the actor is imprisoned by his costume. A designer should know what it feels like to wear a costume and to have to act in it. A good costume makes you feel free and carries you further into the character at the same time. In addition to this, on any given set, it should establish good relationship, in shape and colour, with the background. Sets and costumes, lightly designed, should help the actors and the public to capture the overall character and emotional impact of the production.

There is also the question of lighting, but that is too complicated a subject to be dealt with now. In a classical production with quickly moving scenery, lighting is of first importance. It can help, often unaided, to suggest changes of location as well as mood.

The rest depends upon acting and the strength of your original conception. Discipline, essential when you are at work, is the condition of freedom in acting. Freedom of the director,

---

15   The production Saint-Denis is referencing as an illustration of stylisation is Peter Brook's 1946 *Love's Labour's Lost* and not *As You Like It*. It is not clear whether Saint-Denis is making an error or does not want to reveal the unnamed director. Peter Brook discusses the production and Saint-Denis's reaction in his 1998 *Threads of Time*. Brook did indeed base his visual concept on Watteau's paintings because he felt that *Love's Labour's Lost* 'needed a fresh image' (34). Its reviews were excellent; Saint-Denis was alone in his condemnation. He told the hurt and angry Brook that 'theatre is theatre' and should not be confused with any other art. Brook eventually came to agree with the criticism.

freedom of the designer, freedom of the actor: it's impossible to achieve one without the other. Without this common freedom I believe that complete reality in acting cannot be achieved.

I am not assuming an easy attitude towards the idea of freedom. To attain freedom is a life's work. We mark with a white stone the few productions during the preparation of which we have had the feeling of being free and of making other people free. Four times in the course of my life I have had the experience of leading a company in such a way that the last dress-rehearsal took place without any tension, in a spirit of confidence which was justified by public success the next day. This kind of freedom means mastery.

What concerns me most, in the present state of the theatre, is how to attain this freedom and how to ensure that it is something usual and familiar.

The first condition necessary to create this freedom, without which dramatic reality cannot be complete, is to have a stage in keeping with the style of the play: picture-frame for naturalism and certain forms of realism, or even certain classical plays: all plays which need, more or less, the illusion of life being lived. But for the rest we need a stage of the kind I tried to describe in my last lecture, liberated, openly conventional, where the theatre is theatre, where the actor is an actor and the dramatic action an invention in which the public is made to believe.

There is no possible freedom, I believe, if the people working together on a show have not previously known each other. I come back to that human reality which is indispensable to artistic reality. To me the unity and quality of a performance, particularly if the play is one of style, depends mainly on a quality and a unity which should exist in the company before the work on the play begins. A director must know the elements of his realisation, and the means by which he is going to bring the play to life, before he sets to work on it. He must know his collaborators, particularly his actors, but also all the people, even the least significant, who will take part in the preparation of the show behind the scenes. (Think how important a stage-manager can be.) It's from that mutual knowledge and pre-existing understanding that strength can freely spring and an artistic conception be rooted in firm ground.

I will probably be accused once more of going against the times. I have been accused of training people for a theatre that does not exist. I am aware of that criticism. I am told that the people who work in the theatres of the West End, the Parisian Boulevard, and Broadway are a great family, all of whom know each other—actors say so with tearful voices. And we find that up to a point it is true, especially as we come towards the end of our life.

But it is also perfectly false. The only style this great family can touch is the realistic one. Look, however, at Stanislavsky; look at the American Group Theatre. Did they not bring something new to realism itself? Will not their names go down in theatrical history because they were based on an attempt at permanence and continuity?

What happens with plays of great style?

I do not know if you feel like we French. We often complain that, even in the same show, actors play in many different styles. How could it be otherwise when there is such a variety of styles; when actors have got to be able to move from Shakespeare to Clifford Odets and thence to television?

Unity of style can be obtained only by working together and getting used to each other's physical and emotional reactions. Occasionally one may succeed without it and directors and actors of genius delight in winning against the odds: it's so much more exciting! But a theatre cannot establish an artistic policy unless it gathers together a well composed group of collaborators around a permanent company of actors, with partial renewal every year. Even with a variety of interesting plays the talent of a director is not enough to give expression to a policy without the continuity of the actors' presence. For it is the company that gives the place its spirit. The public is attached to the men and women they can see in the flesh.

That was a digression. To conclude I return to my subject.

What is the working relationship between actors and their director going to be?

This is an embarrassing question. I am at the moment changing my mind towards it and I could not begin to answer it without taking you into my confidence.

I have always been caught between two opposite tendencies: on the one hand to give shape, to give plastic value to a production; on the other to preserve the freedom of the actor.

I believe that the layout of a set, the relative positions of the actors, their movements, attitudes, the expression of their bodies, the sound of their voices, have by themselves a power of direct revelation.

I have studied Greek and Far Eastern theatrical forms. I have a strong feeling for tragedy, enough to want my staging to have formal value. The use of space on the stage has a precise significance for me: two steps to the right, two steps to the left, such a small move can be full of meaning. From feeling strongly the need for such a move to imposing it upon the actors, is a very little distance; but to make an actor appreciate such a need, you must suggest it at just the right moment in just the right way, even with somebody who has absolute confidence in you.

Add to this, that as an actor, I have often practised improvisation, rehearsing and playing in the manner that the Italians call 'alla improvisare'. There is a medium in which the actor invents everything within a given framework. He is not directed, he is rather 'advised' from the front by a director who acts as a kind of mirror. This sort of freedom, as I experienced it on the stage, was the most liberating experience.

How is one to reconcile these two ways of working, to give expressive shape to a production, and at the same time to cultivate the actor's inventive freedom? There lies the secret of theatrical art. But I have not yet put my hand on its solution.

I have been spurred on in my research by a man who is nearly twenty years younger than I am, Jean Vilar,[16] the head of the Théâtre national populaire in Paris.[17] A few years ago he created the Avignon Festival, which is now an important yearly event. He is the man I most admire in the French theatre today. I have acclaimed his two productions of *Le Prince de Hombourg* by Kleist and *Don Juan* by Molière. He has a strong theatrical organisation, the best collaborators on every side, and a permanent collaboration. His theatre, the Palais de Chaillot, is not a suitable one, but it has 2,500 seats. Vilar has taken advantage of this abnormal size to play at popular prices and to reproduce indoors the open and free conditions he finds at Avignon. There is a very large stage which he has enlarged still more by building a forestage over the orchestra pit, thus connecting stage and auditorium. He plays without footlights. His open stage is lit by spots set in the auditorium, and he never lowers a front curtain between audience and actors. When I saw his work for the first time I was very surprised by the daring way in which he makes use of space, limiting it by means of lighting. Scenery for him is only a background.

His costumes are generally designed by painters, not by stage designers; they build up the actor by means of strong blocks of colour without unnecessary details. He makes considerable use of music and sound. For ten years before his appointment to the TNP he played Strindberg, Pirandello, Chekhov, and any number of modern plays. He was trained at Charles Dullin's school in classical disciplines, but by nature he is a Latin realist, born on the shores of the Mediterranean. He interests and puzzles me because he has very often succeeded in achieving that difficult fusion between a realistic attitude and a classical style. Laurence Olivier also did it, for instance in his productions of *Richard III* and *King Lear*, but the French tradition is more strict than the English.

The production, the staging, the whole work of Vilar give an impression of liberty, of freedom of style. How does he do it?

I have never seen him at rehearsals. His actors have sometimes told me that they did not rehearse enough. His stage-director has complained that the sets were not studied carefully enough. In all this, there seems to be some carelessness, some looseness.

Every time I have seen a show, however, it has been in perfect order, never mechanical, always meaningful

---

16 Jean Vilar shared Saint-Denis's basic theatrical values, as attested to by this quotation from *De la tradition théâtrale*, 'The author is the creator in the theatre' (65).

17 [Saint-Denis] Since these talks were given, Jean Vilar's company has been seen both in London and New York.

and full of style–with the occasional failures which are natural to any creative artist. I was the more puzzled.

On the boat coming here I read a book by Vilar which has just appeared. It is called *De la tradition théâtrale.*[18] I was at once struck by the quality of the thinking, the concentration, the density of that little book. It is never commonplace. It is lucid, simple, and precise, never nebulous or philosophical, never pretentious.

Vilar writes that one always tends to work on the stage too soon and too long, giving too much time and care to what we call placing, but which I believe the Americans call 'blocking'. (Remember that his ideas assume a permanent company of talented and well-trained actors.) 'One should', he goes on to say, 'not only give confidence to the actor but have onfidence in him. One never has enough confidence in his professional intelligence and sensitivity. A third of the rehearsal time should be given to word rehearsals, what we call "répéter à l'italienne". When you put an actor on the stage too quickly, his physical reactions are too hastily provoked', and Vilar writes, 'We must rehearse a lot'–in French: 'le corps au repos et le cul sur la chaise', which means 'body at rest and bottom on a chair'. 'Cul' is a very good word.

'It's necessary', he writes again, 'that the deep sensitivity of the actor, guided by the director, should be given time gradually to reach the right level.'

And later, 'There is no part which has not to be characterised. There is no ready-made impersonation, there is no good acting without characterisation.' Very illuminating. And Vilar is not at all a man who caricatures anything. His style is very limpid. He also says, 'Placing (or blocking) and physical expression should be dealt with comparatively quickly by a truly professional actor, taking approximately fifteen rehearsals out of forty.' Is it not striking? I do not yet completely understand how he does it. And again, 'The director's art is one of suggestion, not imposition.' That we know. 'Above everything he must not be brutal. The actor's spirit is as important as the poet's. One does not reach somebody's mind by being brutal. It's on the mind of the actor rather than on his emotional quality that the good interpretation of a play depends.' And again, 'A director who does not know how to detach himself from his work during the last rehearsals, when he is not involved, is only a poor artisan, losing his sight, forgetting, the stupid fellow, that before anything else the theatre is "un jeu"[19] where inspiration and childlike rapture are more important than sweat and fits of temper.'

I like the tendency which such an attitude reveals. I agree with it. Remember once more that it applies to a permanent and well-trained company, where voice, body, and style are practised daily.

---

18 [Saint-Denis] L'Arche, Paris 1955.
19 Two of the meanings of *jeu* are acting and a game.

And all this is related to the idea of freedom which is unattainable without first-rate craftsmanship.

I believe that this freedom is the supreme goal of an artist who cannot be master of his art until he feels relaxed and natural. Classical art helps you on the difficult road to freedom. It helps you to acquire a lightness of touch and a concentration upon essentials. By picking you out of the mud of naturalism it raises you above your work.

I believe that a classical discipline equips you with sharper instruments with which to penetrate to the depths of realism.

To avoid the dangers inherent in classical practice one needs a good, broad, cultured background, and a long training. In my last lecture I shall say something about this training and my work at the Old Vic School.

CHAPTER FIFTEEN

The Stage Manager

WHAT DOES THE STAGE MANAGER DO?

She is the person who holds the show together practically, technically, and emotionally. The director works most closely with the stage manager. The stage manager is the only constant presence in a production from the very beginning until the close of the production. She is the person through whom all information flows as a theatrical piece is created. The stage manager is the liaison between the director, actors, designers, technical director, administrators, and crew chiefs. The only aspect with which a stage manager does not deal directly is the audience.

A stage manager is a very skilled and special individual. The special skills required are organization, multitasking, leadership, and facilitation. This individual must coordinate the production by organizing every aspect and maintaining discipline.

COORDINATING A PRODUCTION

The stage manager works closely with all involved in a production to create a schedule and timeline that will allow the multifarious aspects of theatre to be created concurrently while leaving room for the inevitable adjustments and reworking that are necessary in a live performing arts endeavor. Throughout the design and rehearsal process, artistic discoveries emerge. The stage manager must be attuned to all aspects of the production as she must recognize when one artistic change will affect any other aspect of a production. For example, the blocking may change in a rehearsal that requires two actors to lie on top of a table. This new blocking may affect many things, including:

- The set (insofar as the table must be sturdy enough to handle the weight of these two actors).
- The costumes (the clothing must be flexible enough to allow this type of vigorous movement, and a decision must be made about undergarments if one actor is female and is wearing a dress).
- The lighting (the change in the angle of lighting to illuminate an actor in a prone position).

The director depends on the stage manager to take care of all of the pragmatic concerns of the production and rehearsal process.

The stage manager is required to be incredibly organized and must be good at multitasking. She will need to stay calm when many things are happening at once, and she is being pulled in many different directions. She needs to be a leader who has good facilitation skills so that she can get the best and most creative work out of all members of the production. The stage manager is a person who must be able to think and problem-solve quickly when things go wrong in performance.

The stage manager must be able to organize and maintain discipline with a large group of often energetic individuals. The stage manager calls all meetings and rehearsals to order. She will maintain a prompt book, which is a copy of the performance text, within which all rehearsal work is documented, including blocking, lighting and sound cues, and changes to the script. Stage managers use this book to prompt actors on both lines and blocking during rehearsals. The stage manager attends all production meetings and provides a link between those who are at production meetings and those who are at rehearsal. It is also her job to manage the actors. She relays all information from the director to the actors. She will let actors know if there are any changes to the rehearsal schedule and has to deal with actors who show up late or are absent from rehearsal. She is often the person who deals with personnel problems and acts as a go-between when conflicts arise among members of the company.

Taking care of the actors is one of the stage manager's primary jobs. She will be aware of when the actors need a break and will let the director know it is necessary. The theatre space must be clean and safe for the rehearsal process. If it is not, it is her job to rectify the situation. If it is an equity house, the stage manager is required to report any infractions of union rules to the Actor's Equity Association. The stage manager must be flexible and make people feel comfortable while still getting a production together.

Running the show is one of the stage manager's primary responsibilities. She enters the director's cues in the prompt book during technical rehearsals. Once the show opens, she calls those cues and is responsible for keeping the rhythm and pace of the show consistent. She keeps time for the entire production, making sure actors know when they must arrive at the theatre and giving them warnings at various intervals (one hour, 30 minutes, five minutes) before the curtain goes up and the play begins. In addition, the stage manager must communicate with the house manager, letting him know when things are ready on the stage and backstage, so he can let the audience take its seats at the appropriate time.

She is the person who knows what every technical cue does and how it should look on the stage. She is also aware of how that cue relates to and interacts with the actors. Once the show opens, the stage manager is in charge and is responsible for maintaining the artistic intention of the director, whose job ends on opening night. If it is a long-running show, the stage manager must teach new actors their parts and communicate how the director expects the part to be played.

CHAPTER SIXTEEN

The Technical Director and Technical Support

The Technical Director (TD)—*The technical director is respon-*sible for all things technical in a theatre space and/or for a theatre production. He must be well-versed in all facets of technical theatre. Some of the basic duties of the technical director are the operation, maintenance, and safety of all of the technical equipment in the theatre. He will supervise the use of tools, lighting, sound, communications equipment, and the use and maintenance of stage facilities. He will determine the necessary technical staff needed for a production build and run. The TD also maintains and assists in the setup of lighting and sound systems. He will advise designers on the technical specifications, costs, and usage of technical equipment required for the individual show, and he supervises the build, hang, and implementation of approved technical designs. The technical director may recruit, train, and assign volunteer or paid technical staff for the show. The TD assists with the preparation and control of production budgets and maintains an inventory of stock and orders specialized supplies that are needed. It is imperative that the TD attends rehearsals during tech week in order to supervise and assist in the technical aspects of mounting the show.

A CONVERSATION WITH MICHAEL KATZ, TECHNICAL DIRECTOR

Bio: As Technical Director for UMass Boston Department of Performing Arts, Michael Katz does the technical designs and leads the construction of all of the Theater Arts productions.

He also teaches classes on the world of stagecraft. Michael has had the privilege of holding high-level technical positions in many of the finest Boston area theater companies including: The American Repertory Theatre, The New Repertory Theatre, The Boston Lyric Opera, The Opera Company of Boston, and The Jewish Theater of New England. He has taught at MIT, Emerson College, Tufts University, and Bridgewater State College, as well as presenting a number of seminars at the New England Theater Conference and at the United States Institute for Theater Technology. He is a member of the Board of Directors of USITT (The United States Institute for Theatre Technology) and of USITTNE (The United States Institute for Theatre Technology–New England). Michael holds an MFA in Technical Production from Boston University as well as a BFA in Technical Theater from Carnegie Mellon University.

Mike Katz was among the first generation of TDs to go to design meetings. In prior generations, the TD waited for the designer to deliver the plans to the shop and then building would begin. What became apparent over the years is that choices made in the shop may drastically affect the design. It is important that the TD have an overall sense of the world of the play—and the design concept—as he makes that world a reality in the shop. There are many nuances in design; what is on paper may not exactly represent what the design team really wants. Being in design meetings enables the TD to make decisions in the shop that will give the designers what they really want. Unlike a carpenter or general contractor on a house working with an architect, the TD and theatrical design team are creating a *theatrical reality*. By going to meetings, the TD can participate in conceptual discussions to enhance the design and make the building process more seamless. But, the TD must also step back in those meetings and let the designers do their work. When asked the difference between the mindset of a TD and the mindset of a designer, Mike says, "I see a blank piece of paper, and I get scared. A designer sees a blank piece of paper, and she gets excited about the possibilities. The designer creates the picture of the set. I look at the picture and think, 'how can I make this a reality?'"

When looking at the design, the TD will try to figure out where he can suggest cuts to the design team based on the distance between the set and the audience, where details are needed, or where the design can be simplified. The theatre is a classroom, a place to solve problems.

The TD is the person who is looking at the long view—every choice and action has a consequence: "If I do this, then this will happen." He sees the train wreck before it happens but does not want to inhibit creativity—which is a very fine balance to strike. He is in constant negotiation with the design team, the director, and the administrators—making them aware of the effects of decisions. "If this, then that" is a constant mantra for the TD.

The TD schedules use of the space, so he must be well organized. He must also have the ability to look at a design and available resources in terms of money and staff and be able to determine if a set can be built in time for tech week with the available resources. The first thing he considers is how much there is. He then looks at what is in stock. Many theatres—both professional and educational—have limited stock and limited storage. Basic set pieces, such as platforms and flats, are standard stock elements.

Mr. Katz is a member of USITT—The United States Institute for Theatre Technology. USITT is a membership organization, which aims to advance the skills and knowledge of theatre, entertainment, and performing arts professionals involved in the areas of design, production, and technology. The USITT mounts conferences and exhibitions, promotes awards and publications, and supports research. The rapid changes that occur in technology have a huge impact on technical theatre. Professional development is incredibly necessary. Members of USITT who participate in professional development opportunities can learn new things or give something back. Katz, who has over 30 years of experience as a TD working in both professional theatre companies and educational institutions, will search out new TDs to mentor and support. He will also advocate for them.

Safety is a critical aspect of the TD's job. He must be aware of—and implement—the laws and regulations that have been established by the Occupational Safety and Health Administration (OSHA) as well as building and fire codes. In order to insure that the shop and stage are safe working environments, he must do serious planning before anyone even shows up to start working. He is also the person who usually says "no" when someone is asking someone in the company to do something that is unsafe.

There are times when resources available do not match the aesthetic wants of the director, designers, or actors. The TD must be very good at negotiation and must work towards creating equity and parity. He has the ability to do technical design while the scenic, lighting, costume, projection, and sound designers each contribute artistic design. This means that the TD can make structural and resource choices that will make the most of the resources that are available. While all designers may not get everything they want, the TD insures that they get enough of what they want so that the director's vision can be fulfilled.

THE TD AND THE PRODUCTION MANAGER

Up until the mid-1960s, the TD was the highest-level technical/administrative person in the theatre. Technical directors—beginning with those working in opera—lobbied for the creation of a new position to take on some of the administrative duties that were being placed on the TD. These technical directors stated that they did not have the time and energy to do all of the work required to safely and effectively mount a production. At this time, the position of the production manager was created. With the addition of this staff member, the TD retained the responsibility for the day-to-day workings of the theatre, and the PM took responsibility for the long-term planning

THE SET

Scenic Shop Supervisor—The scene shop supervisor is responsible for getting the materials necessary for the completion of the set and for creating a schedule that will get the set built in a timely manner and within budget.

    Set Build Crew—This crew creates the set under the supervision of the shop supervisor and the technical director. They may build the set from scratch, may pull some pieces from stock, buy some pieces and make adjustments to them to fulfill the design concept, or they may borrow some elements of the set. This crew will also load in the set onto the stage and assist with any of the finishing touches.

    Set Run Crew—The run crew is in charge of the set during the run of the show. It will set the stage before the play begins, check to make sure all moving parts are in working order, and will make any necessary set changes during performance. This crew is also looking out for safety issues or set function issues that may arise due to repeated use of the set.

THE PROPS

Prop Shop Supervisor—The prop shop supervisor oversees the prop shop and the creation of all props for the production. She will see to it that the shop is organized, stocked, and in working order so that the prop build crew can bring the set designer's vision to fruition. Many prop shop supervisors have a background in scenic design and are skilled at finish painting, upholstery, light carpentry, and craft work. The prop shop supervisor may purchase, rent, or borrow props. She will keep an inventory of props that are in stock. If props are rented or borrowed, she will assure that they are returned in good working condition. The prop shop supervisor communicates with the costume and set designers about designs for the props to confirm plans for creating/securing props for a production. She will also instruct and communicate with the prop build and run crews to ensure that all props are ready for the production and that the run crew understands when, how, and by whom props will be used. The prop shop supervisor will often work with the stage manager and director to locate rehearsal props that actors may use in lieu of the production props with which to practice during the rehearsal process. Once the production has finished its run, the prop shop supervisor will return borrowed or rented props, return stock props to inventory, and catalogue new props and place them in the stock inventory.

Build Crew—Some props need to be built for a show. At other times, props need to be bought or pulled from stock and altered. The build crew will create or change the props under the guidance of the prop shop supervisor.

Run Crew—The prop run crew will make sure that props are where they are supposed to be during technical rehearsals and during the run of the show. The run crew is responsible for pre-setting props on prop tables stage right and stage left, on the set, or in actors' costumes before the show starts. At the end of the show, the props run crew must also confirm that those props that belong on the backstage tables, on the set, or in actors' costumes have made it back to their assigned areas. If any of the props are not in their specified locations at the end of a performance, the run crew must locate them and get them in their proper places before leaving the theatre. If any props cannot be located, the run crew must inform the stage manager, who must then solve the problem.

THE COSTUMES

Costume Shop Supervisor—The costume shop supervisor oversees the costume shop. She will make sure that the shop is organized and in working order so that the build crew can make the costume designer's vision a reality. Many costume shop supervisors have a background in costume design as well as expertise in hand and machine sewing, patterning, cutting, and, sometimes, millinery work. Costume shop supervisors will create a schedule for taking actors' measurements, creating or buying patterns, cutting, draping, stitching, fitting, and finishing all costumes. This shop supervisor will also ensure that the shop is well-stocked and may also shop for fabric, notions, etc., with the costume designer or on her own. If costumes are to be rented, the shop supervisor will measure actors, secure the costumes, keep an inventory of the rented pieces, and assure that they are in good repair and laundered before they are returned.

    Costume Build Crew—If costumes are being created for a show, the build crew will construct costumes from scratch using the designer's renderings as a guide. Patterns will be chosen or created, material will be chosen and approved, and the costumes will be cut, stitched, fitted on the actors, and finished by the costume build crew.

    Costume Run Crew—The run crew is responsible for making sure that costumes are clean, pressed, and in good repair for every performance. If a show requires costume changes backstage, the costume run crew will preset costumes that are needed for changes in a predetermined area and will assist actors with costume changes. The run crew will attend dress rehearsals and practice costume changes with the actors. The goal is to assist the actor to change her costume in as quick and efficient a manner as possible. The actor has many things to focus on and must not be overly concerned about making a costume change backstage.

LIGHTING

Master Electrician (ME)—The ME is responsible for taking the lighting plot and making sure that all lighting units on the plot are hung in the correct locations and actually work. Coordinating the numbers of lights and circuits and allocating cabling, gels, and other accessories are the most important aspects of this role.

Hang, Cable, and Patch Crew—This crew assists the ME in making sure all lighting units on the plot are hung, focused, gelled, cabled, patched, etc., correctly.

Light Run Crew—The run crew will run the light board and any follow spots during performance. It takes its cues from the stage manager. This used to be a somewhat stressful and skilled position, requiring an ability to use a light board with sliding dimmer switches. Now that most light boards are computerized, cues are programmed in, and changing cues can be done with the press of a few buttons. Once the board operator knows how to run a computerized board, this job is a relatively easy one.

CHAPTER SEVENTEEN

The Theatre Critic

WHAT IS THE ROLE OF THE THEATRE CRITIC? IS THERE A DIFFERENCE BETWEEN A CRITIC AND A REVIEWER?

Theatre criticism has a long and illustrious history. Written criticism can be traced all the way back to ancient Greece; Aristotle's *Poetics* offers a good deal of valuable criticism about the theatre. Since that time, scholars have written extensive evaluations of written texts and productions of those texts in an attempt to elucidate the value of a play, a theatrical movement, or a theatrical style. This type of criticism can be valuable to both the student of theatre and the theatre practitioner. It may assist the artist in his search for a more in-depth understanding of his art form. It also allows the artist to reflect more deeply on his process and the contributions he may make to an art form that has existed for centuries.

The other type of theatre criticism—which appear in newspapers or magazines or on television or radio—may be, in fact, good theatre criticism, or it may be a review. What is the difference? Most theatre artists benefit from good, well-founded criticism. A good theatre critic has a firm grasp of the history of theatre as well as the collaborative process involved in creating a theatrical production. This critic is able to comment on and evaluate the many factors that go into the making of a performance. A good theatre critic can watch a play and understand why it is—or is not—working. Is it the script? The acting? The directing? Is it the audience?

Theatre has many styles and genres. The well-prepared theatre critic will have some understanding of the various styles and genres that exist—and she will be open to experiencing a new style or genre. An experienced theatre critic is able to respond emotionally and intellectually to a production. She can experience a production and analyze what is valuable and effective about it, as well as what may be the production's flaws. This person is able to make connections between the production that she is experiencing and the tradition from which the production comes, as well as possibly connecting it to traditions from around the world throughout history. She is able to communicate these responses to a production in a clear and concise manner to her audience of readers.

A well-respected theatre critic may help a theatre to sell tickets, or she may close a production. Theatre practitioners—writers, directors, actors, designers, producers, audience—can learn a great deal by reading a well-written critique of a production by a well-prepared critic. Artists learn and grow through evaluation of and reflection on these critiques; they are integral to the artistic process. Exceptional theatre critics have contributed a tremendous amount to the growth and development of theatre around the world throughout history.

A theatre reviewer, by contrast, may not know much about theatre and is focused primarily on her personal response to a production. She will probably not be able to analyze a production very deeply and may not understand what factors contribute to a production's success or lack thereof. She will attempt to make her review entertaining to read and will either recommend or condemn a production based on a visceral, inexperienced response. Like a well-crafted critique, a theatre review may help a theatre to sell tickets or it may close a production, but it will be of little additional value to the artists and collaborators whom it praises or criticizes.

HOW TO WRITE GOOD THEATRE CRITICISM

Now that you have an introductory understanding of theatre, you can embrace the challenge of writing a critique of a theatrical production. Go to see a production, and try your hand at writing a critique of the production. Write it as if you want to assist those who are reading the criticism—actors, director, designers, audience, producer—to discover something new or become a more competent audience member (actor, designer, designer, etc.) by reading your comments. Use the following suggestions as a starting point for your critique.

Your evaluation should include two basic elements—an evaluation of the script or message itself (written script or story) and an evaluation of the production (acting, design, directing, technical support)

The following lists the major points you might want to discuss in your criticism:

- **Provide a brief summary** of the plot and/or major message or theme of the performance (two–three lines). Was the story or message interesting and well developed? Was the action, language, and characterization compelling?

Did you reflect on the play the day after the performance? Did you discuss any elements of the play with friends and/or family? What were they? How did the play make you feel? What did the play make you think? Was there anything in the play that sparked your interest or curiosity, making you want to learn more about something or explore something new in your life?

- **Discuss the performance's direction**. Give the director's name (in the program) and discuss the director's approach. Did the production seem cohesive? Was the production clear and understandable, or were you confused, bored, or lost at any time? Did any elements of the production stand out or seem like they did not belong? Did everything make sense to you? If not, was this on purpose?

- **Review the performances.** What style of acting was used—Presentational or Representational? Were the actors well-trained and well-rehearsed? Were the actors focused? Were the actors convincing in their roles? Were you convinced that the actors were the characters they were playing, or did it seem like the actors were disconnected from the roles they were playing? Were you inspired by the actors? Were you moved intellectually or emotionally by the performances? Be sure to provide the actors' names (in program).

- **Mention the design elements:** set, costumes, lighting, sound, and projection (if any). Be sure to name all of the designers (in program). Discuss the importance of these items to the performance. Did the design match the style of the acting and the script/message/style of the performance? How did the design elements work together to support the message of the play? Did any design elements stand out? Did this makes sense (i.e., was it on purpose)?

- You may also want to **discuss the audience's reaction** to the production, any elements of **technical support/behind the scenes** that were noteworthy, or any aspect of the **front of house experience** that influenced your response to this show.

- Tell your readers whether you would **recommend the play**, and give reasons **why or why not**. Suggest ways in which the performance could be improved, and if you thought the performance was great, tell why. Avoid using terms like "must see" and "thumbs up" as these expressions give the readers very little valuable information.

PART

Five

GENRES AND STYLES OF THEATRE FROM AROUND THE WORLD

CHAPTER EIGHTEEN

Why Should I Learn About Genres and Styles of Theatre?

AS AN AUDIENCE MEMBER

As an audience member attending a theatrical production, there is benefit to knowing what type (genre or style) of performance you will participate in; we know that audience members at the theatre are participants, and make up one of the three necessary components of live theatre (along with story and actor). As an audience member, my reaction and connection to a performance is integral. I will be a more engaged participant if I know what to expect and what my role is as an audience member. Is the play meant to make me make laugh—is it a comedy? Am I supposed to sit relatively quietly and express myself (through laughter, gasps, applause) in a relatively docile manner—as is expected audience behavior in many Western performance styles? Or, am I expected to shout things at the actors on stage—as is expected audience behavior in many Asian, African, and Indigenous performance styles? Will the actors speak directly to me, or will they pretend that I am not there and that they are in a different world? The audience has a role to play in every live production, and if it understands what to expect—if it understands the genre and style—it will be more prepared to play its "role."

Why should I learn about theatre from cultures and time periods other than my own? There are many answers to this question, and you might have one of your own that may feel more relevant than mine. Let's go back to the first question we asked—why theatre? Humankind created theatre to LEARN and to ENTERTAIN. It is quite obvious that experiencing performances of productions that have been developed by those who lived before us will teach us something about them. We can learn a great deal about the past from theatre. All theatre reflects the human condition of the time and place in which it was created. What the playwright writes—or what the performer passes down through oral tradition—enables the audience to experience: a slice of life; a thought; an idea; mannerisms; values; standards; codes of behavior—I could go on ad infinitum about how a great theatrical production can teach.

AS A PERSPECTIVE PERFORMING ARTIST

Many young performing artists have visions of what they want to do and who they want to be—"I want to do musicals;" " I want to do film;" "I want to do realistic contemporary plays;" " I want to do new, cutting-edge productions." Why should a performing artist who knows what he wants to do study anything other than his desired style and genre of performance? This is a question that is difficult to answer in a short paragraph, but it is an important one to address. Some of the answer is revealed in the section above about being an audience member. A performing artist must represent humanity. It is his job to know as much as he can about people, places, and societies—both past and present—in order to honestly reflect and represent life.

There are genre and styles that have been around for thousands of years. Plays that were written or developed over 2,500 years ago can still move, entertain, and teach people something about themselves, the world in which they live, and what it means to be human. Most of the genres and styles of theatre that have been developed throughout history were founded by individuals who had knowledge and experience working in the forms that had been around for millennia; however, they believed that changes needed to be made because life had changed—and society had changed so much that new styles and genre were needed to reflect humankind's experiences. Yet despite the many external changes that have developed in the world—through developments in industry, science, technology, and the social sciences—the basic components of human life and the essence of the stories told through performance have not changed. Humans still grapple with the same core ideas—we are born, we struggle through life, and we die. What is the purpose of life? How should we live our lives and why? Do we have souls or spirits or consciousness that live before and/or after our bodies or forms exist on this earth? How do our feelings, actions, beliefs, needs, and wants affect our own paths in life and the paths of those we encounter? What is the purpose and result of love? Hate? Greed? Fear? Control? Denial? Jealousy?

CHAPTER NINETEEN

Traditional Theatre of Africa

RITUAL/ORIGINS

Indigenous African theatre, like theatre all over the world, grew out of ritual. In fact, it is highly likely that theatre as ritual began in Africa where human civilization began. The first known dramatic presentations occurred in Northern Africa. Indications of ritual performances can be seen in activities of hundreds of African tribal groups dating as far back as 6000 BCE. It is likely that the performances resembled tribal performances widely performed in rural Africa today. These performances, which were comprised of ritual and storytelling, united the two most important aspects of African life: religion and community. African performance activities have persisted despite many obstacles through the centuries. Religious rituals, festivals, ceremonies, storytelling, and various types of celebrations are woven into daily life on this continent.

ELEMENTS OF PERFORMANCE

Languages other than words—especially dance, music, and drumming—communicate more to an African audience than words. To these languages can be added visual imagery, symbolism, gesture, mask, and costume.

Masks are a very important component of most early forms of theatre. They have been important in ritual, religion, and theatre for thousands of years. Archeologists have found 20,000-year-old cave paintings depicting people wearing masks. There is evidence of rituals using masks in prehistoric Africa, Europe, Asia, and the Americas. Masks are especially prevalent in the dance-dramas of native African theatre. Masks can allow wearers anonymity. When a performer wears a mask, he can take on the qualities of a different person, an animal, or a mythical being. Those who feel inhibited can put on a mask and assume the qualities of the mask. Once you change your face, you can change who you are. In traditional African theatre, the mask allows the wearer to identify with and assume the spirit of a mythical ancestor or supernatural being.

Native African performances usually take place in spaces very different than in traditional European theatres. Theatre spaces are often outdoors. Since audience participation is encouraged and expected, there is seldom much of a separation between the audience and the actors. Generally, the audience forms a circle around the performers, singing and dancing along with them. Direct audience participation is usually expected. It is accepted that the dancing, music, and singing would prompt communal responses, such as clapping in rhythm, singing refrains, repeating phrases, and making comments about the action and characters. Because the performers often wear masks, the audience can be part of the performance and yet look different than the performers.

SPECIFIC TYPES OF PERFORMANCE

It is hard to generalize about theatre in Africa, and it is impossible to discuss in a book of this sort native African performance in every country and state on the continent; there are close to 50 states and more than 800 local languages, and local performance traditions do not always travel from one community to the next. I have, therefore, chosen to highlight only a few forms of native African theatre. Northern Africa is dominated by Arab languages and customs; however, in the parts of Africa that are located south of the Sahara Desert, languages and customs are highly diverse. Most of the forms of theatre mentioned here are found in the areas of Africa that are not dominated by the Arab culture.

NATIVE DRAMA IN SUB-SAHARAN AFRICA

In Sub-Saharan Africa, there is an expansive variety of traditional drama in which ritual and storytelling continually interweave. Many African tribes have longstanding traditions of dance-dramas.

The Dogon performers of Mali are celebrated for their stilt walking and brightly colored masks. The Senufo of the Ivory Coast and Burkina Faso have animal masks, with tusks of wild boars, the teeth of alligators, and the horns of antelopes. These masks are meant to frighten witches. Performers also don brightly colored masks for certain female characters (played by men). These masks feature arched eyebrows, visible teeth, and ritual scar marks on the cheeks. The character's hand props often include horsetail whisks. In the Yacouba country of Ivory Coast, traditional performers may wear elaborate beaded headdresses and full-face makeup instead of masks. In the panther dance-drama, performers will cover their entire heads in painted cloth with panther ears. Acrobatics are a feature in Burundi performances and rain-dance rituals are common in Botswana.

NATIVE PERFORMANCE IN NIGERIA

Public performance as a medium of expression and communication has been an integral part of Nigerian culture for centuries. With its more than 250 different ethnic groups, each with its own language and performance styles, native Nigerian theatre is extremely diverse. Various types of performance are presented throughout the country and throughout the year in the many communities that make up this African state.

Nigerian Masquerade

The masquerade of the Igbo people—known as *mmonwu*—is one of the most lasting and popular performance institutions in Nigeria. In the Igbo culture, existence is divided between two worlds: perceptible matter (*the uwa*) and imperceptible spirit (*the mm*uo). *Mmonwu* combines these two worlds through trance performance. In the *Mmonwu* performance, the spirit embodies the material being of the performer's mask. Each principal performer wears a full-face mask and full-body costume, concealing his real identity and allowing him to embody the other-worldly wonder of his character. Spectacle is as important as story in the masquerade dance-drama since the masked characters are understood not merely to represent spirits but to embody them.

The language of the ceremony is a poetic chanting. Many of the words chanted in the performance are often unique to the masquerade style.

The masquerade performance space is quite detailed. The staging area is outdoors and as large as four football fields. At one end is a sacred house, the *ekwuru*, or "home of the masks." This building is richly decorated with colored banners, tassels, staffs, flags, posters, and bunting. The elaborate masks and costumes are made in the sacred house in secret. Masked characters enter the large semi-circular acting area (*ogbo*) from this location. A small raised "platform of authority" within the *ogbo* allows a principal speaker to rise above the others and deliver a poetic chant. There are two additional playing areas on either side of the *ogbo*. One area, known as the *ulooma*, or "house of the yellow palm leaves," is enclosed. A female chorus performs from this area. The *onoduigba*—an area in which the male chorus and orchestra play—is open. Spectators surround the action on three sides. All the spectators may talk to the performers, but they may never touch them.

GRIOTS

Griots are African storytellers who do much more than tell stories. They are actors who mix narrative, impersonation, song, and mime to create highly theatrical presentations of folktales, tribal histories, and myths. Some sing the entire story while accompanying themselves with simple instruments. Because they use very simple staging, these actors must paint detailed verbal images, sometimes called "verbal scene painting," inviting the audience to see the events unfold in its own mind's eye. For the most part, African storytellers perform on their own. If they need other actors, they invite members of the audience into the circle to play the parts.

EFFECTS OF INVASIONS AND COLONIALISM

In the parts of Africa invaded by Muslims, Islam's resistance to theatre often reduced or abolished theatrical activity. In the rest of the continent, sixteenth-century Christian invaders tended to stifle African theatre by imposing their language, customs, religion, and theatre on the indigenous peoples. Early European travelers and missionaries who witnessed African ritual theatre dismissed—and sometimes banned—it because it was so unlike anything they knew. Due to these years of oppression, Africa's mostly oral history and its predominantly tribal indigenous cultures with its indigenous native African theatrical forms weakened. When colonialism began to loosen some of its oppressive rule (between 1920 and 1960), a transition from colonial to post-colonial performance traditions took place and changes in theatre offerings began to emerge. Professional native touring companies began to develop. These groups created adaptations of indigenous theatre forms, using local language and culture. University drama departments were also indispensible in the fight to develop works that included elements of indigenous tribal performance. These drama departments later became the centers for a national theatrical movement.

HOW INDIGENOUS AFRICAN THEATRE
LIVES ON ALL OVER THE GLOBE

Despite years of oppression and the dissemination of its people around the globe through the slave trade, the essential strength and optimism at the root of African culture did not die. In the Americas, enslaved peoples used the tools of the theatre (storytelling, dance, music, and narrative) not only to survive emotionally but also to preserve their cultural heritage. The enslaved Africans around the globe perpetuated their native traditions of telling stories and using theatre to create hope, change, and optimism. Elements of African theatre have survived through the American and Caribbean descendants of slaves. Native African theatre had a very strong influence on the development of the American musical theatre and Caribbean dance and music.

CHAPTER TWENTY

Traditional Theatre of India

Asian drama probably began in India and is sometimes seen as the "river" from which all Eastern theatre flowed. Ritual theatrical dance performance existed in India as early as 2500 BCE. Performance traditions that sprang from these religious rituals have existed in India for thousands of years in one form or another. As language and literature evolved, some forms of theatre with its roots in Indian ritual dance performance became more exclusive (i.e., reserved for the elite). However, the theatrical forms of rural India—puppet theatre, storytelling, and dance-dramas—which evolved as religious rituals and later became secular in inspiration—have had a strong presence in parts of India for centuries.

To appreciate native Indian theatrical traditions, it is helpful to have an understanding of some aspects of the Hindu religion as many of the themes of Indian drama emanate from Hindu beliefs. Hinduism stresses that spirit is the essence of life, and that the goal of all living beings is to be united with the supreme world soul known as Brahma, the Hindu god of creation. Brahma is eternal, infinite, and indescribable.

In the sacred Hindu tradition, Brahma created theatre (*natya*), the fifth Veda (sacred text), which would make the content of the previous four sacred texts accessible to everyone—even the illiterate. The goal of theatre was to both educate and entertain the people.

According to Hindu teaching, the passage of time is an illusion; time is an eternal cycle with infinite wheels of experience, each coexisting in immortal harmony. Each life is only one incarnation of infinite cycles of the soul. Therefore, other-worldly characters—spirits, gods, demons, etc.—play an integral role in indigenous Indian drama.

SANSKRIT THEATRE

The oldest-known native Indian theatrical tradition is called Sanskrit theatre, so-named because it was performed in Sanskrit, the ancient written and spoken language of India, which eventually became the language of the ruling and intellectual classes of that country. Although we do not know exactly how Sanskrit theatre was performed, we do learn an extensive amount about it from the *Natyasastra*, a book of theatrical practice and theory that is akin to Aristotle's *Poetics*. This treatise, dating to about 200 CE, is very wide in scope and contains a detailed analysis of Sanskrit dramatic texts, theatre buildings, acting, staging, music, dance, gestural movement, facial expression, costumes, makeup, scenery, playwriting, philosophy, organization of acting companies, the audience, competitions, and a mythological account of the origins of theatre. The *Natyasastra* states that theatre is a form of religious enlightenment, and the bliss of aesthetic experience is a portal to nirvana, the ultimate bliss. The author of this treatise defines a quality called *rasa*, or flavors. There are eight *rasas* or basic sentiments: the erotic, the comic, pathos, rage, terror, heroism, odiousness, and the marvelous. These correspond to basic human emotions/feelings such as love, sorrow, fear, etc. Theatre permits spectators to submit themselves to a dramatic situation corresponding to some powerful feeling that they themselves possess. Theatre can, thus, lead towards enlightenment as this performing art becomes a way to move toward metaphysics and the divine.

The rise of great Hindu epic literature (*Mahabharata*, *Ramayana*, and *Purana*) that depicts the ancient Indian beliefs and the life of Krishna (incarnation of the god Vishnu) provide the model, if not the actual source material, for much Indian theatre. These epics of Indian literature teach that true pleasure comes through kindness, humility, duty, love, and correct behavior. The *Natyasastra* describes ten major genres of Sanskrit drama, including two primary ones: *nataka*, based on well-known heroic stories of kings or sages, and *prakanara*, based on the theme of love. Sanskrit dramas included at least 2,000 plays between 200 CE–800 CE. The plays are of many scenes, places, and moods, unified not by action but by *rasa*. Sanskrit drama combines the believable with the unbelievable, comic and serious themes, and magical imagery and fantastic stories in which animals and trees can speak. Common sources may also be fables, history, mythological characters, and love stories. In Sanskrit plays, good always triumphs and virtue is rewarded, violence is never dealt with, and there is always a happy ending.

The clown figure is often central as a comic counterpoint to the hero. The often-flawed hero must struggle, suffer, and learn to achieve success. Love and restoration is the persistent truth.

Sanskrit drama was performed with an on stage instrumental and percussion accompaniment from tambourines, lutes, flutes, and zithers. The non-realistic dramatic conventions that exist in Indian dance-drama are too numerous to mention, but some of the most obvious and familiar are:

- **Masks, makeup and costumes**—An elaborate costume and mask or makeup identify each type of character. Heroes wear certain colors and makeup, while villains wear others. Demons and gods use masks in styles dictated by tradition for easy recognition.
- **Dance and gesture**—The performer moves and gestures in abstract rather than realistic ways. The actor learns each step, finger movement, gesture, and expression of face and body to communicate essence rather than everyday reality.
- **Narrator**—Narrators sing, chant, and describe in local dialects the details of the story.
- **Music**—Music is inseparable from the dance-drama, which uses instrumentation, key rhythms, and tempos to express meaning.
- **Time and length of performance**—Traditional Sanskrit drama can last several days or even weeks. Performances start at sunset and continue all night, taxing the strength and endurance of both the performers and audience.

The *Natyasastra* describes an India of professional touring acting companies that include both men and women. Each early troupe had a leader—the *sudtradhara*—who was the chief actor and also managed the others involved in the production. Men were the main performers, but contrary to other traditions, women played important roles, too. They were often central figures, objects of love and devotion, and powerful figures in their own right who changed the nature of the world.

Performers trained rigorously in vocal and physical technique with masters in an intensive, arduous program that lasted years. During their many years of training, performers learned representations of emotions through highly-stylized gestures, six glances of the eye, six movements of the brow, four movements of the neck, five leaps, and ten gaits. They also needed to master dozens of hand gestures with one hand and dozens more with both hands, all of which have precise meaning.

Performances of Sanskrit drama are meant to be like feasts that please the senses. There are various elements to the performance, each meant to satisfy a particular *rasa* (taste, flavor, emotional, or mental state). The goal of Sanskrit drama is to offer a sensual banquet, not catharsis. The standard conventions of Sanskrit drama include *benediction*, which is a prayer that is offered to the gods, and a *prologue*, given by an actor who also serves as a type of stage manager. This segment eases the audience into the fictional world. The actor introduces characters and gives a synopsis of the story. Following these segments, *song and dance*—both pure dance (*Nritta*) and gestural dance (*Nritya*)—are used extensively in the performance to tell the story and create mood.

The *Natyasastra* suggests an India of permanent indoor theatres built of wood and stone, seating 200 to 500 spectators, with elevated stages and close connections to temples. It reveals that the appropriate space for the great epic dramas is the temple, featuring marble-pillared halls with large sweeping roofs. The temple building was rectangular with separate entrances for men and women. Between the two entrance doors stood two large copper drums. The theatre was most likely twice as long as it was wide, divided equally into stage and auditorium. Four pillars in the auditorium—colored white, yellow, red, or blue—indicated where members of the different castes should sit. Carved wooden elephants, tigers, and snakes adorned the pillars, and, perhaps, the ceiling. Scenery was not used. A curtain divided the stage into two parts—one part for the action and the other for the behind the scenes area.

Even as Sanskrit drama spread across the Indian Empire, Sanskrit as a spoken language fell into disuse, becoming the language of elite scholars and poets. However, even though people did not know the language, they knew the stories. As time went on, the plays evolved into an increasingly visual form. Performers danced, gestured, and spoke Sanskrit while a narrator translated the play into the language of the audience. Music and dance provided a universal language that crossed cultural boundaries.

Once Islam became the state religion in northern India, theatre no longer thrived. The Islamic religion did not condone artistic imitations of gods and humans. Followers of Islam discouraged or forbade all artistic representations of gods or humans, including theatrical performance. Beginning around the tenth century, Sanskrit drama began to die out, and regional dance-drama theatrical forms like Kathakali and Kutiyattam became popular in southern India. Despite their differences, all Indian dramatic forms share many of the fundamental theatre aesthetics of their Sanskrit predecessors and reflect the aesthetic theories of the *Natyasastra*.

KATHAKALI

Today, the most popular and widely known of the regional dance-drama forms that were created after the demise of Sanskrit in the tenth century is the Kathakali or story plays. Kathakali is a vigorous dance-drama that was developed in the seventeenth century in rural villages in the province of Kerali in the south of India. It is a popular entertainment of village life. Like its predecessor, Sanskrit drama, it uses stories from the great epic literature of *Mahabharata*, and *Ramayana*. The repertoire consists of about 50 plays that feature kings and heroes in the constant struggle between good and evil, between gods and demons. Their mood is mysterious, cosmic, and often frightening, with stories that center around the passions (loves and hates) of gods and demons. Though good wins in the end, the power of evil forces is fully realized. Dancers bring violence and death—which are forbidden in Sanskrit drama—to the stage.

Although Kathakali has clear connections to classical Indian Sanskrit, it is also designed to delight and appeal to the visceral tastes of a more common, less sophisticated audience. Similar to Sanskrit, the stories revolve around clashes between good and evil, with good always winning.

Unlike Sanskrit theatre, which has both male and female performers, all performers in Kathakali are male. Performances are highly-stylized, and performers use a style of performance that is similar to the traditional gestures and dance described in the *Natyasastra*. Kathakali involves great strength and majesty, alternating huge leaps with perfectly still poses. A distinctive feature of Kathakali is that the actors do not speak. One group of performers sings while the actors dance and pantomime the dramatic action to the accompaniment of loud, fast drumming. By employing precise and elaborate hand gestures, footwork patterns, distinctive eye and eyebrow movements, facial expressions (see Figure 20.1), and postural contortions, the actors reveal subtlety of meaning and characterization that are barely suggested by the text that is recited and sometimes forcefully sung by the small chorus of two or three to underscore the actors' movements. Today, Kathakali has become the most internationally familiar style of Indian dance-drama.

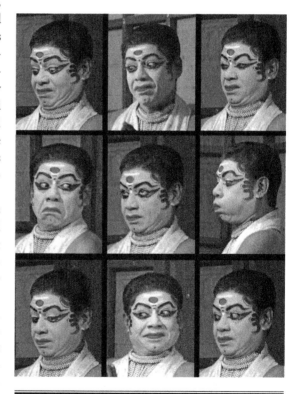

Some of the most dazzling elements of Kathakali are the highly-stylized makeup, elaborate and almost abstract costumes, and ornate crown-like headdresses that are used to convey character and attitude.

Performance training begins around age ten and is long and arduous because extraordinary and powerful movement and vocal skills are required. Actors do not often achieve mastery until they are in their 40s.

The traditional Kathakali performance can take place anywhere, but it

Figure 20.1 Kathakali actor facial expressions. (Copyright © 2014 by Jean-Pierre Dalbéra, (Copyright © 2014 by Jean-Pierre Dalbéra, (CC BY 2.0) at https://commons.wikimedia.org/wiki/File:Acteur_de_Kathakali_(Kochi,_Inde)_(14219962516).jpg.)

is often produced at night on stages about 16 feet square, covered with a canopy of flowers. The stage is surrounded by four poles, one at each corner. A single large oil flame emanates from a metal cauldron placed in front of the playing area. The sense of mystery and other-worldliness of Kathkali is heightened by this fire. It is customarily performed with no scenery. Originally, productions were epic, occurring outdoors and lasting from about ten in the evening until past sunrise on the next day. Audience members were free to leave, take naps, and eat during the performance. Today, performances usually happen within the three-hour time block that is common to Western theatre.

KUTIYATTAM

Only in Kerala, at the southern tip of the continent, did Sanskrit theatre survive in the form of Kutiyattam performance. This performance tradition preserves the custom of actors performing plays in Sanskrit while translators interpret the performances in regional dialects. As in Sanskrit theatre, both male and female actors perform in Kutiyattam productions. Similar to Kathakali, elaborate costumes and headdresses and fantastical makeup are used by actors in performance.

Figure 20.2 The first ever Kutiyattam performance outside Kerala-Madras (Chennai), 1962. (Copyright © 1962 by Sreekanthv / Wikimedia Commons, (CC BY-SA 3.0) at https://commons.wikimedia.org/wiki/File:Thoranayudham-_Madras1.jpg.)

The characters in Kutiyattam are mythological characters, primarily gods and demons. Performers use highly-stylized, coded movements and gestures and exaggerated facial and eye expressions. The text is chanted. Music is an integral aspect of performance. Two female actors play small bell-metal cymbals that sustain the tempo of the production. Drums, cymbals, oboe-like wood instruments, and a conch shell (*snaka*) accompany much of the action.

The stage is equipped only with stools, and some decorative carvings of deities and mythological characters are only faintly visible on curtains that surround the stage. There is a narrow door upstage left used for entrances, and a door upstage right is used for exits. Large pot-shaped drums (*mizhavu*) rest in heavy wooden stands between the doors. The only light on stage flows from a large bell lamp that is placed downstage center.

A typical Kutiyattam performance lasts several days. In the first days, characters and historical incidents are explored in detail. On the final day of performance, the actual text of the play is performed in chronological order. This ancient art is preserved by state and national governments and private institutions. In modern India, these institutions come together to provide the resources to sustain a Kutiyattam performance once a year.

CHAPTER TWENTY-ONE

Traditional Theatre of Japan

There are four major forms of traditional Japanese theater: Noh, Kyogen, Kabuki, and Puppet Theater/Bunraku. Noh and Kyogen are most often studied together. They are very different and distinct forms, but they share the same stage, sometimes share actors, and are usually presented as a part of one performance offering.

Similarly, Kabuki and Japanese Puppet Theatre/Bunraku are often studied together. On the surface, these two forms could not be more different. However, they share stories, characters, and the written works of one of Japan's finest writers, Chikamatsu Monzaemon.

THE NOGAKU STAGE

Noh and Kyogen, which both emerged in the fourteenth century, are most often presented as part of one performance event and called *Nogaku.* Both Noh and Kyogen strive to present the true essence of human nature, but they do it through very different approaches. Noh reveals the nature of life through the use of a symbolic and idealized presentation of an illusory world. Kyogen, in contrast, displays the essence of humanity through humor.

Traditionally, the *Nogaku* stage was built outdoors in a garden, but stages are now generally built indoors in large halls. (see Figure 21.1) The entire playing area is divided into four parts: the bridgeway (*hashi-gakari*); the main stage (*hon butai*), the rear stage (*ato-za),* and stage left of the main stage (*juitai-za).* The audience views the stage from four sides—in front of the

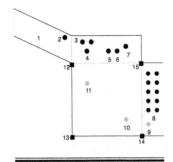

Figure 21.1 Noh stage diagram (1: hashigakari. 2: kyogen spot. 3: stage attendants. 4: shime-daiko. 5: ōtsuzumi. 6: kotsuzumi. 7: shinobue. 8: chorus. 9: waki seat. 10: waki spot. 11: shite spot. 12: shite-bashira. 13: metsuke-bashira. 14: waki-bashira. 15: fue-bashira.) (Menace3society / Wikimedia Commons / Copyright in the Public Domain.)

downstage, stage right and stage left areas of the main stage, and from the downstage area in front of the bridgeway.

The bridgeway plays an important role as part of the playing space and is the place of entrance and exit for the musicians and all important characters. At the far end of the bridgeway there is an *age-maki*, which is a multicolored curtain that can be raised and lowered to allow actors to enter and exit the stage. Downstage of the bridgeway are planted three small live pine trees, which are evenly spaced across the length of the bridge. These pine trees symbolize heaven, earth, and man.

The main stage looks like a medieval Japanese shrine or temple building and is the largest playing area. It is a roofed structure that is open to the audience on three sides. Eaves hang over the three open sides. There are four pillars supporting the roof over the main stage, each having a specific name and purpose. The *metsuke bashira,* also known as "the sighting or gazing pillar," is the downstage right pillar. It helps the actor—who is often masked in the Noh play—to position himself on the stage.

The *shite bashira* is the main character's pillar and is found in the upstage right corner of the *hon butai.* The main character—the *shite*—pauses at this pillar when he enters to announce his name and where he comes from. The *waki bashira is* positioned in the downstage left corner of the main stage and is associated with the secondary character—the *waki.*

The floor of the *hon batai* and *hashi-gakari* are constructed of thick boards polished to a smooth, glossy finish. This smooth textured floor is necessary for the "sliding foot" walk and dramatic dancing of Noh actors who do not wear shoes but wear foot coverings made of cloth. The floor also has hollow "sounding cups" placed underneath. These cups make the rhythmic, forceful stamping of the feet that is an integral aspect of Noh drama.

The orchestra and stage assistants occupy the rear stage (*ato-za*) upstage of the pillars, which allows them to see the main stage and the bridge. It is necessary for the musicians to be able to see the principal actor's performance as they must adapt what they do to his performance.

An important element of the *Nogaku* stage that is not visible to the audience is the mirror room (*Kagami-no ma.*) The mirror room is located behind the multicolored curtain (*age-maki*) that is hung stage right of the bridgeway. This room is similar in structure to the green room found in many European and North American theatres. However, the mirror room of the *Nogaku* theatre carries greater significance than most green rooms, which are seen primarily as a place for actors to dress and wait for their time on stage. Behind this curtain, the Noh actor becomes fully costumed. Once fully costumed and masked, the actor gazes into the mirror to concentrate on his role and "become" his character.

The *Nogaku* stage is simple; it does not have stage equipment—unlike Kabuki and Japanese Puppet Theatre/Bunraku. Scenery—other than the painted and live pine trees—is practically non-existent.

The Nogaku Performer

Occasionally, but not often, the *Nogaku* stage will share musicians between Noh and Kyogen performances. But, it is rare that Kyogen performances use musicians. There is also an actor within a Noh play (*ai-kyogen)* who performs in both the Noh drama and the Kyogen play. This actor will appear after the *shite (*main actor*)* of the Noh play exits the stage. He will relate to the *waki (*supporting actor) the story of the upcoming Kyogen in great detail.

NOH

Noh, considered by most to be the first great Japanese theatrical form, emerged in the late fourteenth century. Zen Buddhism was a major influence on Noh theatre. Acting troupes were under the patronage of the Zen Buddhist shrines and temples. Early Noh performances were considered "sermons" as much as they were "entertainment." The Zen Buddhists believe that ultimate peace comes through the union of all beings and the abandonment of individual, earthly desires. The Buddhists believe that happiness, fulfillment, and enlightenment cannot be achieved unless one is able to let go of their attachment to things of this world as nothing in earthly life is permanent. Attachment to this world—and everything and everyone in it—ultimately brings suffering.

The protagonists of Noh theatre reflect this belief. The main characters in Noh plays are often ghosts, demons, and obsessed human beings. They are souls that cannot be released from this earth and are continually drawn back to the material world because they are/were too devoted to worldly honor, love, or some other temporal ambition.

Noh in Performance

Noh is a very symbolic drama that imparts a graceful aesthetic with an effect of quiet elegance. The beauty of a Noh performance lies in its subtlety, restraint, and simplicity. In this way, it is the direct opposite of the Kabuki theatre. Noh theatre possesses the quality of *yugen*—elegance and refinement. The refined and elegant movements of Noh seek to capture and raise awareness of the Buddhist belief in the fragility and impermanence of earthly existence. Because the performance relies so heavily on indirectness, a Noh performance may be difficult for the novice to understand fully. The character's movements and vocalizations are often a reflection of a past event that stimulates a certain emotional state or mood. That aura is then explored through movement, music, and vocalization. Noh is sometime called "the art of walking," as a great amount of attention is given to the way a character enters, moves around the stage, and exits—all seemingly in slow motion. This type of movement accentuates the feeling of other-worldliness highlighted by Noh performance.

The written script of a Noh play is quite short—shorter than the average one act drama. It supplies a structure for telling the story through movement, music, and vocalization. The performance builds—through dialogue, song, and movement—to a final dance. Classical prose and poetry is used by the playwright: prose is intoned without musical accompaniment, and verse is sung in a rhythmic fashion to instrumental musical accompaniment. Ordinary speech only happens when an actor comes on stage between acts to summarize what has happened in the previous act(s).

Acting in Noh

Noh performers are traditionally male, however, in recent years some female actors have begun to train in Noh and appear on the Noh stage. *Shite* or primary actors take on various roles in a Noh drama. The characters this actor may play include: the main character (*shite*); the accompanying character (*tsure*); the child role (*kokata*); the chorus (*jiutai*); or stage assistants (*kolan*). The actor can portray a wide range of characters within these broad types including: spirits of men, women, plants, or trees; gods; demons; or supernatural beings. The type of character he plays depends on the type of play being performed. There is a Noh mask appropriate for almost every role played by the *shite* actor. The *shite* actor chooses the most appropriate mask based on his idea of the subject matter and his plan for the performance. This actor also wears elaborate costumes that are composed of at least five layers of clothing, which enables him to create a larger-than-life presence. The *shite* is the last to arrive on stage and most often appears from the darkness.

The *waki*, or secondary actor, supports the main actor. He will play a range of characters, including: Shinto priests; Buddhist monks; and Samurai. The roles the *waki* play are always real living men. This actor does not wear a mask and uses a performance style called *hita men*, which means "direct face." With this style, the actor performs without expression as though his face has become a mask.

Masks

The Noh mask (see Figure 21.2) is called *omote*, which means "face." There are five basic types of Noh masks, and each type has numerous variations. They are made of painted wood and are passed down through generations. The Noh mask is sculpted in such a way that the character seems both real and abstract. The way in which

Figure 21.2 Noh masks. (Daderot / Wikimedia Commons / Copyright in the Public Domain.)

the light strikes the mask can seem to change the expression on the mask, and the actors can create these changes through specific movements of the head, neck, and body. These movements can express a wide range of moods. The *shite* actor will often change masks mid-performance, showing the audience his actual face in order to reveal his true identity. When a female mask is worn by a male actor, there is no attempt made by the actor to use a more feminine voice.

Costumes

Costumes for the *shite* and *waki* actors, called *shozoku*, express in a visual way the mood and meaning of Noh plays. The garments are rich in color, design, and texture. Robes are made mainly of silk and very thick materials, which often have various elaborate designs embroidered into them. There are outer robes, which may be broad sleeved or small sleeved. Under these outer robes are inner robes—usually small sleeved—with trousers (*hakama*) or a divided skirt. Some garments may be combined or layered for use in different roles. The actor may also wear a wig, headdress, neck piece (*eri*,) and white socks. The style of these garments is based on the typical fashions of the fourteenth century. In stark contrast to the actors—the chorus, orchestra and stage attendants wear simple black kimonos and divided overskirts.

Properties

Hand properties play an important role in Noh drama, but they are minimal, simple, and conventionalized. Unlike Kabuki, there are no machinery or scenery—other than the painted and live pine trees that are a part of every performance. There are usually no more than one or two stage properties present on the Noh stage at one time. The most important props are the folding fans (*chukei.*) The actor is trained to use these fans in a very skillful way that allows him to represent objects or express emotions. The way in which the *chukei* are manipulated can suggest the blowing of the wind, the ripple of water, the rising moon, falling rain, or a plethora of subtle emotional responses. Meaning is communicated through the actors' movement of the fan as well as the music that accompanies the movement.

Orchestra, Chorus, and Stage Attendants

Four types of musicians make up the Noh orchestra—the flute player, the shoulder drum player, the hip drum player, and the stick drum player. There is a chorus (*ji*) of six to ten men. These performers narrate many of the events during the play. They may sing a character's lines at any time during the play, but they always sing all of the character's lines while the actor playing that character is dancing. The stage attendant is present—on stage—throughout the course of the performance, but he is not considered to be a part of the actions or the stage picture. He assists the main actor in changing or adjusting his mask or his complex, layered costume. The stage assistant will also set and remove stage properties and prompt as necessary. He is a trained, senior *shite* actor and will assume the main role if there is an emergency and the actor scheduled to play the main role cannot perform.

Rehearsals

All of the members of the performance—actors, orchestra, chorus, stage attendants, etc.—usually have only one rehearsal prior to performing together. All are trained in the same tradition and know the plays thoroughly, so there is no need to run through lines, staging, and timing many times. This spontaneity of interaction, combined with well-executed explicit conventions of performance, create a very dynamic event. Each participant in the production must be fully present and able to pick up on the nuances created by his fellow artists in that particular performance. In this way, Noh strives for a perfection through a mastery of artistic conventions and a passionate fusing of each component in a collaborative union.

KYOGEN

Kyogen plays are short, farcical pieces that are often performed during the interludes between individual Noh plays. The Kyogen performance varies—it may explain, in simple terms, the story of the preceding Noh piece, or it may merely offer comic relief. Kyogen literally means "wild words." It is a spoken dialogue drama of encouraging and optimistic words, filled with satire and humor, whose goal is to bring about laughter through physical comedy, mime, and lively language. An audience member at a Kyogen performance will experience witty jokes and tasteful, gentle humor. However, it does not stop at mere realism in its style of acting. Like Noh, it is performed according to strict conventions. The experienced Kyogen actor utilizes an acting technique that incorporates a highly-stylized physical and vocal form of expression. The Kyogen performance usually lasts about half an hour. It may have a short song or dance in the climactic scene accompanied by the drums and flute of the Noh performance.

The subject of Kyogen is most often the everyday life of the ordinary person in Japanese feudal society. Stories often realistically depict a kind of "everyman" character. He is a large-hearted, strong character who evokes joyful laughter. The stories are sometimes based on folk tales with animals, gods, and devils as characters. The plays may also be parodies of the Noh plays that have preceeded them. Kyogen reveals a wide range of comic subjects, and there is more emphasis on situation than on character. It is most common for these plays to have only two or three characters, who speak in the prose dialogue of the lower classes. The characters—both primary and supporting—are mostly nameless and are involved in ridiculous everyday situations. Comic situations arise in these plays because of the unexpected predicaments in which the comic characters—drunkard, cowardly Samurai, ignorant leader, greedy monk—find themselves. The plays breathe life into the amusing situations in which ordinary people in feudal Japan would find themselves on a daily basis. Many of these situations are the same ones in which contemporary individuals find themselves—giving them a timeless, universal appeal. The plays are divided into categories by types of characters.

Masks

Although masks are used, they did not develop as extensively in Kyogen as in Noh. There are about 20 different types of masks, and all are designed to provoke laughter in the audience. These masks are used for characters, such as old people, deities, ghosts, demons, and spirits of animals and plants. Often, however, actors do not wear masks—even male actors who play women express emotion with their own faces.

Costumes

Kyogen costumes are designed to resemble the clothing of common Japanese people of the Middle Ages. The clothing is simple, but it may integrate some outlandish shapes and designs. The material is dyed with light attractive patterns, which reflect the personalities of the characters who will be wearing them.

THEATRICAL GENRES: NÔ AND KYÔGEN

Nô is a highly stylized art in which drama, dance, and music are intertwined. The lyrics are either sung with an energetic instrumental accompaniment or declaimed in unique patterns of intonation, and dances are performed by the main character at the climax. *Kyôgen* is a comedy consisting mainly of dialogue and pantomime. *Nô* and *kyôgen* have been performed on the same stages since the Muromati period (1334–1573). Although *nô* and *kyôgen* have performance techniques in common, music is given less weight in the dramaturgy of *kyôgen*.

HISTORY

Before the Meizi era (1868–1912), *nô* and *kyôgen* were called *sarugaku*—a term deriving from a popular entertainment of the Heian period (eleventh century, at the latest) that was full of farce and pantomime. An element of farce remains in *kyôgen*.

In the Kamakura period (1192–1333), the main repertoire was *okina*, a sacred ceremony, in which three gods called Okina, Titi no zyô, and Sanbasô gave their blessing to humankind. This ceremony is believed to have been derived from the rituals performed in temples in the first or second month of the new year.

At the beginning of the fourteenth century, Kan'ami Kiyotsugu (1333–1384) and his son Zeami Motokiyo (1363–1443) emerged from the Yûzakiza, one of the troupes performing *okina* in the courtyards of Buddhist temples and Shinto shrines, to establish *nô*. Kan'ami transformed *nô* into a musical play by introducing *kusemai*, a narrative song chanted rhythmically with dance. He also contributed such popular works as *Zinen kozi* and *Sotoba komati*, which appeal to audiences because of their eventful stories and witty dialogue.

Zeami, through his acting, directing, writing, and composing, as well as his choreography, poetry, and theory, became Japan's first great all-around man of the theater. Among his numerous achievements, he established the standard two-scene play called *mugen nô*, in which he combined poetry with music very effectively. A typical plot develops as follows. In the first scene, the main character, appearing as a reincarnation, chants an old story concerning his or her past. In the second scene, the character reappears as in life, but just before death, and performs a dance that symbolizes the essence of the play. Most of Zeami's works are constructed in this way, including *Takasago*, *Atsumori*, and *Izutsu*. As a result of Zeami's activities, *nô* developed into one of the world's most sophisticated forms of musical theater.

Takakuwa Izumi, from "Theatrical Genres: Nô and Kyôgen," *The Concise Garland Encyclopedia of World Music*, ed. Ellen Koskoff, pp. 1169–1173. Copyright © 2008 by Taylor & Francis Group LLC. Reprinted with permission.

THE STAGE

Nô and *kyôgen* are performed on a special stage (figure 1), which is not separated from the audience by a curtain but is open on three sides. The main stage, which has an area of approximately 30 square meters (it is about 5.4 meters on a side), is covered with highly polished boards to facilitate the performers' sliding footwork. The back wall of the stage, called *kagami ita*, on which a pine tree is painted, serves as a resonating board; the acoustics are also enhanced by large earthenware jars buried under the floor. At the end of the entranceway is the *kagami no ma* 'mirror room', where the actors put on their masks and the instrumentalists tune and warm up by playing a short melody.

NÔ THEATER

Actors

Nô involves three groups of performers: *tati kata*, the actors; *ziutai kata*, the chorus; and *hayasi kata*, the instrumentalists who provide the accompaniment.

Tati kata is in turn divided into three subgroups: site *kata*, *waki kata*, and *kyôgen kata*. The actors in *site kata* play the main character, called site; and the attendant role, called *ture*. The *site* and *ture* wear delicately carved masks when they play female or nonhuman roles. The chorus, called *zi utai*, belongs to this subgroup. It consists of six to ten members who sing in unison—they present the greater part of the text, describing the situation and the emotions of the main character.

The *waki kata* plays a secondary role called *waki*. He enacts a minister, a priest, or another man who summons the *site* to the stage and draws out his or her story. The *waki kata* never wears a mask and seldom dances. His chanting is less elaborate than that of the *site kata*.

The third subgroup, called *kyôgen kata*, is common to both *kyôgen* and *nô*; it too consists of one actor. In *nô*, he has either an intermediary role, summarizing the story in the interlude between the first and the second scenes; or a minor farcical role.

Repertoire

The repertoire of *nô* is grouped into five categories according to subject matter and the main character. In the first category, called *kami nô* or *waki nô*, the main character is a god or a messenger of a god, who gives blessings to humankind. *Takasago* and *Tikubusima* are popular pieces in this category. In the second category, called *syura nô*, the main character is the ghost of a warrior of the Heike or Genzi clan, who presents a scene of a past battle. *Yasima*, *Kiyotsune*, and *Sanemori* are well-known examples in this category. In the third category, called *kazura nô*, the main character is the ghost of a beautiful woman who reminisces about past love, or the spirit of a plant appearing as a woman. *Izutu*, *Matukaze*, and *Basyô*—all highly elegant—belong to this category, which is considered the essence of *nô*. The fourth category, called zatu *nô*, has miscellaneous subjects and treats them realistically. For example, a woman distraught with grief over her lost child is the main character of *Sumida gawa* and in *Aoi no ue*, a noblewoman jealous of a rival in love turns into a demon (figure 2). In the fifth category, *kiri nô*, the main character is a demon or a supernatural being. *Momizi gari, Kokazi, Syakkyô,* and *Syôzyô* are representative works in this category.

Styles of acting and musical performance are formalized in accordance with this classification, which was established in the Edo period. Even today, the classification remains the standard, and that explains why *nô* can be performed without a director. When more than one drama is presented in the same program, the order of presentation complies with this classification.

Instrumental Pieces

There are many instrumental pieces for introductions and dances. When a character appears onstage, an instrumental piece matched to this character is played. Dances are usually performed by the main character as the highlight of a play. They are divided into three groups and selected according to the type of main character.

The first group of dances—including *kami mai, otoko mai, haya mai, tyû no mai, zyo no mai,* and *sin no zyo no mai*—is not intended for realistic expression; its purpose is to display the beauty of the dancer. Each dance has the same

structure: four or five sections in which a unit of four phrases is played repeatedly by the *nôkan* in eight beats. Although all these pieces have a common basic melody, they are varied by means of inserted phrases and changes in tempo. *Kami mai* is the fastest dance, that of a young god. *Otoko mai* is the second fastest dance, that of a warrior. *Haya mai* is a dance of the ghost of a nobleman. *Tyû no mai* is performed by various characters in a modest tempo. *Zyo no mai* is a slow, delicate piece, the dance of a beautiful woman. *Sin no zyo no mai* is the slowest dance, that of an elderly god. Most of these dances are played in the *ôsiki* mode, but *haya mai* is in the *bansiki* mode, one pitch higher. *Ôsiki* and *bansiki* are terms taken from *gagaku*.

The second group of dances—including *gaku, kagura, kakko, syôzyô midare,* and *sisi*—involves realistic representation. *Gaku* is danced as *bugaku* accompanied by *gagaku*. *Kagura* is a dance of a goddess or a shrine maiden. *Kakko* is derived from popular music of the Muromati period. *Midare* is a dance of a drunken spirit living in the sea. *Sisi,* the most energetic piece, portrays a lion spirit living in the holy mountain. Each of these dances has its own structure, consisting of several sections with distinctive phrases in eight beats. Some of them are connected to the pieces of the first type in the latter half: *kagura* with *kami mai, kakko* with *tyû no mai*.

The third group of dances—including *kakeri* and *inori*—creates many theatrical effects. For instance, *kakeri* is intended to express the restless mind of a madwoman who misses her husband or child, or the mind of the ghost of a warrior who is suffering the aftereffects of a battle. *Inori* accompanies a scene of confrontation between the specter of a woman and a priest who tries to exorcise the evil spirit through prayer. Most of these dances are short pieces with no eight-beat melodic patterns.

Kyôgen

Various types of music can be heard in *kyôgen*. Some plays, called *mai kyôgen*, are structured much like nô, with a chorus and instrumental accompaniment. In *kyôgen*, however—unlike *nô*—not all of the text is chanted, nor do instrumentalists always take part. Popular songs of the Muromati period are often inserted as entertainment in banquet scenes. Some of them are the same pieces as in *nô*, but others are from *kabuki* and are accompanied by the *syamisen* (three-stringed lute). They are chanted in the same modes as in *nô*, but the rhythm is slightly different. Instrumental pieces are sometimes used for dances and as introductions. Most of them—such as *sandan no mai, gaku, sidai*, and *issei*—have the simplified structure of those in *nô*. It may be said that music is not always closely related to the dramaturgy but is only a part of the performance.

There are about 260 works in the *kyôgen* repertoire, performed by one or both of two *kyôgen* schools: Ôkura and Izumi. These plays can be classified according to the type of main role: for example, there are plays in which the main character is a Shinto god or Buddha; a landowner, or *daimyô*, who is mocked; a foolish or clever servant, *tarô kazya*; a jealous or affectionate wife; or a ridiculous monk. This typology, however, is more flexible than the classification of *nô* plays, which fall into five fixed groups.

As in *nô*, the vocalizations and body movements of *kyôgen* are highly stylized. Although *kyôgen* consists mainly of musically stylized speech, it also includes songs and instrumental ensembles. Songs, called *kyôgen utai*, may be specific to a particular *kyôgen* or may be used more generally. For instance, the song *Nanatugo* or *Nanatuninaruko* 'Seven-Year-Old Child' can be performed during any scene where *sake* is being drunk. Interestingly, this particular piece is derived from a medieval popular song, indicating that *kyôgen* is related not only to *nô* but also to other musical genres. *Kyôgen* uses the same two scales (*yowagin* and *tuyogin*) and the same rhythmic structures as *nô*.

Kyôgen also uses the same instrumental resources as *nô*. As in *nô*, one instrument (the *nôkan*) or combinations of two instruments (*nôkan* and *kotuzumi*), three instruments (*nôkan, kotuzumi*, and *ôtuzumi*), or all four instruments are used, depending on the nature of a scene. However, the way the instruments are played suggests different aesthetics. The players sit face to face, at right angles to the wooden wall, and play rather softly. Drum calls are also softer than in *nô*.

Thus, *nô* and *kyôgen* complement each other, using music and drama to illuminate different aspects of human nature.

—Adapted from an article by Takakuwa Izumi

BIBLIOGRAPHY

Bethe, Monica, and Karen Brazell. 1982. *Dance in Nô Theatre*. 3 vols. Ithaca, N.Y.: China-Japan Program, Cornell University.

Bowers, Faubion. 1974. *Japanese Theatre*. Rutland, Vt.:Charles E. Tuttle.

Keene, Donald, and Kaneko Hiroshi. 1990. *Nô and Bunraku: Two Forms of Japanese Theater*. New York: Columbia University Press.

Nakamura Yasuo. 1971. *Noh: The Classical Theater, trans*. Don Kenny. New York: Weatherhill; Tokyo: Tankosya.

Ortolani, Benito. [1990] 1995. *The Japanese Theatre: From Shamanistic Ritual to Contemporary Pluralism*. Princeton, N.J.: Princeton University Press.

Yoshinobu Inoura, and Toshio Kawatake. 1981. *The Traditional Theatre of Japan*. Tokyo and New York: Weatherhill.

KABUKI AND PUPPET PLAYS/BUNRAKU

During the Edo period (1603–1868) these two forms of theatre—Kabuki and Puppet Theatre—were the most popular entertainments in Japan with the common people. Kabuki theatre, which highlighted the physical and vocal talents and charisma of dynamic actors, dealt most often with conflicts within a great lord's (*daimyo*) household and sometimes with the struggles of the commoners. Kabuki is an actor's theatre; it provides numerous opportunities for "star" actors to demonstrate their virtuoso acting techniques. Puppet Theatre—later called Bunraku—paid more attention to the lives of ordinary people. Because this theatre used puppets, it exploited the special capability this format afforded in presenting scenes of chaos, violence, and superhuman feats.

The texts performed in both theatres were the same. There are two primary types of texts used in these forms of theatre. The gossip play or domestic play (*sewamono*) dealt with common ordinary people and not heroes from the past. The most popular of the *sewamono* plays is the "love suicide" play. The period play (*jidai mono*) dealt primarily with historical events. Originally, the managers of the theatres who created the scripts for Kabuki and Puppet/Bunraku theatre were not particularly interested in creating long-lasting dramatic works—they just wanted to fill seats. However, this was changed by Chikamatsu Monzaemon, often considered Japan's most significant playwright.

Chikamatsu Monzaemon wrote plays for the Kabuki stage and the Puppet Theatre. He is lauded for the way in which he portrays the everyday townsperson in his writing. The common people of his plays are much like the heroes of contemporary plays who are trapped by financial and other ordinary life circumstances that they feel unable to change. In developing characters in his works, he went beyond the limitations of good and evil characters who had existed in earlier works and created characters of some moral ambiguity and significant complexity. His plays highlight members of the middle class, who speak as they would if they were happened upon in real life. In his work, Chikamatsu reveals the ability of human beings from all walks of life to experience powerful emotions—something that did not appear on the European stage until 150 years later. He is best known today for the *sewamono* plays he wrote for the puppet theatre—especially his "love suicide" (*shinju mono*) scripts, a genre that he invented. In his love suicide plays, his protagonists conclude that the only noble choice they have is to commit suicide rather than kill their oppressors. In addition to his sensitive characterizations, Chikamatsu is admired for his subtle, beautiful, and complex use of language—especially the rhyme patterns and puns he uses in his works. He is noted for a writing technique known as "pivot word." This form of literary dexterity involves using more than one meaning of word in a single line. The word functions one way in the beginning of a line and another way in the remainder of the line.

Puppet Theatre/Bunraku

The puppet theatre—most commonly referred to as Bunraku—can be traced back to 1100 when Oe Tadafusa published his *Book of Puppeteers*. From this point forward, some form of puppet theatre was always practiced by traveling entertainers. Even before puppet theatre became prominent, a variety of entertainment in which stories, folktales, and legends were recounted or chanted to the accompaniment of a stringed instrument (*biwa*) was common.

For some time, the puppet theatre was the most popular form in Japan. It catered to the tastes of the audience and capitalized on all of the feats that the lifelike puppets could achieve more successfully than live actors. The puppet theatre had the advantage of eliminating the complication of the Kabuki play that focused on the presence of the actor rather than the play itself. It also indulged the audience's desire for the trick stage business known as *karakuri*. During the early part of the eighteenth century, the types of visual effects that were possible with the puppets were similar to what is possible today with computer-generated imagery in animated and live-action films. Impossible situations like operations, quick transformations, or dismemberments could be enacted with puppets but not with live human actors. Eventually, Kabuki prevailed over puppet theatre/Buraku in popularity, but by the time this occurred, the puppet theatre supplied Kabuki with about half of the plays in its repertory and Japanese literature with many of its dramatic masterpieces.

The Puppets

The puppets used in traditional Japanese puppet theatre have undergone many changes, and some have become more complex. Originally, the puppets only had heads, and the head of each puppet was painted in such a way that it signaled to the audience whether it was a good or evil character. Later, hands

(a) Sanbaso puppet face detail with moveable eyes, eyebrows, and mouth. (Shinobo / Wikimedia Commons / Copyright in the Public Domain.)

(b) Bunraku puppet doll and costume (Copyright © 2008 by Ellywa / Wikimedia Commons, (Copyright © 2008 by Ellywa / Wikimedia Commons, (CC BY-SA 3.0) at https://commons.wikimedia.org/wiki/File:Bunraku_doll_in_national_theatre_Osaka_2.JPG.)

Figure 21.3 Saga Dainenbutsu Kyogen festival.

and feet were added. In the 1700s, many changes were made to the puppets, which made the most of their adeptness and potential. These changes included: a mechanism that was introduced to allow the puppet's eyes to move, open, and shut; moveable eyebrows were added; moveable mouths were created; jointed and moveable fingers were affixed; and hands that could grasp objects were developed. (see Figure 21.3a and 21.3b.) Today, puppets vary in size and complexity, depending on the importance of the character in the play.

As the puppets continued to become larger and more complex, the number of operators increased. Originally, the puppets had one handler who was hidden from view. After the 1730s, the figures grew in size to their present three to four feet and were operated by three men, all in view of the audience. One puppeteer gives life to the head and the right arm, one manipulates the left arm, and one controls the feet. (see Figure 21.4.) Training for handlers is long and arduous, taking over 20 years.

The Stage

Just as the puppets that inhabit the realm of the traditional puppet theatre have grown in size and complexity over the years, so has its stage. The current stage is about 36 feet wide and 25 feet deep and is divided into three levels, from downstage to upstage. Each section—again, from downstage to upstage—is designated by a low partition between which the handlers work. Productions utilize painted scenery that suggests realistic representations of the various locales depicted in the drama, and they change as required by the story. Moveable stage settings began to be used after 1715, which led to the invention of stage machinery that was later adopted throughout the world. For example, the revolving stage device was developed for the puppet theatre about 100 years before there was any similar device used on the stage in Europe. In 1727, elevator traps were invented to raise scenery through the floor. Many properties are used in traditional Japanese puppet theatre.

The Samisen Player

The samisen is a three-stringed instrument with an extremely versatile sound. The sound this instrument produces can replicate the rise and fall of the voice; it can give special emphasis to words or enhance, punctuate, and intensify narration and action. The samisen player is considered one of the two most important performers in the traditional Japanese puppet theatre. He brings the text to life by adding punctuation and musical accents to the words of the chanter and the actions of the puppet

Figure 21.4 Bunraku puppet, showing handlers dressed in black to the right and left of the puppet. (Copyright © 2007 by Boonrock / Wikimedia Commons, (CC BY-SA 3.0) at https://commons.wikimedia.org/wiki/File:Osonowiki.jpg.)

with a wide range of sounds. In this way, he helps to define the emotional quality of each moment of the production.

Acting

The handlers and the chanters aim to create a kind of realism that is achieved through the imaginary conditions of performance. The puppets are very elaborate and are, therefore, capable of expressing considerable emotion—especially when accompanied by the samisen musician. The audience is expected to "suspend disbelief" and accept the awkward artistic movements of the puppets as reality. The three-person puppet enables the handlers to create surprising effects and subtle and amazing movements. This requires considerable coordination among the puppeteers.

The Chanter and the Handlers

In the Japanese puppet theatre, the puppeteer/handlers do not speak. The Chanter, whose voice is very well trained, sits or stands to the side of the stage and vocalizes all of the dialogue. He also acts as a narrator, both commenting on and advancing the action. He will tell the story and express the feelings of the puppets through vocalization, facial expression, and gesture—smiling, crying, jolts of shock, gasps of fear and astonishment. His interpretation is guided by musical notations in the text that indicate accents, changes, and inflections throughout.

The handlers and puppets perform center stage. They silently bring the text to life, creating powerful, lifelike, and dramatic movements out of words—even when the movements are not described by the text of the play. The handlers of the puppets are usually in a lowered section of the stage so that they remain unobtrusive. In modern performances, they are most often dressed in black and wear black face masks so that from a distance, they are almost imperceptible (see Figure 21.4). They try to become one with the puppet and absorbed in the drama—physically and emotionally. Because these handlers do not speak, all expression is communicated through their integrated movements with the large dolls they manipulate in coordination with their co-artists.

THEATRICAL GENRES: BUNRAKU

The word *bunraku*, once the name of a specific theater (the Bunraku za, established in Osaka in the early nineteenth century), has come to mean, more generally, a puppet play accompanied by *gidayû busi* (narrative singing) and music. *Bunraku* is performed collaboratively by people who have three different functions: narrator, *syamisen* player, and puppeteers. Normally there is one narrator, one *syamisen* player, and three puppeteers for each puppet. However, there are several exceptions to this rule. One exception occurs in *mitiyuki* (poetic journey) scenes or *keizi* (dance drama) scenes, where the narrative is shared among two or more performers and there is also more than one *syamisen* player. Another exception occurs when there are two platforms and two sets of performers, one on either side of the stage, as in the *yama no dan* 'mountain scene'. A third exception is the occasional

appearance of an extra *syamisen* player. Fourth, sometimes a different kind of instrument—such as a *koto*, the thirteen-stringed long zither; a *kokyû*, a long-necked bowed lute shaped like a *syamisen*; or a *yakumogoto*, a two-stringed long zither—is added to the performance, making a trio. In such cases, the additional instrument is played by a young *syamisen* player. However, the focus of the genre is not just on the *syamisen* player, narrator, and puppeteers, but on the essential relationships between them.

Puppets and Stage

In the early days, the puppeteer would simply set up a large oblong box and hide behind it, holding the puppets above it. The puppets had no legs, so the puppeteer moved the doll with his hands from underneath his *kimono*, a long robe with wide sleeves. Later, many technical advances were made.

Motegi Kiyoko, "Theatrical Genres: Bunraku," *The Concise Garland Encyclopedia of World Music*, ed. Ellen Koskoff, pp. 1176–1177. Copyright © 2008 by Taylor & Francis Group LLC. Reprinted with permission.

The three-man manipulation was first introduced in 1734 and it is still used to this day. The principal puppeteer inserts his left hand into the body of the doll and manipulates the doll's right hand with his right hand. The second puppeteer is in charge of the doll's left hand; the third puppeteer is in charge of the feet. This method requires the three puppeteers—or at least the upper parts of their bodies—to be visible to the audience.

The contemporary stage has two parts to differentiate between indoor and outdoor scenes: the *hon tesuri* has a rail marking the boundary of the indoor scenery; the *ni no tesuri* has another rail for outdoor scenery. The railings allow the puppets to appear to be standing on the ground, whether indoors or outdoors. At each rail, the floor is low, so that the operators can usually be seen only from the knees up. This means that the dolls are fully visible above the rails where their feet are placed by the third puppeteer. Another feature of the *bunraku* stage is a platform placed at an angle at the right side of the stage, where the narrator and the *syamisen* player sit. This small revolving platform enables players to make their entrances already seated after the curtain opens and allows a second group of players to revolve into place when the first group is finished.

A *bunraku* doll consists of a wooden head, a body, two hands, and two legs. The puppeteers assigned to each role assemble and dress the doll. Puppeteers build special relationships with their dolls, treating them with great respect

and even a sense of tenderness. There are heads made specifically for various types of roles. The broadest division is between male and female heads, which can then be further categorized as old, mature, and young; and as good characters and villains. The head called *bunsiti*, for example, is a virtuous middle-aged warrior, a typical prudent hero. The head called *musume* 'girl' is often used for a sweet adolescent. The head called *gabu* is used in special cases, when a character must suddenly change into a demon. The dolls are made to perform not only realistic actions but also many formalized movements expressing various emotions. They are said to have a beauty possible only with wooden puppets.

Music

Because *bunraku* is theater, its music must serve the needs of dramatic expression. As a result, the off-stage music of *kabuki* (*geza ongaku*) was introduced into *bunraku*. Above the entrance curtain on the left-hand side of the stage, behind a bamboo blind, is a small room called the *hayasi* room. The *hayasi* instruments used in *bunraku* are practically the same as those of *kabuki*; the *syamisen* is the primary one. Formerly, a single performer would play all the instruments—a feat requiring not only musicianship but also acrobatics. Today, however, two or three performers share the work. There are rules about melodies and playing techniques, but these are not applied very strictly; their purpose is to enhance the appropriate atmosphere and the expressiveness of the puppets.

At present, there are a few contexts of folk art in which puppet plays are performed with *gidayû busi*. The best-known performers are the Awaji puppet troupe, which has a permanent theater on Awaji Island, and the Awa puppet theater in Tokushima. There are puppet performances with *syamisen* music other than *gidayû busi* in various parts of Japan.

Style and Structure

Bunraku includes both historical plays (*zidai mono*) and contemporary plays (*sewa mono*). It also includes *zidai sewa*—plays that have elements of both *zidai mono* and *sewa mono*.

The historical plays are set in the times before the Edo period (1600–1867), and the major characters are mainly of the *samurai* class. In the contemporary plays, the major characters are common people of the Edo period; these plays realistically depict the emotional conflicts of everyday life. The first *sewamono* play written by Chikamatsu Monzaemon (1653–1724) was *Sonezaki Shinzyû* 'Love Suicide at Sonezaki'; it was first performed at the Takemoto za theater in Osaka in 1703, by Takemoto Gidayû (1651–1714).

Traditionally, a historical play has five acts (*dan*). Later, plays with more acts were written, but musically these can be reduced to the five-act format. The first act presents an incident that sparks the drama. The second act contains a conflict. The third act is the tragic climax. The fourth act, which is elegant and lyrical, includes or is preceded by a *mitiyuki*—a poetic

journey. The *mitiyuki* is a dance scene that depicts the scenery through which the characters are traveling as a kind of procession. The fifth act resolves the original conflict.

In the five-act structure, each act—except for the fifth act and the *mitiyuki*—has an opening scene (*haba*) and a closing scene (*kiriba*). The *kiriba* is important both dramatically and musically, and it is recited by a senior narrator. The *haba*, by contrasts, is an introduction depicting an incident that leads up to the *kiriba*, and musically it less flamboyant than the *kiriba*. If an act is divided into three scenes for dramatic purposes, they are called *kuti*, *naka*, and *kiri*; in this case, the *kuti* and *naka* correspond to the *haba*.

A contemporary play consists of three acts. Because it dramatizes events in townspeople's lives, the music is simpler and more realistic than that of a historical play. In a contemporary drama, the *mitiyuki* occurs in the last act; typically, the journey is undertaken by two lovers who are on their way to commit a double suicide. With regard to the structure within each act, contemporary plays are virtually the same as historical plays. There are also one-act plays called *keizi*. These are dance dramas, often based on pieces from *nô*, *kyôgen*, and *kabuki*.

Audience members become deeply involved in the dramatic content of the plays; they buy and read scripts as the play progresses, applaud the virtuosity of the narrator, and gasp with delight at special effects, such as when a genteel-looking puppet suddenly reveals a demonic side through the transformation of a head of the *gabu* style. Audience members also burst into tears as, for example, a man sacrifices his own son so that his lord's son's life might be spared. In each case, the conflict between duty and desire is drawn publicly in a performative catharsis that audiences come to expect, and to need.

—*Adapted from an article by Yamada Tieko*

BIBLIOGRAPHY

Gerstle, C. Andrew, Inobe Kiyoshi, and William P. Malm. 1990. *Theater as Music: The Bunraku Play "Mt. Imo and Mt. Se: An Explanatory Tale of Womanly Virtue."* Ann Arbor: Center for Japanese Studies, University of Michigan.

Keene, Donald. 1961. *Major Plays of Chikamatsu.* NewYork: Columbia University Press.

Keene, Donald, and Kaneko Hiroshi. 1990. *Nô and Bunraku: Two Forms of Japanese Theater.* New York: Columbia University Press.

Scott, A. C. 1955. *The Kabuki Theater of Japan.* London: George Allen and Unwin.

KABUKI

Kabuki theatre can be traced back to 1603 in Kyoto when Izumo Okuni—a female dancer/shrine maiden/prostitute—and her troupe of female dancers began to give public performances on an improvised stage. In this original style of kabuki—*Onna Kabuki*—the performers were all women, and the performances, which took place just outside of a Buddhist temple, were obviously erotic and an expression of an optimistic, sensual society. Izumo Okuni was known to be a provocateur. She is said to have worn men's clothes and to have imitated the costumes and makeup of the most extreme Kabukimono of her time. The origin of the word Kabuki is the verb *kabuku*, which means eccentric, slanted, offbeat, eccentric, extraordinary, or outside the limitations of common sense. During the Edo period in which Izumo Okuni lived, the Kabukimono were people who had extreme hairstyles, wore high fashion clothes, and resisted the controls and conventions of society. The dances and simple skits that she and her troupe performed were also provocative—depicting aspects of activities that would occur in a brothel, showing relations between men and women, titillating the audience, and advertising the troupe of female dancers who were also sex workers.

In 1629, because the form had come to be associated with prostitution, women were banned from the stage and were replaced by young men. This style of kabuki, known as *Wakashu Kabuki,* included the skits and dances of the previous form, with the addition of acrobatics. It was also this incarnation that brought about the evolution of the art of the female role specialist (*onnagata.*) When young men played these roles, looks were the primary component—the "prettiest" young men would be called upon to play the role of the ingenue. This factor created a certain homoerotic element to the performances, which brought about another ban. In 1652, young boys were banned from the stage because authorities felt that the large number of men who were gathering to admire the boys who played the *onnagata* roles created a threat to public order and the moral fiber of society. These bans left a limited pool of performers—older men only—to create the wide variety of characters who peopled kabuki plays.

Yaro Kabuki

Yaro Kabuki, which utilized more mature male actors instead of women or boys, gradually changed from review-like dancing and skits to performances that put a greater emphasis on serious drama with real artistic content. Clearer divisions were established between the *onnagata* actors and the male role players, and within these two main categories, training was established that allowed actors to become increasingly specialized. Actors trained to become experts almost exclusively in one role—the clown, the older woman, the villain, the warrior, etc. At this time, the art of *onnagata* developed extensively. Because older men were now playing the roles, they could not rely on a pretty face to carry them through. In order to be more convincing and effective, actors incorporated stylized gestures and higher-pitched voices into their characterizations. Dance, which had been a part of Kabuki since the start, shifted almost exclusively to the realm of the *onnagata* for whom dancing was seen as the central expression of femininity and eroticism. In the eighteenth century, dance became an essential part of all roles, and professional choreographers became customary members of the company.

Form

Kabuki performances are long. During the height of its popularity in the Edo period (1650–1850), performances would usually last about 12 hours. These performances were arranged into four parts, which would relate thematically: a historical play (*jidaimono*) which glorified the traditional values of the samurai; a dance with a strong emotional component, which may or may not tell a story; a domestic drama (*sewamono*) set in the environment of merchants, traders, or artisans; and concluding with a humorous one act dance-drama. Over the years, the running time of the performances has been greatly reduced, although the four-part arrangement is still kept. Complete full-length plays are seldom performed; instead, the four-part arrangement may include as many as ten acts from a variety of plays.

Dance is, and always has been, the centerpiece of Kabuki. Kabuki dance includes any type of rhythmic movement, deliberate posture, or stylized, coded gesture. The dance performed in Kabuki reflects the text and distills the essence of the emotions.

Music

Music helps to establish character in Kabuki theatre, but it takes a subordinate role. In some plays, there is music both on stage and off stage. In the dance-derived plays, actors do not sing. However, on stage, traditional instruments, such as drums, shamisen and flutes, accompany the on stage narrators to add power and emotion to their delivery. A chorus sings lyrics that describe the scene and narrate the story. These melodic forms of singing are accompanied by rhythms of percussion. The chorus may also sing lines that are being said by the character—almost as if the chorus' voices go through the character.

Acting

Kabuki acting is a combination of stylized speaking and rhythmic movement; it is not realistic. Various techniques are used in Kabuki by different characters:

- The *aragato (which translates as "wild stuff")* style of kabuki acting is used for the masculine hero roles. When performing in this style, the actor will paint colorful lines on his face and body. He will use grand poses (*mie*) to create larger than life moments. A *mie* is a strong pose that is struck by the male heroic character. It outwardly expresses a powerful emotion or conflict through a physical pose, gesture, or facial expression. It is a stop-action tableau accompanied by loud beats of wooden clappers for emphasis. This technique is a way of expressing—visually and aurally—a specific feeling and presenting it to the audience. The moment is frozen—almost like a snapshot. His expressions will also include shrill screams. All of these devices combined create a thrilling, spine tingling performance that is difficult to forget.
- The *wagato* style is used for gentle romantic men. They are likable and charming to watch.

The female roles (*onnagata*) are played by men. These actors use a special theatrical convention based on an idealized artistic interpretation of a woman.

There are also stylized fight scenes in Kabuki called *tachinawari*. In these scenes, a group attacks a single hero with carefully choreographed steps, acrobatic leaps, and somersaults.

The dances that are performed are a combination of physical motion, music, and acting. The sensuous movements allow the actors to flow from one moment to the next, using subtle and meaningful gesture. Actors learn a vocabulary of specific and codified mime that communicates actions—like writing a letter—or setting—like scattering petals in the wind. The movements, along with the lines and the music, bring the poetic imagery of the text to life.

The language in Kabuki is expressed in a very presentational and external way. Language is not commonplace or naturalistic. Eloquence in language is demonstrated in a speech called *tsurane.*

The main actor directs the kabuki play. Because it is repertory theatre, most of the plays and dances are performed continually and are well-known to the actors. The lead actor will choose which version of the play will be performed based on his family's performing conventions (*kata.*)

All of the actors already know their roles (see training), so very little rehearsal time is required. Of course, brand new works or revivals of plays that are not performed regularly would be an exception and would require more rehearsal time.

Makeup, Costumes, and Wigs

Costumes, wigs, and makeup range from the simple to the very outlandish and extraordinary. Masks are not worn by actors in Kabuki theatre. However, the makeup used in this traditional Japanese theatrical art form is often very elaborate and may make it seem like the actor is wearing a mask. The most basic makeup is a white base. Upon that white base, various details will be added to signify character. The *onnagata* (see Figure 21.5) draws in false eyebrows and adds rouging from the corner of the eye to the mouth. Other than that, this character's face is completely white. Basic characters will have red and black designs painted on the face. Demons and evil characters will use blue or brown paint.

The most gorgeous costumes and wigs belong to the top-ranking courtesans. Historical accuracy in costume design is not important in Kabuki. Each role has a traditional costume that has its base in a historical garment, which is then altered for dramatic effect. Fashions from many different eras will often be seen in a single play. The costumes are not always easy to wear, and actors must train to manipulate them with grace and elegance. Some of the costumes weigh as much as 50 pounds,

Figure 21.5 Sagimusume (Heron Maiden) dance performed by onnagata Akifusa Guraku. (Copyright © 2011 by Fujisaki Tomoya, (Copyright © 2011 by Fujisaki Tomoya, (CC BY-SA 3.0) at https://commons.wikimedia.org/wiki/File: 日本舞踊_長唄「鷺娘」.)

which makes it necessary for stage attendants to assist actors on stage with their costumes.

Properties

Props used in the Kabuki theatre range from the symbolic to the realistic. Like in Noh, the fan is an important prop, especially in the dance plays. The way the fan is used may indicate riding a horse, shooting a bow and arrow, the rising of the moon, the opening of a door, or a variety of other actions. The scarf is also used extensively in Kabuki and can serve a large number of purposes.

Training

Kabuki actors train diligently for many years. Most begin training at the age of six or seven. Dance is studied first, followed by instruction in diction, intonation, and wearing of costumes. Students may appear on stage early in their lives as there are many children's roles in Kabuki. An actor is not considered a master until after he has reached middle age. Since actors get so much performance experience from an early age, they are expected to learn a great number of plays and dances; by the time they are mature performers, they just need brief reviews (and very little rehearsal time) to be prepared to perform. Kabuki is predominantly a hereditary profession. Lead performers are drawn from a few acting families (see Figure 21.6).

The Stage

The Kabuki stage is unique and is populated with a variety of machines that were invented

Figure 21.6 Kabuki acting family: Danjuro Ichikawa I, II, III, IV, V, VI, VII, VIII, IX, X, XI and XII. (Copyright in the Public Domain.)

Figure 21.7 Kabuki theatre looking toward the stage. (Copyright © 2013 by urasimaru / Flickr, (CC BY-SA 2.0) at https://www.flickr.com/photos/urasimaru/11490910863.)

to create dramatic special effects. Some of the mechanical stage devices that were invented by the Japanese for the Kabuki theatre include: a small trap door in the floor; the larger elevator stage; and the revolving stage. The principal acting areas of the Kabuki stage include the fore-stage and the *hanamichi. (*see Figure 21.7) The *hanamich*i is a raised walkway that goes through the audience, connecting the fore-stage to a small room at the rear of the house. It is used for all major entrances and exits and for all important scenes.

Scenery

Kabuki has a great deal of scenery, which serves both decorative and functional purposes. Every locale in the play is suggested scenically. Settings are changed in full view of the audience by means of the revolving stage machinery, elevator traps, or visible stage attendants. The revolving stage allows for very rapid set changes and dramatic scenes in which people or things, such as boats, can seemingly move across the stage without assistance. The *suppon* lift allows the actor to appear suddenly in the midst of the audience. Other lifts allow whole buildings to rise up out of the ground or huge roofs of dilapidated palaces to crash to the floor.

Scenic painting is flat and not intended to appear three-dimensional. In most productions, the stage is enclosed upstage by flats painted with a scene of a distant view. There is no effort made to create a sense of reality in the scenic design—cracks between flats are exposed, black curtains are used to mask the top of a flat, and detailed finishing is not required. Many scenic pieces are incomplete or are used symbolically. The scenic design in Kabuki constantly reminds the audience that it is watching a play.

Audience Interaction

Kabuki is a popular entertainment, and because of the configuration of the stage, the actors and the audience are in close proximity. One of the fundamental principles of Kabuki is that it is presentational—all stage action is directed toward the audience, which makes the audience feel as if it is an integral part of the performance. During the performance, some members of the audience will shout out at the actors. This is a traditional practice called *kakego*. The shouts of the audience are meant as a kind of applause and encouragement for the actors. They add atmosphere to the play and can stimulate both the actors and their fellow audience members, making for an exciting theatrical experience. Kabuki actors are very popular "stars" who are admired for their acting skills as well as the spirit of individuality and freedom that they embody.

THEATRICAL GENRES: KABUKI

Kabuki theater combines, drama, dance, costume, and music. It is a colorful, lively genre that has been popular for centuries and is still followed with tremendous enthusiasm by a cadre of devotees, particularly in cities such as Kyoto and Tokyo. *Kabuki* is an emblematic form that for many represents

Motegi Kiyoko, "Theatrical Genres: Kabuki," *The Concise Garland Encyclopedia of World Music*, ed. Ellen Koskoff, pp. 1174–1175. Copyright © 2008 by Taylor & Francis Group LLC. Reprinted with permission.

a sense of premodern Japan. Most Japanese people have never seen, and never will see, a *kabuki* performance, but tickets sell quickly, *kabuki* performers are treated almost like nobility, and most conventions of performance practice and audience behavior remain similar to their seventeenth-century antecedents.

The essential characteristics of *kabuki* theater derive from its foundation as a popular entertainment form during the Edo period (1603–1867), when Japanese society included a samurai class (the subject of many of the plays) and a merchant class (the sponsors of many of the plays). Its content was—and is—primarily feudal, including stories of loyalty, hierarchy, and internal conflicts, as humans struggle with divided needs and desires and for political control. The audience engages noisily with the actors, shouting encouragement and compliments in a way that is as guided by unwritten rules as what is taking place onstage. Actors draw from a complex repertoire of poses, vocal expressions, stylized gestures, and ways for moving across the stage, all known collectively as *kata* 'form, pattern'. Because the three primary theatrical genres of *nô*, *kabuki*, and *bunraku* draw from similar literary traditions and conventions, each influences the other. Movements drawn from *bunraku* puppetry appear in *kabuki* in the *maruhon* or 'puppet style', while stories from *nô* theater are used in both *kabuki* and *bunraku*. Dance in *kabuki* can be as delicate as a young woman dancing with a parasol or as lumbering as rustic farmers at work; the intention

of the scene dictates which dance *kata* are used. *Kabuki* is famous for its transformative costumes in which an entirely different costume is revealed with a single movement, but most costumes reflect traditional wear of the Edo period.

Present-day *kabuki* theater makes use of many instruments that have been incorporated over the course of the genre's history. In its infancy, at the beginning of the seventeenth century, *kabuki* music was played on a handheld flat gong (*kane*) that the performers struck as they danced and chanted Buddhist prayers. In the early seventeenth century, the four instruments (*si byôsi*) used in *nô* drama— *nôkan* (transverse flute), *ko tuzumi* (shoulder drum), *ô tuzumi* (side drum), and *taiko* (stick drum)— were incorporated, as was the *syamisen* 'samisen' (a three-stringed plucked lute), which had been introduced to Japan in the mid-sixteenth century from China by way of Okinawa. By the mid-seventeenth century, the *ô daiko* (a large barrel drum) and *take bue* (a transverse flute) had been added, completing today's basic *kabuki* ensemble. Three musical forms are the foundation of *kabuki* music: *gidayû busi* (narrative singing); *nagauta* (lyrical singing); and *hayasi* (instrumental music).

Gidayû busi was introduced around 1684 and was strongly influenced by the *zyôruri* narrative style used in puppet theater. It is performed by musicians who specialize in *kabuki* and are independent of their colleagues in *bunraku* puppet theater. The content of the stories is the same for both theatrical genres, but because the actors onstage are given primacy in *kabuki*, they are free to cut or extend portions of the text that normally would be presented in *gidayû busi* style in *bunraku*.

Nagauta is a vocal genre accompanied by *syamisen* (three-stringed plucked lute) that developed within the *kabuki* tradition of Edo (now Tokyo) during the second half of the eighteenth century, although the first mention of it is found earlier, in a program of the Edo Nakamura troupe dated 1704. Compared with the *syamisen* used in *zyôruri* (narrative style of *syamisen* music), the instrument used in *nagauta* has a more slender neck and a lower bridge and is played with a thinner plectrum, resulting in a high, piercing tone that many Japanese perceive as somewhat showy. *Nagauta* serves two main functions: background music performed from behind the *kuromisu* screen at stage right; and music, known as *de bayasi*, used as an accompaniment to dance and played by performers seated in rows at the back of the stage, facing the audience.

Hayasi can be traced to the assimilation of the *nô* ensemble in the early 1700s, but Buddhist and secular instruments continued to be added through the 1930s, producing a unique sonic world that has evolved continuously to accommodate improvements in stage construction and changes in narrative content and directorial methods. *Hayasi* music is played almost exclusively on wind and percussion instruments, many of which were borrowed from other performance genres such as *nô* and *gagaku*. Perhaps the sound in *hayasi* most familiar to *kabuki* lovers is that of the *ô daiko*, a large barrel drum that is struck with beaters of various lengths and sizes to suggest psychological states, depict lively festival music, or evoke natural phenomena such as rain, wind, rivers, waves, snow, and thunder.

INSTRUMENTS AND ENSEMBLES

As noted above, *kabuki* has made use of instruments from *gagaku*, *nô*, Buddhist ritual, Shinto ritual, folk music, chamber music, and the instruments developed for the genre itself. In short, it has made use of almost every type of instrument found in Japan since the 1600s. Experiments continue today, with some groups incorporating synthesizers and other modern instruments in an effort to stay true to the mission of *kabuki*: to create sounds that communicate with contemporary audiences. These various voices and instruments are selected and arranged in ways that best match the drama unfolding onstage. In sharp contrast to the meticulously planned musical structures of Western opera, *kabuki* concerns itself with overall musical progression, while leaving room for unplanned combinations of sonic materials. Though unplanned, these combinations are by no means accidental. Through their experience with and understanding of the overall musical characteristics of a given piece, the performers possess detailed knowledge concerning the timing and nature of the sounds they must produce to fulfill their intended role within the larger context of the work. Experience, understanding, and knowledge constitute a tradition that defines the context in which unplanned or improvisational events are allowed to occur.

—Adapted from an article
by Motegi Kiyoko

BIBLIOGRAPHY

Gunji Masakatu. 1969. *Kabuki—Yôsiki to densyô* (*Kabuki*—Style and Transmission). Tokyo: Gakugei Syorin.

Halford, Aubrey S., and Giovanna M. Halford. 1956. *The Kabuki Handbook*. Tokyo: Charles E. Tuttle. Kageyama Masataka. 1992. *Kabuki ongaku no kenkyû* (Study of *Kabuki* Music). Tokyo: Sintensya.

Leiter, Samuel L. ed. 2001. *A Kabuki Reader: History and Performance*. Armonk, N.Y. and London: M.E. Sharpe. Malm, William P. 1963. *Nagauta: The Heart of Kabuki Music*. Rutland, Vt.: Charles E. Tuttle.

Scott, A. C. 1955. *The Kabuki Theater of Japan*. London: George Allen and Unwin.

CHAPTER TWENTY-TWO

Traditional Theatre of China

*The theatre of China has its roots in the song, dance, acrobatic spec-*tacle, puppetry, visual art, poetry, storytelling of folktales and legends, and music that was created by the various ethnic groups who have inhabited the region throughout the centuries. The dominance and popularity of various performance modes waxed and waned as leaders from each new dynasty or government championed distinct forms. However, many of the various ethnic group's traditions and techniques were kept alive and often flourished in their local communities after their genesis.

During the Tang Dynasty (618–907), comedy skits and puppet shows were popular forms of performance art. It was also during this period that progress was made toward creating a theatrical form that incorporated music, dialogue, dance, and acrobatics and saw the development of the first formal training school for actors, "The Pear Garden." The Emperor Xuan Zang set up this school to train singers and dancers to become entertainers at his court. This school trained young artists in both popular and innovative forms rather than traditional ethnic forms from any specific region. After the creation of this school, "Student of the Pear Garden" became synonymous with the term actor or thespian.

Some of the most extensive developments in Chinese theatre occurred during the Song Dynasty (960–1279). These earliest dramas expressed the struggles of the people. One of the most popular forms of performance in the Northern region of China early in this period was the *zaju*, also known as mixed form. These were short, comic variety shows that included poetry, song, dance, singing, and mime. The oldest existing Chinese dramatic text, *The Doctor of Letters*, which has its roots in the drama of the Southern region of the country, is believed to have been written during this time period. The play includes a prologue, which summarizes the main action and story of the performance, which is then told through dialogue and songs.

Another development during this period is the performance of popular Chinese novels that had been written over the centuries as well as folktales passed down through oral tradition. These stories were told by professional storytellers at teahouses, a common location for social gathering. Puppet shows and shadow plays were also popular forms of theatre at this time. The characters in shadow plays are brought to life through the use of flat, jointed, cut-out figures attached to sticks. These figures are often very detailed, finely crafted characters that are works of art in and of themselves. However, when these figures are placed between a source of light and a screen or scrim and are manipulated by a puppeteer, the shadows that they create make the characters come to life in front of the audience.

The traditional Chinese theatre, known today as Beijing Opera, began to emerge in the twelfth century as a union of a variety of highly-evolved methods of artistic expression. When the southern and northern feudal regimes merged, the northern *zaju* variety shows were the first to blossom and develop in Bejing. The shows were expanded to four acts, each with ten to 20 arias sung by the protagonist. All other characters would speak or recite their lines. Strict rules or conventions were developed:

- All songs in a single act must use melodies from the same mode.
- All lyrics must use the same rhyme scheme,
- The mode and the rhyme for one act could not be used for another act in the same play.
- If the dramatic action could not be completed in four acts, prologues or interludes could be added in the form of wedges (*chie jie*). *Chie jie* are short (no more than two arias), and they can be sung by a character other than the protagonist.
- At the end of the play, the story is summed up with a rhymed couplet or quatrain.

The action of the play took place over the span of months or years and occurred in many locations. Sometimes the play ended happily, sometimes unhappily, but poetic justice always prevailed.

In the Yuan Dynasty (1279–1368), there was a burgeoning of Chinese literary drama. The writers from this period, who were most likely well-educated intellectuals who had been excluded from their usual work in the government by the new Mongol regime, are considered the creators of the written foundation of classical Chinese theatre. These dramatists culled stories from history, legends, folktales, novels, and contemporary events. The pieces presented a wide range of Chinese life, often based on the past while made relevant to contemporary civilization. Although characters represented the entire spectrum of life, the most important roles in these dramatic works were emperors, scholars, government officials, and generals, as well as rebels, students, wives, daughters, and concubines. The major themes in the plays include: loyalty to family and friends, honesty, devotion to work, and duty. The dramatic structure of these plays showed a world in conflict, but, in the end, justice would prevail. There was not always a happy ending. The play may end unhappily for the protagonist; however, the villain was usually discovered and would pay for his crimes.

Staging practices for these plays were strictly adhered to. The stage was open on three sides to the audience (thrust stage) and was essentially bare. There were two doors on either side of the rear wall—stage right for entrances, stage left for exits—on either side of an embroidered wall piece that was purely for decoration. Costumes were extremely colorful and contained a great deal of texture and detail. The costumes had long, extremely wide sleeves, referred to as *water sleeves*. Makeup was very dramatic and colorful, and some male characters wore long beards. Performers during this time period were both male and female (notable because women would later be forbidden by law from performing in public). In fact, acting companies during this period were often named for the leading actresses of the time. One of the best-known dramatists of the period, Guan Hanqing, is often referred to as the father of Chinese drama.

In the middle of the fourteenth century during the Ming Dynasty (1368–1644) this *zaju* style was preempted by the more literary, poetic southern style of drama known as *nanxi*, which is renowned for its poetry, pathos, and beautiful songs. Hundreds of new plays grew out of local ethnic songs and dances.

The mid-sixteenth century brought changes to *nanxi*, based primarily on a new musical form, and it also acquired a new name, *kunque*. This new style was so successful that it dominated Chinese traditional theatre from 1579 to 1779. *Kunque* may have 50 or more acts, each with its own title. The opening act is an argument or prologue in which a secondary character explains the story and the author's message. The ensuing acts introduce various plot strands, all of which are happily resolved by the end of the performance. In contrast to the previous style in which only the protagonist sang, in this new form, any character could sing, and performances included solos, duets and choral pieces. The most famous dramatist of this period was Tang Xiazu, whose collection of four plays—*The Four Dreams*—was very popular. Eventually, *kunque* lost favor among the public because the scripts were too long to be produced in their entirety, and the language of the plays was too formal and filled with illusion to be understood and appreciated by the uneducated. Also, the rules circumscribed by the form limited the writers' in their creativity and spontaneity. Now, the plays from this period are recognized primarily as literary works rather than as scripts that are appropriate for performance.

BEIJING OPERA

Beijing Opera as it is most often experienced today first came into being in 1790 when performers from various regions of China were brought together in Beijing (then known as Peking) to perform at the 80th birthday celebration of Emperor Qian Long. After the celebration, many of the performers stayed on in the capital and worked together to combine features of the various regional styles into a new form called Capital Drama, or *jinqxi*. *Jinqxi* is characterized by conventions inherited from earlier periods and developed into a strict system. It incorporated the best that local dramas had to offer and developed highly-sophisticated and subtle conventions of performance. It is closely related to the lives of the common people and has wide popular appeal. This style is predominantly theatrical and performance-based rather than literary. The audience goes to SEE a production rather than HEAR a play. The focus of the performance is on strictly-controlled codes of acting, dance, movement, music, and singing rather than text. When an audience attends a Beijing Opera production, the expectation is not that it will see a single work but rather a series of selections, often acts or portions of longer, complete works that are combined with acrobatic displays.

In Beijing Opera, there are two main types of plays: civilian and military. Civilian plays deal with social and domestic themes. Military plays present the adventures of warriors. It is possible for both types of plays to be blended together. As in previous manifestations of Chinese opera throughout the country and history, stories are taken from history, historical novels, epic legends, fairy tales, mythology, folklore, anecdotes, and legends that are well known to the public. Some stories are taken from plays created centuries before. Also, like previous versions of this traditional style, all the plays end happily.

As the text is not integral to the production, it is not strictly followed. Actors are free to make changes to the text at certain points in the production. Each performance troupe may have a slightly different interpretation of standard works. The texts and the stories are meant to be merely an outline for performance.

At times, when watching a performance of the Beijing Opera, the dramatic action may seem obscure and be difficult to follow as it is a section of scenes, dances, songs, martial arts, and acrobatics that are chosen to accentuate the high points of a story. As in previous incarnations of this traditional performance style, the actor is the main focus of the show. The stage is mostly bare, and few properties are used. The stage is an open, roofed platform raised only a few feet above the ground; it is usually square. The surface of the stage is covered by a carpet.

The only permanent set pieces are a wooden table and a few chairs, which are moved about the stage by stagehands into various configurations in order to symbolically create various locales. Dialogue and the actor's physical movements help to establish time and location. Symbolic movements express a great variety of actions: opening and closing doors, riding a horse, rowing a boat, etc. (see Figure 22.1.) The environment is evoked in the audience's imagination— a very powerful tool. Space and time in the structure and arrangement of the play is very flexible. There is no curtain or light change between scenes, so the actors must convey the passage of time and change in location. A few actors may symbolize a huge army. At times, *double scenes* may be performed simultaneously on stage—one upstairs and one downstairs, one inside the city and one outside the city—creating a sense of suspense. The sense of time and space may seem to be shifting, which imparts an unusually heightened sense of drama.

Figure 22.1 Beijing Opera "Qiujiang" (京劇「秋江」), performed by actress SHIOZAWA Tomoko (塩沢伴子) and actor TOMITA Masahisa (冨田正久). (Copyright © 2011 by Kimura Takeshi, (CC BY-SA 3.0) at https://commons.wikimedia.org/wiki/File:Beijing_Opera_Qiujiang.jpg.)

This symbolic mode of expression afforded by conventions and strict codes allows for great flexibility in the conveyance of time and space. Almost any action or scene may be expressed in a Beijing Opera performance.

In traditional Beijing Opera, both stagehands and musicians, who are dressed in nondescript clothing, are present on the stage throughout the performance to support the actors. Stagehands help actors with costumes and handle the shifting and placement of properties on stage. But, they become almost invisible; the audience's eye is constantly drawn to the colorful, lavish costumes worn by the actors and to the seemingly magical physical and vocal prowess demonstrated by these expertly trained performers who move and vocalize according to strict conventions mastered over years and years of arduous training. In contemporary China, with the switch to proscenium stages as the venue for performances, musicians are often seated in the wings rather than on stage.

Most Beijing Opera plays are full of sympathy for the oppressed. Since the plays are often devoted to political and military struggles and social problems, they tend to incorporate the legends of heroes and heroines who personify the high ideals of the people. These individuals arouse the people's concepts of good and evil, right and wrong throughout the ages. Characters are taken from all walks of life and are divided into four main types, with subcategories. These subdivisions determine a character's age, profession, and personality. The main categories and their subdivisions are as follows:

- **Main category—Male or *sheng*.** The subcategories within this main type are: old men; young men; and warrior types. Actors playing these roles wear simple makeup and all—except the young men—wear long beards.
- **Main category—Female or *dan*.** The subcategories within this main type are: quiet and gentle; vivacious; warrior maidens; and old women. Originally all of these roles were played by women, but from the late eighteenth century until the early twentieth century, women were forbidden from performing, and female roles were played by men.
- **Main category—Painted face or *jing*.** Actors who play painted face characters have elaborate and colorful patterns painted on their faces, which signify what type of character they are. Painted face characters may be warriors, bandits, supernatural beings, gods, or government officials. The basic qualities of these characters are enormous confidence, bluster, and exaggerated strength. Painted face roles are subdivided into: major or minor characters; fighting, acrobatic and gymnastic characters; or singing and acting characters.
- **Main category—Clown character or *chou*.** The *chou* is the most realistic character in Beijing Opera. He speaks prose (not poetry) in a common dialect. He improvises, tells jokes, and pokes fun throughout the performance. The subcategories within this main type are: a civilian clown with emphasis on singing and acting (*wen chou*); and an acrobatic and stage fighting clown (*wu chu*), who is often an expert mime and acrobat.

The format of the Beijing Opera is very stylized and follows strict conventions and codes of symbolic gestures, movements, and intonations, which are modified in accordance with the traditional aesthetic of the Chinese people. The technique is similar to that used in Chinese painting in which a few swift, sparse strokes of the painter's brush can convey the whole form and meaning of the subject. Upon entering the stage, characters will describe themselves and explain the story. These speeches clarify the situation and characters quickly, allowing more time to develop moments of high interest.

All stage movement is rhythmic, symbolic, and represents or imitates reality, but it is not realistic. Every gesture that an actor makes is part of a systematic code. There are seven basic hand movements, more than 20 pointing gestures, more than 12 special leg movements, and a myriad of sleeve and beard movements—each communicating a message to the audience about character and plot. The conventions are integral to the aesthetic principle of the performance and must be adhered to. These conventions epitomize the national identity of Chinese traditional drama.

As was briefly mentioned earlier, costumes are extremely important to character and story. There are over 300 standard items that are designed to describe a character's personality, social status, and age through color, design, ornamentation, and accessory. Each item is made of luxurious material (see Figure 22.2) with the exception of those clothes worn by poor characters and clowns, which may be comprised of cotton or linen. All costume designs have great symbolic significance. Headgear is as diverse and intricate as clothing. There are approximately 100 various types of headgear, and each conveys a unique meaning.

Makeup is also very explicitly designed according to strict rules. Some characters wear very little makeup. The faces of other characters are painted with a white base and simple coloring around the eyes. Clown types are differentiated by black markings that are painted on their faces. *Jing* roles have the most complicated makeup, with bold patterns that are symbolic of the character they are playing. (see Figure 22.2.)

Actors who perform in Beijing Opera commit to a lifetime of rigorous training. Children enter training schools between the ages of seven and 12 years old. They then engage in an arduous and disciplined training program under the tutelage of experts for a period of six to 12 years.

Figure 22.2 Actors in the role of "bad guys" in the Chinese Opera. (Jean Norwood / Library of Congress.)

It is important to note that the conventions are not fixed and unchangeable. The codes can be applied flexibly according to variations in character and play. Outstanding actors throughout the years have brought their own expressions of creativity to the form. The extensive physical and vocal training actually offers an actor greater freedom, as the body responds spontaneously to create the form and energy, thus affording him the unfettered ability to communicate the spirit of the character. In performance, these highly-trained performers are able to combine their life experiences with artistic expression to reanimate the characters through conventions and, perhaps, even create new conventions. They *create people*, they do not *act parts*.

CHINESE OPERA: AN OVERVIEW

Chinese Opera exists in a great variety of forms and styles and has a long history. Although the best-known in the West is Peking opera (known as *jingju* 'capital opera' in the People's Republic of China; known as *guoju* 'national opera' in Taiwan), some 350 different kinds of musical drama were found in a survey conducted in the 1950s. Each is identified with a particular province, district, or dialect; they can all be called "traditional" in so far as they developed during the past several hundred years as an integral part of the Chinese cultural fabric and share many features of content and structure with one another.

Zaju

In order to convey the scope and complexity of Chinese opera, a brief mention of a few operatic genres from the past is helpful. It is generally recognized that a sophisticated form of opera called *zaju* had developed in northern China during the Yuan dynasty (1279–1368) and, significantly, became a vehicle for creative output by the literati. More than 160 complete opera scripts have been preserved to this day; most of these can be attributed to known writers. The scripts do not contain musical notation (although they provide the titles of the tunes), but they reveal much about the rigid formal structure that almost all the operas followed. With few exceptions, each had four acts plus an optional interlude. Musically, the nucleus of an act was a suite of arias (solo songs) unified by the same tonal mode and by a single rhyme running through all the verses of the text. The general practice was for all the arias in an opera to be assigned to a single performer, who played the principal male or female role.

Although we know little about the tunes themselves, we do know that they were as a rule not "composed" by individuals but were preexisting tunes, each identified by a literary title. The vast repertoire of tunes used in *zaju* came from a variety of sources, including folk tunes and other kinds of vocal and instrumental music. The poet-scriptwriter selected the tunes appropriate to the dramatic and structural demands of the scene, wrote texts to them, and arranged them into suites. Some tunes became extremely popular among poets; a single tune might be chosen for a large number of verses in the same opera or in different operas. This was feasible partly because flexibility of the tunes, and partly because the poet-scriptwriter chose the words carefully so that the text conformed to a prescribed prosodic structure, one that could be readily fitted into the tune. This basic compositional process of *zaju* is found in all operas of later ages and styles.

Little information is available today on the musical instruments used in *zaju*. Paintings and occasional document suggest that the performance may have been accompanied by an instrumental ensemble consisting of a *dizi* (a side-blown bamboo flute), *ban* (wooden clapper), *gu* (drum), and *luo* (hanging gong). Other instruments, such as the *sanxian* (a three-stringed plucked lute and the *pipa* (a four-stringed pear-shaped lute), may have been used.

An important feature of *zaju*, which is still found in most contemporary operas, is *jiaose*, or role types. The characters in all the operas were categorized into a limited number of *jiaose*, each with its own style of acting, speaking, singing, costume, and makeup. These aural and visual means of expression define the gender, approximate age, social status, profession, and personality of the *jiaose*, and thus the identity of the character. In *zaju*, there were more than twenty *jiaose*, only a few of which were singing roles. And today an actor or actress is usually trained in a particular *jiaose* and enacts the characters in different operas belonging to this *jiaose*.

Nanxi

While *zaju* flourished in the north, theatrical activities also developed in other parts of China. The most prominent was *nanxi* (southern dramas) in the south. Sixteen complete scripts of *nanxi* and a large number of fragments have been preserved from about the same period as *zaju*. They show that the southern style differed from its northern counterpart in having a more flexible structure. The number of acts

was not fixed and often ran up to forty or fifty; and at times more than one performer sang in an act. The pattern for the sequence of arias was also more flexible, and the choice of arias was not restricted to a single tonal mode within an act. But the aria, which uses preexisting tunes of southern origin, is still the basic musical unit. *Nanxi* was later influenced by *zaju* and developed into a kind of opera called *chuanqi* during the Ming dynasty (1368–1644).

The association of *zaju* and *nanxi* with the literati explains their relatively high social status, their prominence in historical documents, and the proliferation of drama scripts, all of which contribute to their visibility today. However, there were doubtless more than these two kinds of opera in China. Other kinds, differing from one another in several respects, especially in musical style and dialect, flourished in many areas of the country, although little is known about them, because of the lack of written source material.

Shengqiang and Juzhong

Before continuing with this overview, a word of explanation is needed for the Chinese terms *shengqiang* and *juzhong*. *Shengqiang* (or *qiang*), though it means different things in different contexts, principally refers to systems of tunes, it also implies general modal characteristics and vocal ornaments. *Juzhong* refers to types of drama that differ from one another mainly in dialect, but often share plots, styles of costume, and styles of acting. A large number of *juzhong* share the same *shengqiang*, and some *juzhong* combine more than one *shengqiang*. Local dialects and aesthetic preferences introduce regional flavors into the music and into performance practice, so that the same *shengqiang* may be manifested in different guises. Among the major *shengqiang*, *kunshanqiang*, later known as *kunqu*, eventually became the most popular during the middle of the Ming dynasty; it exerted the greatest influence on other *shengqiang* and *juzhong* throughout China from the sixteenth to the nineteenth centuries.

Kunqu and *Jingju*

Kunju—meaning the (musical) drama of Kun, or Kunshan—is a post-1950 Chinese official designation for a style of drama that arose in the Kunshan–Suzhou area of Jingsu Province during the mid-fifteenth century. It is also commonly known as *kunqu* 'song of Kun[shan]', a pre-twentieth-century term that is still prevalently used and is the one used in this text.

As theater, *kunqu* rose to a dominant position over other regional theaters during the mid-Ming dynasty around the sixteenth century and continued its dominance on the national stage well into the the mid-Qing dynasty of the late eighteenth century. The eventual dominance of *kunqu* over all other operatic styles is largely attributable to one of the greatest performers in Chinese history, Wei Liangfu, who was active in the mid-sixteenth century. Wei introduced important musical innovations in his performances: he paid special attention to matching the tonal movement of a melody with the linguistic tones of the text, emphasized the accurate enunciation and projection of the text, and executed his melodies in a particular style known for its intricate ornamentation and its exceptionally slow tempo.

A standard *kunqu* troupe is made up of five basic categories of actors and their subcategories: *sheng* (actor or male role), *dan* (actor or female role), *jing* (actor of painted-face role), *mo* (actor of subsidiary male role), and *chou* (actor of comedic role). A *kunqu* actor is expected to be a good singer and to master many modes of speech, ranging from recitation and heightened speech to appropriate delivery of everyday language. In addition to singing and speech, a *kunqu* actor must master complex gestures and dance movements involving elaborate manipulation of the head, eyes, hands, and feet, as well as complex movements with long sleeves and other props.

Performances of *kunqu* are accompanied by a small instrumental ensemble that, though, never standardized, consists of a melodic section and a percussion section. The principal melodic instrument, the *dizi*, is a transverse bamboo flute with six finger holes, a mouth hole, and another hole covered by a thin membrane that gives it a characteristic buzzing sound. Other subsidiary melodic instruments that add layers of heterophony to the *dizi* melody include the *sheng* free-reed mouth organ and an assortment of plucked strings such as the *sanxian*, a three-stringed plucked lute with an oval sound box; a *pipa*, a four-stringed plucked lute with a pear shape, and the *ruan*, a round-bodied lute with four strings played with a plectrum. The principal percussion instruments include a wooden clapper and a small flat drum used in conjunction with the *dizi* to punctuate the meter and rhythm of the songs and a small gong, a cymbal, and a barrel drum to punctuate movements and to indicate dramatic situations.

During the mid-eighteenth century, the national dominance of *kunqu* was challenged by other, more popular regional theaters and by the late nineteenth century, *kunqu* was seldom performed anywhere exept the lower Yangtze region, where it had first been given shape. Nevertheless, aficionados have continued performing it and it remains highly regarded in Chinese opera circles.

Several of the rival *shengqiang* spread to many parts of China and spawned a large number of *juzhong*. Among the *shengqiang* that were important in the course of the next two centuries were *yiyang-qiang, bangziq-iang*, and *pihuangqiang*.

Around the end of the eighteenth century, *pihuangqiang* was introduced into Beijing, the capital, and soon became the most popular of the various *shengqiang;* significantly, it won the royal patronage of the Qing dynasty (1644–1911). Known since then as *jingju*, or Peking opera, it soon spread to the other parts of the country. Peking opera is a dramatic art in which

Figure 1 Peking opera performed at the Taipei Military Theater in Taiwan, 1978. *Photo by Terry E. Miller.* (Copyright © 1978 by Terry E. Miller. Reprinted with permission.)

Figure 2 An imprisoned female character (*dan*) with a comedian (*chou*) keeper in a performance by a youth troupe at Taipei Military Theater in Taiwan, 1978. *Photo by Terry E. Miller.* (Copyright © 1978 by Terry E. Miller. Reprinted with permission.)

Figure 3 Battle scene in Peking opera performed in Taipei, Taiwan, 1978. *Photo by Terry E. Miller.* (Copyright © 1978 by Terry E. Miller. Reprinted with permission.)

The makeup, in a variety of colors and designs, also reveals personality—heroic, temperamental, comical, and so on (figure 2). Although all dramatic movements are dancelike, there are also scenes of real dance, sometimes with a sword or long scarves and ribbons. The most spectacular are the battle or fighting scenes, which are, of course, an opportunity to display acrobatic feats (figure 3).

The stage setting for Peking opera is reduced to a minimum. It is mainly through the gestures and movements of the performer that we see or imagine the surrounding conditions in the drama, such as whether he is supposed to be on a boat in a stormy sea or stepping into a room by crossing a threshold.

The aural aspect of Peking opera includes singing, instrumental interludes, speech, and percussion patterns. Singing can occur at any moment of the drama. It can be the main feature of an act, or it can simply serve as a routine structural element concluding a scene. A long passage often can be sung by just one person expressing his or her feelings, narrating a sequence of events, or expounding a long argument. Alternating dialogue singing between two characters is also frequent. The amount of singing that occurs in an opera depends mainly on the nature of the story. Some operas feature singing almost throughout, whereas others may have spoken dialogue and acting, with some singing inserted here and there.

both the visual and the aural elements are highly systematized. The various kinds of singing and speech, the body movements, and the costumes and makeup are all standardized and have symbolic meanings. Complicated as it is, the artistic language of Peking opera is familiar to a good part of the audience, whether a piece is an established work or newly written. Within certain limits, such operatic elements can be manipulated creatively by experienced performers and readily appreciated by knowledgeable members of the audience.

The actor's facial expressions—anger, joy, surprise, and so on—are all codified. The bodily gestures with their various meanings invariably develop into a dancelike routine (figure 1). The costumes are symbolic in both design and color, so that through a costume one can immediately recognize a character's social or official position.

At the peak of their popularity, *kunqu* and *jingju* were performed in many places and enjoyed by people at many social levels. *Kunqu* was particularly cultivated by the literati, and as noted above, *jingju* had the patronage of the Qing court. Their association with the privileged classes enabled these two kinds of opera to reach a high level of refinement and sophistication. Social prestige and financial rewards, unmatched in other kinds of opera, attracted performers and scriptwriters of exceptional talent; the performances came to be appreciated as more than entertainment. Aesthetic theories were proposed and established. Repertoires were stabilized and systematized; scripts and, to a certain extent, musical notation were published; biographies and histories were written. In short, each of these two operas evolved into a generally recognized "high art."

Despite the dominance of *kunqu* and *jingju* over the past four centuries, a large number of regional operas also developed and flourished; they have mostly served as entertainment for the masses, and have little in the way of formal aesthetic theory attached to them. They have two other important social functions. First, dramatic performances have always been an integral part of religious ceremonies, calendrical festivities, and rites of passage in Chinese society. Indeed, opera and ritual developed hand in hand. In some parts of China, at least, these ritual functions, such as thanksgiving to gods and exorcism of evil spirits, remain largely unchanged today. Second,

for centuries these operas served as a source of information and an arbiter of moral standards and social behavior for audiences, the majority of whom were nonliterate or semiliterate; the operas were thus an important medium for mass communication and, to some extent, education. In recent decades, the importance of this function has been reduced by a rise in literacy and by the flourishing of other mass media, such as radio, film, and television.

Opera Productions

Opera productions developed in particular geographical regions and in some instances among a particular social stratum, making them distinct in several ways. The size of the troupes and the scale of performances can vary greatly, ranging from a handful of performers to as many as fifty or sixty. Foremost among the differences is the dialect used in performance, which is usually that spoken in the area where the drama flourished. Musically, the operas are different if they belong to different *shengqiang*; the differences include the repertoire of tunes, scale, tonal mode, ornamentation, accompanying instruments, and the manner of accompaniment. Operas belonging to the same *shengqiang* share (to a large extent) a repertoire of tunes and other musical elements; but regional aesthetic preferences and regional dialects result in different treatments of the same tune by the singers. Thus, on a more detailed level, each regional opera belonging to the same *shengqiang* has its own musical style as well:

knowledgeable audience members can easily identify the differences. Regional operas differ less from one another in terms of costumes, makeup, and movements. They share a repertoire of stories drawn from legends, myths, and historical and semihistorical narratives that are known nationally.

Despite the fact that a large repertoire of a particular kind of drama, such as *jingju*, is often divided into categories according to principal mode of performance, such as singing plays, fighting plays, acting plays, and comic plays, most operas involve and combine various forms of speech, song, mime, dance, slapstick, and acrobatics. A generous display of visual splendor: makeup, costumes, and sometimes backdrops, stage sets, and props is indispensable. Dramatic coherence often gives way to pure entertainment and spectacle. An accomplished performer must be simultaneously an actor, a dancer, and a singer; most performers must also have rigorous training in acrobatics.

Music has a central role in a performance of Chinese drama. In fact, before the introduction of Western theater, purely spoken drama was not known in China; all stage performances involved some form of singing and instrumental music. Even when opera performers "speak," the delivery almost always departs from ordinary street speech in its stylized tones and rhythmic patterns. Even nonverbal utterances such as laughing and sighing are for-malized. The noted dramatist and scholar Qi Rushan correctly observed that in Chinese operas "all utterances are a form of singing."

The intrinsic musicality may be generalized to a more basic principle of "theatricality" that seems to underlie all aspects of performance in traditional operas. In telling a story onstage, there is no attempt to imitate the sights and sounds of real life literally, even though the characters portrayed and the emotions expressed are lifelike. Instead, a performance seems to deliberately depart from the familiar in order to remind audiences that they are witnessing something fantastic. Everyday colloquial talk is often considered too "real" for the stage (except in Cantonese opera where colloquial language and archaic language are frequently intermixed). Through rhythm and melody, a performance projects a desired artistic effect and seems to say: we are play-acting.

The theatricality of Chinese opera is enhanced by the staging, which traditionally involves a bare space with no realistic backdrop or scenery. The props are very often limited to a simple table and two chairs, which, in different scenes, may be used to represent anything from a mountain to a bedroom. The illusions are achieved through the performers' formalized miming, their occasional use of props, and the accompaniment of percussion music. The performers don elaborate, colorful costumes and wear equally colorful and exaggerated makeup. Their design and color, though, are seldom intended as direct representations of real-life images.

The highly stylized, symbolic movements and gestures of the performers also contribute to the effect of theatricality. For example, a trembling arm denotes fear; a palm outstretched and raised deliberately in front of the face suggests weeping. Very few movements are directly representative of real-life gestures. Qi Rushan has noted that, just as song is ubiquitous, "all movements onstage are dance." His point is that movements and gestures onstage are formalized and stylized according to theatrical tradition and a sense of beauty and design. Even mundane movements, such as sitting or walking, and everyday gestures, such as looking or pointing, must be stylized. Consequently, these movements and gestures are not solely vehicles for telling a story but means of artistic expression in their own right. That is, they are "dance" in the traditional sense of the word.

*—Adapted from articles
by Bell Yung, Rulan Chao Pian,
and Isabel K. F. Wong*

CHAPTER TWENTY-THREE

American Musical Theatre

ORIGINS

Some people who consider themselves theatre "purists" tend to draw a strong distinction between *real drama* and musical theatre. However, what these individuals might fail to appreciate is that music has always been an important part of theatre. Drama has always been at least partly musical. Aristotle, in his ancient treatise, *Poetics*, considered music the fifth most important element of drama (after plot, character, theme, and diction or language). The classical plays of ancient Greece are filled with song and dance. The Greek chorus is meant to sing (not speak) the choral odes while dancing. These choral odes create a strong connection between the audience and the events that occur in the play. The chorus in ancient tragedy was a group of people whose role was to reflect on and react to the events that took place in the drama while also moving the play forward. In ancient Greek drama, these choral odes were accompanied by the aulos—a type of flute—and other instruments. The majority of lines in ancient Roman comedy were accompanied by music.

Wholly sung operas were developed in Italy. Shakespeare incorporated many songs into his plays. In fact, 25 of Shakespeare's 38 plays contain some singing. Most Renaissance and Commedia dell'Arte plays include songs, movement, and dance. In the eighteenth century, a number of popular musical forms, including ballad opera and comic opera, were introduced. The melodrama, which was developed and became so popular in the nineteenth century, used music to underscore and heighten the action of the play. The operetta—a romantic story-based play with music—was a very popular performing art form by the early nineteenth century in Paris.

In London, by the last quarter of the nineteenth century, the operettas of William S. Gilbert and Arthur Sullivan dominated the British stage. And, finally, in all major Asian and African dramatic forms, music, movement, and dance are often more integral to the communication of message and meaning than is spoken text.

AMERICAN MUSICAL THEATRE

From these roots, sprang the style of drama known as musical theatre, or, sometimes more specifically, American musical theatre. What we identify now as the Broadway musical first began to develop in the United States in the early nineteenth century, with singing and dancing shows. One form of show was known as the *extravaganzas*. (see Figure 23.2) These shows, which traveled the country, were grand, spectacular, operatic, dancing entertainments. In working class areas, music halls grew out of public houses (saloons). The music hall became a term associated with lower class musical variety, which included a master of ceremonies, singers, dancers, and comedians. These two forms of favored entertainments—the extravaganza and musical hall entertainment—were soon joined by the increasingly popular burlesque and vaudeville as the most popular forms of entertainment during the first half of the twentieth century.

Burlesque began as loose comic parodies of serious musical works. They often involved cross-dressing. Burlesque was originally seen as respectable entertainment, which attracted men, women, and families. However, in 1869, Lydia Thompson's *British Blondes*, a burlesque troupe that featured women performing in various stages of undress, toured the U.S. After this, burlesque—which featured spectacle, song, dance, and scantily-clad female bodies—attracted overwhelmingly male audiences. Striptease became a prominent feature of burlesque after World War I, and so it was pushed even farther to the outskirts of respectability and became identified as a seedy and unsavory—yet still popular—entertainment.

Vaudeville had a somewhat opposite trajectory. Originally, vaudeville was a collection of musical and variety acts performed in brothels and drinking parlors. It later flourished as it developed into a family entertainment. As vaudeville evolved and became more popular, the musical and variety acts—a non-story mix of comedy, music, dance, and lavish spectacle—began to present more and more acts that were appropriate for and appealed to all members of the family. Many stars from vaudeville later moved on to careers in radio in the 1930s when vaudeville died due to the Great Depression and the draw of movies. Many of these same stars—including Judy Garland, Burt Lahr, Jack Benny, Milton Berle, Lucille Ball, The Marx Brothers, Mae West—later moved on to television and film.

We can begin to see the distinctly American musical form rise from the influences of European operetta, vaudeville, and burlesque after about 1900. At this time, some productions with an inkling of a musical theatre production begin to appear as we witness these shows begin to separate from the European operetta, on one hand, and the musical review, on the other. From the beginning, these entertainments had a double appeal in music and spectacle, the latter often being the female body, gorgeously costumed, often dancing (the chorus girl).

However, it took some time for the American musical form as we know it today to fully emerge and take hold. Burlesque and vaudeville lasted well into the twentieth century. Florenz Ziegfeld became one of America's greatest showmen with his annual *Ziegfeld Follies*, a musical review dedicated to "Glorifying the American Girl." (see Figure 23.1.) The increasing popularity of these two forms of performance rapidly led to a growing number of performers who were adept at singing, dancing, acting, and comedy. This plethora of experienced and talented performers provided the performing talent and set the stage for the burgeoning American musical theatre during its golden age.

Musical comedy began to emerge in the United States in the late nineteenth century. Early musical comedy usually emphasized the romantic appeal of far away, exotic places and outlandish situations. Stories were primarily excuses for songs and ensemble chorus numbers. These chorus numbers were often sung and danced by beautiful young women. Around World War I, ballroom dancing and ragtime music became popular in the United States. These two forms of popular entertainment were introduced into musicals. In this time period, musicals also became more "American," incorporating more familiar characters and surroundings rather than relying on those far away, exotic places and outlandish characters. However, at this time, the storyline in these productions continued to be relatively unimportant. The emphasis of the entertainment continued to be on luscious settings, songs, dances, and attractive chorus girls. (see Figure 23.2.)

Figure 23.1 Sheet music cover with "Tulip Time" referencing Ziegfeld Follies and the New Amsterdam Theatre. (Copyright in the Public Domain.)

Figure 23.2 A poster advertising the Gaiety Dancers of Rice & Barton's Big Gaiety Spectacular Extravaganza Co. in 1900. (The Courier Company / Copyright in the Public Domain.)

THE INTEGRATED MUSICAL

Gradually, the American musical began to take shape as a theatrical entertainment that integrated a coherent story, believable characters, song, music, and dance. The relationship between music, dance, and story became more important. The musical and choreographic elements, sources of pleasure in their own right, were also used to facilitate storytelling. In addition, music, through such conventions as the reprise—the repetition of musical phrases or fragments of lyrics—was used to connect or recall moments separated in time. Music and dance also worked to condense time. Songs, musical passages, and dances were used to quickly show a progression of events that in reality would occur over a long period of time. Music and choreography helped to establish mood and build expectations. Many musicals begin with an overture that establishes the general mood of the work before any actors—or design elements, if the show is being presented on a proscenium stage with a front curtain—appear on stage. As the play evolves, songs, choreography, and musical underscoring help to establish the emotional tone. Modulations in tempo, key, and volume assist in the building of individual scenes and in the piece as a whole.

In the integrated musical, song and dance also began to be used as a tool to convey and develop a character's psychological motivation. These musical plays often centered on romantic love, and songs and dances became part of the action, arising from characters in a heightened emotional state. At pivotal moments in the story, singing and dancing (which may be seen as heightened speech and movement) helped the character to express feelings that could not be expressed by mere words. The lyrics of the songs would contribute to the clarity of the character's circumstances by expressing emotional responses and intentions directly, much as soliloquies and asides did in earlier drama. These songs would also move the plot along. In this way, the songs and dances became integrated into the story and did not stand alone. Singing and dancing were not just inserted randomly, which would have served to pull the audience out of the moment. Instead, the music, lyrics, and movement were meant to give the character—and the audience—a way to go deeper into the emotions and events of the play.

The integrated musical was introduced in the late 1920s through Jerome Kern and Oscar Hammerstein' s *Showboat*, a musical that grapples with the themes of racial prejudice and tragic, enduring love. It was followed by the development of seriocomic musicals with happy endings. *Of Thee I Sing!* (1931), with music by George and Ira Gershwin and a book by George Kaufman and Morrie Ryskind, is one of the best examples of this development of a seriocomic theme in American musical theatre. A play that satirizes American politics and politicians, *Of Thee I Sing!* is also the first musical to win the Pulitzer Prize for drama. The Pulitzer is awarded for a distinguished play by an American playwright, preferably original in its source and dealing with American life. For a musical to win this award was an indication that the American musical had finally reached the stature of a well-respected genre worthy of serious consideration.

By the 1940s, the musical had gradually become distinctly American. During this decade, a more serious dramatic purpose began to emerge more consistently in musicals, such as *Pal Joey*, *Oklahoma!*, and *Carousel*. By this time, the American musical had emerged as a coherent integration of story, music, and dance. *Oklahoma!* (1943), by Richard Rogers and Oscar Hammerstein II, brought this integration even further by setting the standard for the book musical of the period. In book musicals, songs and dances are a logical extension of the libretto's dramatic action.

ELEMENTS OF MUSICAL THEATRE

Composers

Composers are at the heart of musical theatre. Most of the top Broadway composers of the first half of the twentieth century wrote for operetta or review (or both) while helping to create the new, story-based form that became American musical theatre. Some composers write their own lyrics, but most musical theatre composers work closely with lyricists (writers of words to songs) and librettists (writers of the play script). Although many of the major composers of musicals who were at the forefront of the creation of the American musical were classically trained in Europe, what distinguished the music they created for this new form of theatre—and what made it seem "American"—was the adoption of the rhythms that were the rhythms of the popular dance music of the late nineteenth and early twentieth century. This music (including ragtime, jazz, and blues) had its roots in nineteenth-century African American musical forms.

Unfortunately, the creators of ragtime, jazz, and blues (with the exception of Will Cook and Eubie Blake [see Figure 23.3]) are rarely credited for the lasting influence they have had on the cultural landscape of the American musical theatre.

Lyricists

The lyricists who wrote the lyrics to the melodies composed by the early twentieth century musical theatre composers were integral to the development of a new form of drama. The top composers often collaborated with the same lyricist in musical after musical. These lyricists helped to shape

Figure 23.3 Composer, Eubie Blake (1887–1983). (Copyright in the Public Domain.)

the tone and the style of the script and, often, even influenced the songs for which they provided words.

Characters

The new American music of the musical theatre was sung by new American characters. The characters of operettas had been stock, upper class European characters. The characters of American musicals were often common, everyday Americans. Sometimes they were rich, but they were not considered royalty.

POPULARITY

Both the musical revue and the operetta faded after the 1920s and the book musical took their place. Over the past 150 years, musical theatre has become a distinct genre, the most popular theatrical form, and the most popular theatrical export of the United States. Originally, these musicals were lighthearted. Songs and dances were inserted into the play for entertainment purposes rather than as tools used to progress the action. These musicals were meant to be pleasing to the ear, and scripts were merely excuses for showcasing beautiful melodies. The first third of the twentieth century was the great age of musical comedy—a genre that emphasized comedy, singing, and youthful romance. These entertainments featured sexy and lightly-clad female chorus girls and spectacular dancing (often a flashy tap dance accompanied by a jazzy ragtime beat). Most of the musicals were meant to lift up the audience members and allow them to leave the theatre singing the songs and dancing the dances with a smile on their faces. The popularity of the early musicals is probably due to their multiple appeals. Performances contained the winning combination of a simple plot, a cast composed of comedic and romantic characters, an unchallenging theme, lots of pretty women in revealing costumes, and cheerful singing that had no connection to the plot. Musicals also usually provided considerable visual stimulation. Scenic, costume, and lighting designers were offered extensive options to showcase their talents. There were usually several changes in time and place and a large cast—often with much doubling[1]—which required multiple sets and costumes.

The popularity of musical theatre grew exponentially during the twentieth century. By the 1920s and 1930s, tourists from all over the country traveled to Broadway to see the works of the famous composers and lyricists who wrote the music that they themselves played on their pianos and heard on the radio. They also came to see the stars—many of whom had become household names through vaudeville and performances on the radio—bring the shows and characters to life.

---

1   "Doubling" means that one actor plays more than one role in a production.

By 1925, the American musical was beginning to dominate New York's cultural life. The 1920s through the 1960s are the years known as the golden age of musical theatre. By the end of the Second World War, seriously-themed Broadway musicals dominated the commercial American theatre. Many of those elements mentioned above that made musical theatre popular remained consistent. The best of these musicals during Broadway's golden age were commercially successful beyond anything the world of theatre had ever known.

Before this period in history, if a play ran for weeks or months, it was considered a great success. Now, for the first time, a hit musical could be expected to run for years. Theatre tickets for Broadway musicals were sold months in advance. Touring companies brought many of these musicals around the nation and, eventually, around the world. Most Americans during this period had their first live theatrical experiences attending *bus and truck* tours of some of these successful musicals. Due to its enormous popularity and the way in which it has changed the theatre landscape the world over, American musical theatre has now become a world-renowned cultural phenomenon.

CHAPTER TWENTY-FOUR

Political Theatre

One of the purposes of theatre is to educate. One way that theatre educates is by giving voice to all members of society. One of the fundamental conflicts of human existence is the difference between how we perceive ourselves and how others perceive us. Theatre can increase communication and understanding by celebrating differences, by highlighting similarities, and by allowing everyone a voice. Political theatre provides a forum for everyday people to express themselves; it gives a voice to those who are seldom heard in the mainstream media. Because the basic elements of theatre—actor, story, audience—can be attained at low- or no- cost, theatre can provide a platform for anyone who wants to communicate a message. Political theatre gives a voice to the voiceless in society. These individuals or groups are intentionally or unintentionally neglected or stereotyped by those in power and in the mass media.

Theatre should reflect the life experiences of all people. However, art and entertainment have predominantly reflected, been controlled by, and given voice to the dominant culture throughout history. Those in power—members of the upper class, government, religious institutions, and, in particular, men—have dominated the development of theatre. For thousands of years, the dominant culture has controlled playwriting, directing, design, and acting through racism, sexism, discrimination, economic power, and social and religious customs. Throughout the centuries, women and minority racial, religious, and ethnic groups have been left out. Political theatre addresses and looks to change that disparity.

Figure 24.1 Brazilian theater director and writer Augusto Boal presenting his Theatre of the Oppressed at Riverside Church in New York City. (Copyright © 2008 by Thehero / Wikimedia Commons, (CC BY-SA 3.0) at https://commons.wikimedia.org/wiki/File:Augusto_Boal_nyc5.jpg.)

Figure 24.2 Brazilian theater director and writer Augusto Boal. (Copyright © 2008 by Thehero / Wikimedia Commons, (CC BY-SA 3.0) at https://commons.wikimedia.org/wiki/File:Augusto_Boal_nyc2.jpg.)

The goals of political theatre are openly political. The individual aims of political theatre vary, but all political theatre shares the assumption that awareness can be heightened through art. Those who engage in political theatre seek a theatrical experience that can explore a group's experiences and difficulties in society. Some political theatre groups favor intense political statements in performance. Other political theatre ensembles avoid argumentation and debate altogether in performance; they hope that will occur later when the audience reflects back on the message and meaning of the performance. Some companies keep the audience separate from the production. Other groups actively encourage the audience to become performers and join their artistic and political movement to effect real change.

Many political theatre groups encourage a separation of their companies from the mainstream; others work to integrate their own art and artists into the commercial theatre as quickly as possible. Some political theatre ensembles perform in traditional theatre buildings and charge audience members an entrance fee. Other groups perform in streets, parks, malls, subway stations, or retail stores—wherever crowds may be found or people congregate—and charge nothing for the performances. Groups whose primary goal is to have a political impact may work on a shoestring budget and disregard costly production values. They may create their own works through improvisation, often interviewing and incorporating elements of multimedia. Other groups whose mission is political have huge budgets and produce works with high production values and traditional dramatic texts. Some seek modest social change, others advocate revolution.

This type of theatre is what Brazilian director Augusto Boal called *theatre of the oppressed*. (see figure 24.1) Ideally, theatre and all art should reflect the experiences of all cultures; however, since it is doubtful that that goal will be realized, political theatre will most likely be an important element of the landscape of theatrical styles for the foreseeable future. The following is an essay by Brazilain director Augusto Boal (see figure 24.2) about his life's journey: creating political theatre.

HISTORY

The Theatre of the Oppressed Returns to Its Roots—Brazil and Politics

For the first time in the history of the theatre, and the history of politics, an entire theatre company enters the Legislature. How did this miracle come about? Coincidence as a category of luck. We must persevere. Our desire, our goal: to go further!

In 1982, less than a year after coming to power, the French government invited 200 intellectuals from all over the world to a large seminar at the Sorbonne to discuss the nature of the relations between culture and the modern world. Was socialism being instituted in France and, if so, how was this happening? They were not asking our advice; they wanted us to debate the subject. Among the invitees were various Nobel prize winners, a number of famous artists of the cinema, along with more humble folk, including Darci Ribeiro and myself.

Darci had just been elected vice Governor of Riode Janeiro. He was fascinated by the idea of creating Integrated Centres for Popular Education (CIEPS), a project which was, at that time, only at the planning

stage. The idea was simple: to enrol as pupils the maximum possible number of children (every child, if it could be done), to keep them in school for as long as possible (the child, if it could be done), to keep them in school for as long as possible (the whole day, including breakfast, lunch and supper, if this was achievable), lending them support in every area of their lives: medicine, dentistry, sport and—thank God—cultural animation, including theatre.

That was where I came in, or might have come in, since I had told Darci about the work the Center o fthe Theatre of the Oppressed (CTO) was doing—and is still doing, 19 years after its inception—in Paris, working right across France and in various other countries.

The CTO is engaged in the application and development of the methods of the Theatre of the Oppressed, which is founded on the conviction that theatre is the human language *par excellence*. The being becomes human when it discovers theatre. The difference between humans and other animals resides in the fact that we are capable of being theatre. Some of us 'make' theatre—all of us 'are' theatre.

What kind of theatre? The theatre which is, in its most archaic sense, our capacity to observe ourselves in action. We are able to see ourselves seeing! This possibility of our being simultaneously Protagonist and principal spectator of our actions, affords us the further possibility of thinking virtualities, of imagining possibilities, of combining memory and imagination—two indissociable psychic processes—to reinvent the past and to invent the future. Therein resides the immense power with which theatre is endowed. This is the theatre which fascinates me, and the method which I have developed and elaborated over the past 25 years, the Theatre of the Oppressed, tries to systematise these potentialities and render them accessible to and useable by anyone and everyone.

I founded the Paris CTO in 1978, when I was living there and lecturing in the self-same University of the Sorbonne at which we were to participate in the seminar three years later. Since then, this centre has organised numerous courses, seminars, interventions, shows and festivals with community groups. Darci wanted me to do the same thing in the CIEPS, throughout Rio de Janeiro. He extended an invitation to us, to myself and Cecilia Thumim, my wife, and urged us to move back to Brazil.

It was a dream. I had always wanted to go back and live in Brazil, but without abandoning the work I had been doing abroad through so many years of forced exile: five in Buenos Aires (then along came Videla...), two in Lisbon (till the Revolution of Carnations withered away...) and, finally, in Paris, which is still my second home. I felt welcome in Paris, and the minimum material conditions obtained for me to be able to work in a systematic way.

Had we been able to, we would have said 'yes' and returned to Brazil in time to be present at Darci's official investiture as Vice Governor. However, so many times in the past circumstances had obliged us to pack our bags in a hurry, leaving even essentials behind, that my family and I preferred to do things at a more measured pace.

When we did arrive back in Brazil, with only the bare necessities, it was in the middle of 1986, the end of the mandate, and the next elections were about to take place: Darci was standing for Governor. He kept his promise: he contracted us for six months, so that we could try and see if it would be possible to set up a project in Rio similar to the one which was working so well in France. At that point we did not want a longer contract, since this was only an experiment. In the event of a positive outcome, then of course we would want a long-term contract.

It worked like a dream: we assembled 35 cultural animators from the CIEPS, people who, for the most part, had never done theatre—some had never even been to a play—and did an intensive workshop, demonstrating our exercises, games and techniques of Image Theatre, Forum Theatre and Invisible Theatre. Rosa Luiza Marquez, a professor at the University of San Juan in Puerto Rico, who had worked at the CTO in Paris, came over from the Caribbean to take part in this adventure.

By the end of six weeks we already had a repertoire of five short shows around the issues of most concern to the cultural animators (and their families and neighbours in all the areas we were working in): unemployment, health, housing, sexual violence, incest, the oppression of women, of young people, mental health, drugs etc.

With this repertoire, we initiated a series of presentations in the CIEPS. As the venues for these performances were usually standard municipal school buildings, we soon learnt to construct a 'functional theatre' in the dining rooms, using whatever was to hand: two rows of audience sat on the ground, with the next two rows on seats, one row on tables and, finally, one row perched on chairs on top of tables— when there was a real crowd, another row of audience stood on tables at the back. We arranged a white tarpaulin on the ground, with a sheet by way of cyclorama.

Between 200 and 300 people came to each show; sometimes there were over 400—students, teachers, students' parents, friends of the teachers, cleaners and kitchen staff, people who lived near the schools. The performance used to open with a brief explanation by the 'Jokers' of the show (myself and Cecilia—Rosa Luisa accompanied us on percussion)—of the uses of theatre

and the function of the Theatre of the Oppressed; afterwards, we would do exercises with actors and audience not only as a 'warm-up' but also to establish a degree of theatrical communion—and then we would present the five short scenes which had been created during the workshop. This was the first part of the show.

In the second part we would ask the audience which two or three subjects had most interested them, and this led to the 'foruming' of the relevant two or three scenes: i.e., the theatrical debate which constitutes Forum Theatre, with the improvisation of possible solutions, the intervention of members of the audience, the search for alternatives for an oppressive, unjust, intolerable situation. The audience members would come on stage one at a time, to act out their own ideas on the subject, voicing their thoughts and acting out their opinions theatrically. And, still within the theatrical frame, there would be discussion about what it was possible to do, and these possibilities would be rehearsed. Theatre helping to bring about social transformation.

The Forum shows—apart from the artistic activity which they represented in themselves, the aesthetic pleasure which they offered *per se*—helped the citizens to develop their taste for political discussion (democracy) and their desire to develop their own artistic abilities (popular art). The shows contained precious moments of dialogue, of exchange, of learning, of teaching, of pleasure. These theatrical gatherings came to an end only when we were completely exhausted. But the audience, the spectators, our 'spect-actors'—those who observe (*spectare*, in Latin—to see) in order then to act—they never seemed to tire. They always wanted more.

It was at this time that I began to feel the desire to invent some form of theatre which could channel all the creative energy awakened by Forum Theatre in these men, women and children eager to change the world—their world, perhaps only their small world, their part of the big world—and to use this energy beyond the immediate duration of the show. One could not help feeling that ideas as good as those thrown up in the Forum could usefully be applied in other settings.

1. 'Playing, whose end, both at first and now, was and is, to hold as 'twere the mirror up to nature: to show virtue her feature, scorn her own image, and the very age and body of the time his form and pressure.' Hamlet, III.2.20–24.

Forum Theatre is a reflection on reality and a rehearsal for future action. In the present, we re-live the past to create the future. The spect-actor comes on stage and rehearses what it might be possible to do in real life. Sometimes the solution to the spect-actors' problems depends on themselves, on their own individual desire, their own efforts—but, equally, sometimes the oppression is actually rooted within the law. In the latter case, to bring about the desired change would require a transformation or redrafting of the law: legislation. How could that be done? There ends the power of the theatre. We did not have an answer.

Hamlet says in his famous speech to the actors that theatre is a mirror in which may be seen the true image of nature, of reality. I wanted to penetrate this mirror, to transform the image I saw in it and to bring that transformed image back to reality: to realise the image of my desire. I wanted it to be possible for the spect-actors in Forum Theatre to transgress, to break the conventions, to enter into the mirror of a theatrical fiction, rehearse forms of struggle and then return to reality with the images of their desires. This discontent was the genesis of the Legislative Theatre, in which the citizen makes the law through the legislator. The legislator should not be the person who makes the law, but the person through whom the law is made (by the citizens, of course!).

Seldom have I felt so happy in the theatre. I took enormous pleasure in working with the citizens of Rio, in the suburbs and the nearby towns, São João de Meriti, Duque de Caixas, Nilopolis, Angra dos Reis, and many more, spurring them to go on stage and exercise their theatrical citizenship: stimulating them to discover theatre, and the theatre within themselves, to discover that they were theatre.

We did more than 30 shows, and then the year came to an end. Darci lost the elections. In Rio de Janeiro, the policies adopted by an incoming government tend to destroy everything the previous government was doing. Everything good, that is. The bad things they leave in place. The good things they ruin.

The following year, we still tried to carry on, without the slightest help from the new government, which did not even bother to honour signed contracts. We launched into a second workshop which stopped in the middle. Our last show was dispiriting: we merely showed our pieces to each other. Some actors dropped out because they did not have the money to pay their bus fares…it was a disaster.

We tried for private patronage. The big businesses were beginning to use a new law, the so-called 'Incentive for Culture'; in place of part of their tax liabilities they could subsidise theatre, dance or music companies. We went to see them, almost all of them. One company suggested we do some work in their personnel department, using our techniques to help in their staff recruitment. Obviously, we turned the offer down; not for this did we develop the Theatre of the Oppressed. Others made no bones about their lack of enthusiasm for sponsoring a theatre company whose audiences were not part of 'the market'. An oil company has nothing to gain from an audience of passengers of the Central Railway. And then there was the question of image: a silk manufacturer would not want to associate its image with a bunch of scruffy actors. A manufacturer of Italian pasta would feel sadistic offering art to malnourished spectators.

We tried. In vain.

Seeds grow.

Even in arid ground, in dry barren soil. And many Theatre of the Oppressed groups had grown up in every place we had been to, organised by the people who had been the cultural animators.

In 1989, a small group of obstinate survivors of the CIEPS experiment sought me out to propose the creation of a CTO in Rio. An informal body, working from time to time, with internal meetings to study the 'arsenal' (the collection of techniques, games and exercises) and external work when a contract could be obtained.

Informally, we began a new phase—ever-hopeful of better days, believing in promises. The next elections came around and Darci was returned to power but— for reasons which it would be in-appropriate to analyse here—his plans no longer coincided with our proposals.

By 1992, having lost the link with the Department of Education and the CIEPs, the CTO was living a pinched existence—a few contracts with the Bank Workers Union, a couple with the small cities of Ipatinga or São Caetano, events like 'Land and Democracy', organised by Betinho, some workshops for the general public and some for people from abroad. Groups came over from Germany and from New York University to study in Rio. After the workshop with the Germans was over—I tell this story to give an idea of the climate we work in—they were on their way back to Rio one night, returning from a visit to the mining towns in the hills, when their bus was ambushed by marauding outlaws and bombarded with stones: a medieval ambush! Fortunately, the driver was an old hand and he put his foot down and everyone got away safely.

Even so, we lived in great hope, which is, as the saying goes, the last thing to die.

It died.

One day we decided to put an end to the Centre, to carry out compassionate euthanasia on our moribund dream. How best might we lay this dream to rest, after its death? We didn't want a sad, tearful burial; we preferred something in the New Orleans style. A musical funeral, a funeral which would have a joyful aspect—a bang not a whimper. We wanted a flamboyant funeral with lots of rhythm and colours and people—and people of all colours, dancing in all rhythms.

By coincidence, 1992 was an election year and elections in Brazil—in marked contrast to many European and North American countries—are an erotic moment in the national life. Elections here always have something of carnival about them—carnival is a form of eroticism which transgresses all ideologies. And the electoral campaign here is politicised eroticism, or politics eroticised. The people dance and sing and parade and shout—and do everything under the sun, literally and metaphorically.

We wanted to lay to rest the dream of the CTO by helping either a party or a coalition to realise a larger dream: to change the country. And we went to see the Workers Party, the PT, to offer our collaboration. We were given an attentive hearing. We wanted to take part in the campaign on the streets and in the squares, singing our songs, doing forum theatre on the events of the day, using masks, aestheticising the streets. We wanted to theatricalise the campaign.

Our offer was accepted without reservation, but with one additional element: to make our participation more effective, it would be advantageous if one of us were to present him or herself as a candidate for *vereador* (legislator).

This was unexpected, but we accepted the challenge: we would go away and consider which of us would be most suitable to play the part of candidate. And we returned to our base, happily confident of our new role.

We sat round in a circle talking, trying to choose the best candidate—I sat there, looking carefully at each member of the group, trying to make my own choice. And as I looked at everybody I realised that everybody was looking at me. I was caught completely unawares.

'No, not me! No way can I be the candidate!', I protested. 'I wouldn't be able to do the campaign, I'm always travelling, my schedule is already overloaded, I have agreed commitments, I'd be an absentee candidate.

I would never win these elections. It's impossible: there are 1,200 candidates from 22 parties for only 42 seats. No, not me: it would be better if it was someone else.'

They continued to look at me and I continued to resist with bravura, in a mixture of indecision, desire and fear. Till eventually someone asked:

'Who said that we were running to win? The idea is just to take part in the elections, to give the CTO a festive send-off. No-one is asking you to give up your travelling, because no-one has the least expectation of your winning…'

I breathed more easily.

'Fine, well, if it's like that … if we are not going for a win … then I am willing to be the candidate.'

And we relayed our decision to the leadership of the party: I would be our candidate…seeing as I did not have the slightest chance of being elected.

We dived head-first into the campaign. Inspired by the task at hand, the small initial group grew. We did various plays, with a new song every day. Every day fresh script was added. We took an active role in the popular movement against the President of the Republic, a champion of corruption whom we helped to remove; we assisted in the campaign of our candidate for mayor, and every day we went out into the streets. When I say 'we' went into the streets, I mean 'they' went into the streets, because more often than not at that time I was on my way to or from the airport.

Our campaign was developing and becoming better known. Photographers and cameramen love images. And so do newspapers—they have an enormous appetite for pictures. One good photo is worth a lot. And our campaign was a source of good photos. For example: in a musical piece we did against the raising of fees for students at the University of Santa Ursula, on the beach at Ipanema, 10 women were dressed as nuns—and they got dressed in their religious habits in the middle of the beach, with bikinis and black garters underneath, showing their legs, in front of the bathers and the photographers. Then a lecturer held a class on the sand, complete with blackboard, school chairs and desks—all unusual, theatrical, 'photo opportunities'. Not surprisingly, we began to take up space in the papers. And with this came publicity for my candidature.

Another example: a group of women (mostly teachers), dressed in pinafores with scarves on their heads and carrying pots and pans, paraded through the streets and along the beaches singing a song they had written called: 'Maria Sem Vergonha … de ser feliz': 'Agora com Boal, Maria esta total/na rua afinal/em cena teatral./ Agora com Bene/Maria e mais mulher/com todo o nosso axe/pro que der e vier.'

As the campaign gathered steam, a few individuals left because they did not want to take part in a party political campaign, but this was offset by the many more who joined us: people who had never given any thought to the idea of making theatre—their considerations were political, they had political goals, either they were already involved in politics or they were simply fed up with the situation in the country—people who welcomed with open arms the opportunity to try this new way of engaging in politics. Or simply believed in me.

4. 'Coragem de ser fellz'.

Though impoverished, our campaign grew. To give an idea of our poverty and our creativity, our campaign badges were painted by hand, one by one, on beer bottle tops. Papier-mâché hats, with my caricature in harlequin form, were also painted by hand, one by one. Our colours, girl and boy, blue and pink, came ready-dyed on the material we made our banners with— we economised on dye … but not on ideas: our campaign sashes were loud, literally and metaphorically, with bells hanging from ribbons accompanying the demonstrators' voices. We had to be faithful to our slogan: 'Have the courage to be happy'.

Our campaign grew much larger than we expected. So much so that one day some leading members of the party called and spoke to me in grave tones:

'Boal, you are running a risk, a serious risk … .'

So grave was the tone that I took fright. My mind was filled with thoughts of assassination and the like … after all we were in Rio de Janeiro … that sort of thing is a mere trifle here.

'Risk of what?'

'You run the risk of being elected … .'

Stupefaction. Me, a *vereador*?! Never! Not because I place a low value on that function—quite the contrary—but because I could not, at my time of life, change professions, habits, direction, methods, everything—I mean to say! I had a whole programme ahead of me— theatre plans—I was not about to suddenly change direction and take up the career of *vereador*, when I was sure that I did not have the right qualities—or the experience—to be a good *vereador*. The party was full of better candidates. Why me of all people?

'No way! If I run the risk of winning, then I am standing down!'

I was categorical! Absolutely categorical!

And I went back to the CTO, related my conversation and communicated my decision: I would stand down. General consternation. It was all going so well. Every day, we were appearing more in the papers, on the television, we were talking on the radio stations. Every day, more people were coming into our campaign, more people wanted to participate, to practise the Theatre of the Oppressed. What a pity … .

Then someone had an idea: 'Listen Augusto, if you ask me, you are in no danger of winning. But, suppose you did win? Wouldn't that be a good solution?'

'Who for?' I asked angrily, 'Not me!'

We reflected: we had wanted to bury the CTO in a joyful and useful way, but, actually, a burial was not what we really wanted—we wanted the CTO to live, but we did not have the right material conditions for this to be possible. If I was elected as a *vereador*, I would be entitled to contract advisers. As the CTO we needed job security, but our interlocutors, our public, did not have enough money for themselves, let alone enough to pay professional rates for 'Jokers'. Once elected, I would be able to contract all the cultural animators of the CTO and realise our experiment: to go beyond Forum Theatre and invent Legislative Theatre! As the function of *vereador*s is to create laws and to ensure the proper enactment of those that already exist, the people's participation in this process could be achieved by means of theatre: transitive democracy.

Chance and intention had collided: by chance, yes, but more than anything by virtue of our desire, our intense desire, we were now facing the possibility of going further with the Theatre of the Oppressed, of moving beyond simple reflection on reality and rehearsal of the transformation of reality: we were facing the palpable possibility of creating and transforming laws.

For the first time in the history of the theatre and the history of politics, there opened up the possibility of a whole theatre company being elected to a parliament.

Many artists before me had been elected to legislative office (Glenda Jackson, for example, a marvellous actress who became an MP in England), or to executive office, such as Ronald Reagan in the USA (not a good actor, but the holder of an American Equity card—a union card—therefore, *ipso facto*, an actor) or the playwright, Vaclav Havel, who went from prison to occupy the presidency of his country, the Czech Republic. Without forgetting the Italian politician La Cicciolina, star of a form of show business ... at least she was better at striptease than Erroll Flynn was at duelling: respect!

For all that, I was clear that my case was different: I would not have to give up my previous theatrical activity to start a new life as a parliamentarian. The one would be the extension of the other: anyone who voted for me would know what they were doing—theatre and politics!

And I was also clear that, if elected, I would be able to realise something we had sought from the beginning: ways of making a Forum Theatre performance have practical and visible effects beyond those contained in the show itself. Not merely to rehearse for the future, but to begin to realise it. To try something beyond reflection and rehearsal.

Throughout my life I have been engaged in politics (though not party politics) and I have always been engaged in theatre. This was what seduced me in the proposition: to make 'theatre as politics', instead of simply making 'political theatre', as I had done before.

In reality, I think that I first contemplated the idea of one day becoming a legislator, for a certain length of time, when, in 1991, I received the title of 'Benemeritus Citizen of the State of Rio De Janeiro', at the Assembly of Deputies (MPs). Instead of a normal session, we organised a popular reception at the Chamber, entitled 'Be an MP for Three Minutes', during which representatives of Rio's society had the right to three minutes each in which to propose laws to be enacted: street cleaners, trade union workers, prostitutes, domestic employees, black students, slum dwellers, peasants, intellectuals, doctors, lawyers, journalists, everybody was allowed to take the floor—the session lasted five hours, instead of the usual one and a half!

So seduced was I by the idea of winning that I returned to the lists, back to the hard fight—I went back to the streets, the demonstrations, the shows, the rallies. Back to politics! We all threw ourselves back into it with renewed courage, with more determination and greater desire to win.

Now I wanted to win and this changed the way I behaved. I felt like Shakespeare's Coriolanus, somewhat ashamed to ask for votes for myself. Sometimes, I couldn't bring myself to mount my own platform. Or, by contrast, I sometimes had an urge to accuse part of the population of stupidity in voting for certain candidates, of basing their choice on looks. It was very difficult to say 'Vote for me!' It seemed like egoism: with so many good candidates ... I felt as if I was taking someone else's place.

One day, a boy from Morro de Saudade asked me for a set of 11 shirts for his football team. I explained that my candidature was honest, that it had a project, that it was different from others he knew of, and he answered me: 'If you give nothing to the people, how do expect people to vote for you? You must have something to give ... .'

It was difficult to explain that whenever the elector accepts a *presentinho*, a bribe, from the candidate, s/he has to pay later. For instance, amongst those sitting in parliament there are the lobbyists for the bus companies, to give only one example, who will always vote in favour of fare increases. The elector ends up paying dearly for presents from politicians!

Another voter, a woman, wanted me not only to preside over, but to sponsor, a launch of candle-bearing balloons, which are traditionally used in the festival of São João (24 June): call the fire brigade! And all the while offering in return to deliver tens of *favelas* as 'electoral corrals' (the virtually feudal delivery of whole areas into the hands of one candidate, with the effect that no other candidate will be welcome there).

For many people like those we work with today in our community nuclei, it seems only natural for candidates to give tangible gifts, rather than make abstract promises, because it is only in the period leading up to the elections that the people and the politicians get to meet on a daily basis; afterwards they don't meet again till the next elections. There are completely shameless candidates who go as far as giving out sets of false teeth—the upper set before the election, the lower set after, subject to a favourable outcome; in many cases the people who want the dentures still have a few teeth of their own, and as these dentures come in a more or less standard model, the candidate offers the services of a dentist to extract any healthy teeth which are in the way of the false teeth. Others offer wooden legs for amputees and glass eyes for the blind, or sacks of cement and tiles for house-building. One is even in the habit of offering unsigned cheques with the sum filled out; 'I will only sign them if I am elected'. Or half a 100-dollar bill—the other half after the elections. Or, even worse, they give each half to different people living in different parts of the city, people who will never meet after the election.

For many people it is difficult to believe that anyone might want to be *vereador* for a genuine political, aesthetic, social reason. As far as a good part of the population is concerned, politicians are all the same.

Even with these problems, my campaign was creating theatre groups: ecologists, women, university students, black people, all explaining our ethos and our theatrical-political proposition.

Until finally election day came. From early in the morning my campaign officers were already at the entrances to the polling stations, trying for last-minute conversions.

We won. Ours was not among the candidatures which got the most votes, but the votes it got were spread right across the whole of Rio de Janeiro: people who knew me only by way of our theatre, our shows. People who believed in us. People who believed in the Theatre of the Oppressed.

On 1 January 1993, I took my seat as one of six PT *vereadors*. That was how our Legislative Theatre experiment began. An experiment which, I hope, will never end.

CHAPTER TWENTY-FIVE

Written Genres and Styles in Europe and The Americas

GENRES AND STYLES IN THE WRITTEN TRADITION

What is genre? Genre is a way to categorize or group plays together by their structure. Styles of theatre are those types of performances that arise out of a particular time and place as a result of cultural norms and influences and major events that occur in society. Theatre and drama serve to entertain, but they also serve as a way for both the theatre practitioners and the audience to examine and reflect on the human condition.

The written tradition—which is the dominant tradition in Europe and North America—makes sense of a written play's emotional impact and point of view. Genre in the written tradition implies the kind of attitude the playwright brings to the subject as well as the attitude the audience should bring to the experience. The rules of genre reflect the values and concerns of a particular society. The ancient Greek, ancient Roman, and French and Italian Neoclassical playwrights created plays that followed very rigid rules. Playwrights from other eras used some of these rules, added new rules, or disregarded rules of the past and created a whole new form. What has resulted is a variety of theatrical genres and styles that have survived over the generations. The major theatrical genres and styles that developed in Europe and the United Sates are explained in the remainder of this chapter.

MAJOR THEATRICAL GENRES

Tragedy

Tragedies do not end well. They are plays about how humans struggle with and confront their limitations in the world. Tragedies address the meaning of life and are designed to help the audience understand the reasons for the suffering and daily conflicts of life. In experiencing a tragedy, the audience can learn that both integrity and wisdom can grow out of hardship. Tragedies are not meant to make an audience feel sad but, rather, are meant to enable it to experience emotional release, known as catharsis.

The protagonist in a tragedy is a hero of some sort; we root for and look up to him. The tragic hero is a complicated character. He makes choices, takes action, brings trouble on himself, and eventually takes responsibility for those choices and actions. He often begins the play successful and happy. He is then confronted with some preordained fate, and the choices he makes in dealing with that situation trigger the drama that ensues. He often refuses to accept fate and protests against the limitations of what it means to be human.

The protagonist of a tragedy is often on a journey to achieve self-fulfillment, but the choices he makes along the way lead to (at best) failure or to (at worst) disaster. During a tragedy, the audience will often feel pity for the main character, who unwittingly makes very bad choices. The audience members may also experience fear as it dawns on us that we may blindly make similar mistakes at some point in our lives. In this way, the tragic hero becomes a symbol for our conscience.

Tragedy is one of the oldest forms of theatrical genre. For thousands of years, tragedy was considered the preeminent and worthiest theatrical genre. In ancient Greece, the government sponsored an annual theatre festival, the Festival of Dionysus (as previously discussed in Chapter Three). Each year, the whole community would gather to watch a competition in which the best playwrights in the land would submit three tragedies by which they would be judged. The winner of the competition would receive a monetary prize and a great deal of honor. The plays were seen by thousands of citizens over the course of the festival. It is hard for contemporary audiences to imagine what this event was like. Attending a performance today at the ancient theatre of Epidaurus (see Figure 25.1), you can

Figure 25.1 A performance of the tragedy *Philoktetes* by Sophocles, Theatre of Epidaurus, Greece. Photo by Kate Caffrey, 2014.

begin to get a sense of what it was like to attend a single performance in the festival. Contemporary analogies to the festival include events like the Super Bowl, a Fifa World Cup final, or a concert presented by one of the most popular musicians in the world, except that the Festival of Dionysus lasted for many days.

The tragedies were indeed "popular entertainment." The characters in these plays were heroes similar to the present-day athletes or performers cheered by fans at sporting events or concerts. Like the professional athlete and entertainer of today, the characters in these tragedies seemed larger-than-life superstars whom their fans admired and sought to emulate. But the heroes in ancient Greek tragedies were not athletes. They were individuals who had attained high social status, usually as leaders (kings and queens). The action of these ancient tragedies focused on the downfall of these heroes.

In his *Poetics*, the ancient Greek scholar Aristotle analyzed the greatest tragedies of his time and explained what made them so engrossing. Each ancient tragedy had a tragic protagonist. The character was good, worthy, and affluent. He would commit some tragic misjudgment or error, a result of an innate "tragic flaw" in his temperament, which led to misery and disaster and his ultimate collapse (often death, but sometimes mere maiming as in *Oedipus Rex* by Sophocles). As the protagonist is making mistakes, he is not aware of it but the audience is. This is called dramatic irony. The audience empathizes with the protagonist because he is essentially a good person.

This empathy enables the audience to experience both pity and fear as it witnesses the snowball effect of the protagonist's actions. This emotional response to the events that take place in the tragedy take the audience on a spiritual and psychological journey that focuses attention on the moral lesson of the play. The spectator experiences a moment of catharsis when the hero's fortunes reverse, and the hero has a moment of recognition and begins to take responsibility for his actions and move from ignorance to self-knowledge. In the end, the hero suffers some terrible consequence of committing the tragic error, either death or a life worse than death. The punishment seems undeservedly severe, creating pity and fear in the audience, leading to catharsis and release so that the spectator can absorb the moral lesson of the tragedy.

As tragedies have continued to be written throughout the long history of theatre, these main principles of tragedy have not altered greatly since Aristotle evaluated what makes a tragedy great back in 335 BCE. Additional guidelines and rules have been added or emphasized through the ages, which has brought about sub-genres of tragedy—including Roman tragedy; Neo-Classical tragedy; Elizabethan tragedy; Jacobean tragedy; and modern tragedy. Some have suggested that tragedy cannot be written about modern humans because there is no longer a fixed value system by which human behavior may be measured. However, American playwright Arthur Miller argued against this idea in his essay *Tragedy and the Common Man*. In this work, Miller, who wrote *Death of a Salesman*, considered by many to be the greatest modern tragedy, argues that the tragic experience is independent of a universal value system. Miller explains that tragedy could indeed reflect the life of "the common man" who was willing to lay his life down to secure his sense of personal dignity. He argued that when viewing *Death of a Salesman*, the spectator's response is fitting with that of tragedy.

The one significant difference is that the protagonist, Willy Loman, is not a "hero" in the traditional definition (i.e., a person of high status). Miller asserts that Willy, though not of high social status, IS a hero. Willy is a flawed, good man who makes bad choices that lead to his demise. He is searching for self-validation despite economic and social forces working against him. He measures himself against the elusive "American Dream," and finding himself coming up short, chooses death as his only worthy action.

UNDERSTANDING TRAGEDY

Hamlet, King Lear, Macbeth, and Othello

Literary criticism uses the word *tragedy* differently from the way we use it in normal conversation. In normal use, any untimely death is 'tragic'. This is not the way the term is used in literature, however. In literary criticism it is used with a specific, technical meaning.

The first tragedies were written by the ancient Greek dramatists, most notably by Aeschylus, Sophocles and Euripides, who wrote in the fifth century BC. They were imitated by the Roman writer Seneca, whose plays were studied at grammar schools in Shakespeare's time. The conventions of classical tragedy had been identified by the Greek philosopher Aristotle in his *Poetics*. For Aristotle, a tragedy has a main character, a protagonist. This protagonist must be 'noble': not only rich, powerful and strong but possessing certain admirable personal qualities. The play will tell the story of their fall. To have its appropriate effect on the audience this fall must be from a position of eminence and must affect other people who depend on the protagonist. If the protagonist is a monarch, then a whole people are affected. Though fate plays a strong part in these plays, the downfall of the protagonist must be due to some personal error of judgement (*hamartia* is the Greek word). The tragic spectacle depends on the audience being aware of the capacity of even the most powerful of individuals to destroy themselves through their imperfect understanding of our condition in the world, he thought. The experience of this insight, which Aristotle believed conferred moral benefits upon the audience, would not occur if the protagonists were wicked, or if their fall came about by accident. In the first case the audience would feel no regret at their fall, and in the second no perception of mortal frailty would be granted. The point of tragedy, then, was to provide some form of moral and philosophical education for the audience.

There is no evidence that Shakespeare had any direct acquaintance with the *Poetics*. Early modern English tragedies on the public stages of London took the name and an approximation of the tragedic form. These plays did not necessarily set out to explore a moral, social or religious issue, as the Greek writers, and their Roman imitators, sought in their plays. They set out to tell a story in a recognized dramatic genre that would be attractive to London theatregoers, only a minority of whom would have come across classical tragedy in its Senecan form. There was no coherent contemporary idea of what tragedy should be, even if aristocratic writers like Sir Philip Sidney recommended going back to the classical rules.

In telling these stories within the genre of tragedy, the playwrights made statements about many aspects of human life, but perhaps principally about the nature of political power and the problems of the powerful in the world that they knew. They were aware that the feudal society of the fairly recent past had been very different in its organization and in its ideas about how life should be lived (see above, pp. 176–7). They could see a new world coming into being, a world in which individuals had much more opportunity to make their own way; where new forms of power were competing with old ones, and where the role of women was changing.

When powerful historical forces come into conflict, individuals are sometimes the site of that conflict and are destroyed by it. A protagonist who is living within one system of ideas or beliefs has to struggle to come to terms with the forces of another system. But the protagonists cannot understand this other system (usually) because they can see the world only from where they are. Yet, standing outside of the drama, as members of the audience, we can see their predicament and perhaps also see how things could have been different. From the outside we can see that men and women can transform society because the conditions that produce tragedy are shown to be man-made not divinely ordained, as many critics thought in the past. Some critics find the experience of watching the end of a tragedy to be a gloomy confirmation of human powerlessness. Others see there a pointer to a more just world which is perhaps the product of, but separate from, the conflicting forces which have destroyed the protagonist. There is death, waste and destruction at the end of a tragedy; but there is always some hope.

Comedy

Comedies make us laugh. They can be—and often are—about serious topics, but in comedy, the characters are lucky. They triumph over fate and/or obstacles to find happiness. Comedy is a celebration of humankind prevailing over the odds. It is many times an examination of human excess, but it always has a happy ending.

Figure 25.2 New Comedy mask made of marble. 2nd c. BCE. Athens. Photo by Kate Caffrey, 2014.

Comedy is one of the ancient forms of genre. At the outset of a comedy, the social fabric of society is often unraveled. In the course of the play, there is a great deal of conflict and disruption, but in the end, order is restored, couples come together, and all is right with the world.

Comedies were written and performed in ancient Greece as part of the Festival of Dionysus. Dionysus, as you already know, was the Greek god of wine and fertility. As was fitting to a festival celebrating sex, reproduction, and libation, the humor in Greek comedy is often quite bawdy. Aristophanes, one of the best of the Greek comic playwrights, filled his plays with lewd jokes, giant padded phalluses, and the singing of raucous songs. The actors of ancient Greece wore masks that had ridiculous and grotesque expressions, adding to the visual sense of humor. (see Figure 25.2.)

Because comedy makes us laugh, it can be very matter-of-fact and "tell it like it is." The audience can watch the events in a comedy from a safe distance, enabling it to see the truth about human behavior and laugh with relief. Comedy, like more serious genres, deals with how humans cope with struggles in life. It teaches the consequences of uncommon or abnormal behavior in an amusing way.

Most comedies showcase at least one character who is a clown, fool, or trickster. This character has a certain freedom to disrupt the normal rhythm and standards of life. The fool is allowed to disobey social bans and restrictions. In doing so, he makes us laugh at our own social restraint and repression.

All of these elements of comedy, which were developed in ancient comedies as long ago as 500 BCE, have existed throughout history and still exist today. However, funny people have added new elements to this genre over the years. Ancient comedy dealt primarily with social and political concerns. Today's comedies often deal with the personal neurosis of individuals. In addition, those who write comedy use tools or comic devices to make the audience laugh. The tools used in comedy range from broadly physical movement to subtle intellectual language. Different mechanisms are used in diverse sub-genres of comedy, with varying levels of intensity. All of these instruments of comedy launch comic action, which, in turn, invites the audience to respond in a lighthearted manner.

Some of the tools of comedy are as follows:

Surprise is often used to get a reaction from the audience. The action in a play will deviate from normal expectations. The audience will anticipate an action or reaction to take place and, instead, something incongruous will occur. This contradiction and surprise will turn a serious situation into a comic one.

Exaggeration of character, action, language, dialect, emotion, and situation can accentuate the ridiculousness of life. This mechanism of exaggeration is often used with parody, a type of comedy that imitates and pokes fun at individuals or artistic styles. As presented in a very overblown way, the characters or artistic styles seem ridiculous.

Characters in comedy often have some kind of **obsession**. These comic characters lose control and perspective in their journey to attain one single desire.

Slapstick is very broad physical comedy. It is a very ancient comic tool that is named for the fool's slapstick, a wooden device that was used to "torture" the fool or clown of the court, thereby creating a loud slapping noise. Slapstick comedy includes pratfalls, chases, collisions, comic beatings, practical jokes, and semi-acrobatic feats.

Transgressions offer laughs by violating social taboos. Jokes about physically eliminating waste (excrement, passing gas, urination), sex, violating moral codes, and violating society's religious values would fall into the realm of transgression.

The **language** of comedy has its own subset of devices. Some elements of comic language include puns (play on words), jokes, understatement, sarcasm, nonsensical rhythmic exchanges, witty repartee, and peculiar accents. Writers of comedy will also make use of malapropisms (the laughable misuse of words, often by confusing them with similar sounding words) and misuse of language (for example, mistakes in pronunciation or grammar).

The broad genre of comedy may then be broken down into sub-genres, which include: satire; situation comedy; farce; romantic comedy; and comedy of manners.

Melodrama

Melodrama is a genre that speaks directly to the emotions. It stages humankind's deepest and sometimes most unrealistic anxieties and appeases our fears with idealized, fantastical endings. This genre is easily accessible and is, therefore, one of the most popular in film, TV, and gaming. Melodrama includes crime series, horror movies, children's cartoons, and interactive video games like *Dragon's Lair*.

Melodrama has three "s" qualities that make them popular—they are simplistic, sensational, and sentimental. The world of melodrama is emotionally satisfying and morally simplistic. Characters are not complex or conflicted; they are simple and straightforward—they are merely good or bad. The conflict between good and evil is represented in the extreme. And what about the disasters and misfortune that befall the good characters? Unlike tragedy, these setbacks do not come from any flaws within the protagonist. They are the result of outside forces beyond the control of the hero.

Tragicomedy

If you walk out of a play feeling somewhat confused, anxious, bewildered, and not quite sure what genre of play you just experienced, you probably just viewed a tragicomedy. A tragicomedy has elements of both tragedy and comedy, but an audience does not come out of a tragicomedy with a reaction that is overwhelmingly related to one or the other. There are tragedies that have comic scenes; for example, some of the scenes between Juliet and her Nurse in Shakespeare's *Romeo and Juliet* are very funny. But, the overriding feeling the audience experiences during the play is one of a tragedy, the emotions of pity and fear.

There are also serious situations and moments in comedy. For example, when the pious and foolhardy Orgon disowns his whole family and almost ends up in jail in *Tartuffe*, we have pity for him and feel fear that we could suffer the same fate by believing in someone who may really be a hypocrite. However, all is set right at the end of the play, no one is harmed, Orgon sees the error of his ways, and the audience can laugh at this misguided man's folly.

Tragicomedy, however, is different than either of these other genres, and it combines elements of both. Tragicomedy often includes a serious plot in which the expected tragedy is replaced by a happy ending. And yet, the events in tragicomedy are not usually the result of cause and effect. Some tragicomedies—especially those works that belong to the style of Theatre of the Absurd or Avante Garde theatre—seem to have no plot or ending at all.

Tragicomedy is bittersweet. It expresses the concurrent feelings of the pain and pleasure of human existence. It began to develop as societies became more complex and started to move away from the notion of a singular worldview and value structure. Over time, as education became more widely available, more people learned to read with the advent of the printing press, and the Industrial Revolution gathered people from diverse backgrounds into closer proximity, more and more people began to question the authority of God, religion, and government. The old ideas of absolute good (and bad) no longer satisfied the masses. Humankind began to struggle in its search for a meaning to life. Especially in Europe, people's perceptions of society started to change by the beginning of the seventeenth century. Artists began to question the nature of reality and look inward at the human condition. The more structured tragedies and comedies of ancient times, which had previously offered clear and ordered examples of good and bad behavior, no longer seemed to reflect life experiences. Theatre artists began to explore the idea that comedy and tragedy are not separate experiences but co-exist at all times, creating a dramatic tension to the journey of life.

Modern tragicomedy was developed primarily in Europe in the early and mid-twentieth century following the two world wars. Artists were responding to a time when human relationships seemed ineffective, language was imprecise, and the traditional genres of theatre did not reflect the anxiety and ridiculousness of a baffling and illogical society. After living through the devastation and atrocities of World War II, playwrights in Europe created drama that was dark and pessimistic. In these tragicomedies, the world was seen as a place where people could no longer communicate because they were surrounded by a void of meaninglessness.

MAJOR THEATRICAL STYLES

Classicism

Classicism in the theatre is a style that presents a world that is idealized, graceful, and perfectly balanced. The classical worldview is one of order and perfection. The Classicist believes in reason. Truth may be discovered if humans use their intellect and rationality to create an ideal world. Classicism rejects excess and advocates for a life that celebrates moderation in all things. This style of drama celebrates balance and proportion and the control humankind can assert on the world through the application of reason.

The roots of Classicism can be found in ancient Greece and Rome. As the Catholic Church became the dominant force in European society, access to arts and culture that had been developed by the Greek and Roman pagans was restricted, and Classicism disappeared for centuries.

Classicism resurfaced again in Europe during the Renaissance and was developed into a more rigidly systematized style of theatre by playwrights and scholars of this period. Like the ancients before them, Classicists of this period emphasized society and often wrote theatre about honor and duty. Their plays revolved around a rationally-guided catharsis and avoided overt emotionalism. Classicism demonstrated a respect for decorum, which meant that certain subjects were left to narration. Scenes of excessive cruelty or violence took place off stage and were described later rather than being depicted on stage.

Additionally, the Classicism of the Renaissance was more restrictive than the original works of the Greeks and Romans. It had more overtly structural overtones of orderliness and predictability. There was a prescription for the structure of the play that playwrights were advised to follow. All plays were to be written in five acts. They also needed to adhere to the unities of time, place, and action. The unity of time required the playwright to ensure that the entire action of the play (i.e., all of the events) took place in a single day (one 24-hour period). The unity of place demanded that the action take place in one location. The unity of action meant that the play should be built around a single plot line with no subplots.

Classicism also introduced the concept of verisimilitude (an idealized truth) as a main component of the message of the play. All plays should uphold "poetic justice" in which the good are rewarded and the evil are punished. Plays were meant to teach a moral lesson, and the focus of a play as a means of education, rather than as entertainment, took dominance. A play written in a classical style teaches us what and who we can be and lets us imagine what life would be like in a more perfect, orderly world. Design in classical plays is often perfectly symmetrical and balanced. The visual style is simple, formal, and unadorned.

The central characters in Classicism struggle to maintain control over their natural impulses. Characters who are not balanced and who are guilty of extreme behavior are beset by bad fortune. In addition, the Neo-Classicists—who revived the classics during the Age of Enlightenment—dictated that genres should be limited to tragedy and comedy, and the two should not be mixed. Characters in tragedy should be limited to the upper class, royalty, and individuals of high birth. Comedies should be populated with individuals from the middle and lower classes. All characters should behave in a manner appropriate to their gender and social status (in accordance with the theme of decorum).

The language that characters speak is elevated in tone and form. They do not speak the language of everyday realism but in formally-structured sentences. The result is discourse that indicates how people should speak and would speak in an idealized, perfectly-ordered world. Reason dominates over emotion in dialogue and action. Characters often engage in debate, voicing opposing viewpoints and moving toward an ideal that is the centrist point between their differing positions.

Romanticism

Romanticism, like Classicism in the theatre, is a style that presents a world that is idealized, glorified, and graceful. The Romantic artist sees life in an unrealistic, glamorized way. However, where the Classicist views an idealized world of order and rules, the Romantic artist focuses on the freedom of nature and the idea of following the impulses of instinct. The Romantic sensibility is one that is rife with sentimentalism and warmth of feeling, seeing the world "through rose-colored glasses." Romantic plays focus on emotions because emotions are more natural than the rules and reason of Classicism. To the Romantic artist, reason and education are suspect because they are not natural and are, therefore, corruptible. Unlike the Classicists who believed that truth could be found in "norms," the Romantics looked for the truth and meaning of life in the boundless variety that existed in the natural world. Romantic theatre glorifies the "natural man" or the "noble savage," the unrefined character who lives a simple and genuine life.

Romantic plays tend to reflect on the unique and independent experience, not the common and universal. In this style of theatre, all creation is unified and has a certain oneness, but it is the details of existence that are most important.

These artists search for the ultimate truth of life by focusing on the specifics and individuality of human existence. They quest for an idealized truth and believe it may be discovered through feeling the emotions of our idealized image of human perfection. However, the Romantic artist senses that he will probably struggle to discover that idealized truth and never find it, which leads to a melancholy strain in these works of art.

There is a subjectivity to the art of the Romantic style because the artist, the audience, and the evaluator of art are all necessarily subjective and personal in their reflections of life. The Romantics, unlike the Classicists, believed that there was no objective set of rules by which art could be created or evaluated. The ideal is that art serves an exalted purpose, which is to lead people to recognize the root universal nature of all existence. Once this harmony is recognized, conflict is eliminated, and mankind can be "made whole" again.

Plays of this style are inclined to focus more on the mysterious, the spiritual, and the supernatural. The visual and sensational predominates over the verbal and intellectual. The sensual (that is—what is seen, felt, heard) is more consequential than the intellectual meaning of words. In this way, Romantic drama appeals to the intuition, the senses, and the heart: aspects of life that are innate to all human experience. It is not focused on the structural rules of the intellect and education, which are aspects of life that are restricted in some ways to the realm of the upper classes. Therefore, Romanticism is a more representative art form than Classicism. It led to the democratization of theatre in many ways, meaning that one person's feelings were seen to be as valid as any others.

In this way, the Romanticism that emerged as a reaction to Classicism in the late eighteenth century led to the burgeoning of the theatre of the common person. It is an individualistic style of theatre that frees the artist to express his vision of the world and send his message to his fellow human beings. In Romanticism, the artist's imagination and feelings are his law, and in order for the artist to truly express his feelings, the art must come from his subconscious with as little interference as possible from artificial rules that prescribed what a work of art should consist of. The Romantics believed that there were natural laws of creativity. A good creative artist would freely and instinctively give rise to his vision through artistic inspiration if unencumbered by rules and models from other works. There was a belief that exposure to these models of other works through education would obstruct the artist's own imagination and limit his ability to be original and truly inspired.

Characters in Romantic plays tends to be heroes, exceptional human beings, who are headstrong and yet sensitive. They are isolated from society, and yet their goal is to do good for others and society. They are individuals who never compromise their ideals and are swept up by the adventures with which life challenges them. They are not interested in personal gain but strive to be the *perfect* being in their service to others. They often struggle for a goal that they could never attain in real life. The language that the Romantic character speaks is idealized as well. He will speak eloquently and poetically. His speech will be filled with beautiful imagery and elevated language.

The action in Romantic plays are often thrilling adventures, moving from one location to the next. There is a main plot with several subplots, and the mood of the play is filled with many reversals—happy scenes coming right on the heels of sad scenes, ultimately moving to a great emotional climax. This swirling and expansive twist and flow of action and emotion enables the audience to feel the protagonist's crusade for a perfect reality.

Glamorized natural settings dominate plays in this style. The staging—set, lights, costumes—of Romantic plays present idyllic and detailed expressions of the human experience. Scenery of plays in the Romantic style are glorified representations of real life—locations that exist often in exotic locales or places "long ago and far, far away." Romantic plays are escapist; they are set in a better time and place where an idealized truth exists, a place where life is the way we want it to be. Costumes in Romantic plays focus on the details and distinct nature of character.

Realism

Realism is a movement in art that originated in the late nineteenth century. It is the most common type of theatre in modern society. Realism is also the theatrical style that most people are familiar with because of its substantial influence on film and television. Charles Darwin, Karl Marx, and Sigmund Freud significantly influenced the development of Realism in theatre and other forms of art. The research and writings of these three scientists have had a profound impact on both society and the way in which human behavior and human nature are understood.

Darwin's studies found that progress and change are a part of a natural process involving trial and error that works toward improvement and refinement of the species. Heredity, as well as environment, has a great influence on all species, including humans. Playwrights who wanted to write about real people and the actors who would portray those characters realized that in order to depict a realistic character, they would have to understand the character's environment and heredity.

Marx was convinced that environment impacted human behavior and that society must accept some responsibility for learned behaviors. He wrote about the negative aspects of Capitalism and the Industrial Revolution with moral indignation over the plight of the working class. Realistic playwrights who are strongly influenced by Marx's research and writings pen realistic stories that call attention to human oppression. These plays question society's values and explore the social and domestic challenges of the middle class. Early Realistic plays tend to be more political as Realistic playwrights of the late nineteenth century felt that their roles were to incite change through art and attempt to improve society by exposing its failings.

Freud suggested that change, rather that permanence, is the norm and that moral standards are relative to each culture. He found that concepts of right and wrong can vary widely from one culture to the next. Before Freud, Christian societies predominantly believed that human beings had an instinctive grasp of the difference between right and wrong and that conscience was an innately God-given virtue. After Freud's studies began to have an influence on society's understanding of the psyche, that belief changed. Modern societies tend to agree with Freud's findings that a sense of right and wrong is not innate and does not come from God. Values must be taught, and a person's behavior and moral beliefs are relative to the individual, family, or society that have raised him. Freud actually utilized characters from plays—Hamlet and Oedipus, for example—in his deeply-detailed analysis of the human mind. This type of character analysis began to take hold in both playwriting and acting preparation with the development of Realism. Realistic playwrights and performers strive to reveal characters who are complete and whole. These characters' unconscious and conscious motivations are often well-justified through the combined skills of the playwright and those who bring their words, thoughts, and actions to life on the stage.

The new understanding of humankind and society, which Darwin, Marx and Freud championed, brought alterations to the ways in which experiences are reflected through plays created in the style of Realism. Theatre artists working in Realism create Realistic characters as products of their genes (Darwin), environment (Marx), and psyche (Freud.) The details of environment, action, and character in Realism are meant to be so fully realized that they convince the audience that they are watching life itself—that what they are experiencing is *real*.

Characters in Realistic plays are everyday people who speak in ordinary language. These plays take place in real locations that are specific environments. Writing, acting, and production values strive to represent characters and events as they are observed in real life. Realism is based in the scientific outlook of cause and effect and that truth can be realized through examination of a subject through the five senses. Truth in Realism is knowledge of the real world that can be discovered through direct observation. Playwrights write about what they know—the world around them—as objectively as possible.

Because the Realistic character is determined, in large part, by his surroundings and environment, settings and scenic design take on a more important role. The character's surroundings are not just background, they have an effect on the action. Scenic designers in Realism create what have come to be known as realistic box sets—true-to-life interiors with a room or rooms. With this type of set, the proscenium opening is treated as the imaginary *fourth wall* of a room, which is removed so that the audience has the feeling of looking in on a character's private life.

Technical inventions of the late nineteenth century also contributed to the evolution of Realism. The emergence of limelight, gaslight and, then electrical light allowed actors to move back deeper into the stage. Electrical light also allowed for realistic lighting effects, which could be controlled, and directed light. The audience could now sit in darkness, more removed from the action of the play. This development also meant that the actors did not have to play a scene on the front apron of the stage to be seen. This improvement in lighting called for more detailed and authentic scenery and costumes. Lifelike, accurate scenery, lighting, and costumes became the norm.

Theatricalism

Theatricalism is a style of theatre that was developed in the twentieth century in response to Realism. Both Theatricalism and Realism reflect the scientific focus in society and the arts that developed after the Enlightenment and then with the widespread acceptance of the theories of Darwin, Marx and Freud. Theatricalism, like Realism, creates a reflection of life on the stage that is evidence-based and objective. In Theatricalism, scientific analysis is the major influence on the way in which a creator of the play reflects on life. This is true for Realism as well.

How, then, is Theatricalism a response to Realism? It is in the type of reflection. Theatricalism creates a perception of life that is obviously an illusion. A play in the style of Theatricalism persistently reminds the audience that it is in a theatre watching actors on a stage using various types of stage technology to communicate a message. In Theatricalism, one of the goals of the production is to constantly remind the audience members of their roles as viewers and critics of the artwork in progress in front of them. The production does not attempt to convince the audience that what is happening in front of it is reality but, rather, a creation by actors who are real. Many of the techniques practiced in Realism are meant to create an illusion of reality. The fourth wall and passive audience created by the proscenium stage, naturalistic acting, realistic scenic design, realistic/natural language and dialogue, curtains that hide lighting and sound instruments and other theatrical technology, were purposefully discarded. Instead, a play performed in the style of Theatricalism might:

- Be presented on a platform projecting into the physical space of the audience.
- Reveal lighting and sound instruments so that they are visible to the audience.
- Use projections and placards announcing time and place of a scene.
- Utilize direct address from actor to audience and the expectation of audience participation.
- Employ the use of scenery and costume pieces that do not feign authenticity.

The goal of a creator of a performance done in the style of Theatricalism is to make the audience aware that it is in a theatre watching a play. This would allow the audience to maintain the emotional objectivity it would need to learn the truth about the play's subject. One of the greatest theorists and practitioners of Theatricalism is the German playwright Bertolt Brecht. He rejected Realism, believing that it seduced the audience into believing it was watching real life, which led to an uncritical acceptance of society's values. He felt that by constantly reminding the audience it was watching actors perform a play in a theatre by utilizing the techniques of Theatricalism, the audience could maintain the emotional objectivity necessary to learn the truth about society. You can learn more about Theatricalism and the work of Bertolt Brecht by reading the following article.

BERTOLT BRECHT

LIFE AND WORK

Bertolt Brecht (or 'Bert Brecht', as he liked to style himself) was born in Augsburg, Bavaria, on 10 February 1898. He was christened Eugen Berthold Friedrich, and his father was a Catholic, while his mother was Protestant. The father, 'a typical representative of the solid and respectable on hot afternoons [Brecht and his friends] would go swimming in the Hahnreibach, lie naked in the Wolfsahn meadow, bourgeoisie', worked in the Haindl paper factory, and became a director there in 1914. Brecht and his father occasionally quarrelled - Brecht recorded in his diary in September 1920 that after some apples had been stolen from the family orchard he defended the thief, maintaining a tree's produce could not be private property. His father flew into

a rage, accusing him of communism and shouting that his literary work amounted to nothing. But usually he took pride in his son, and supported him financially for many years. Brecht's mother, who died in 1920, dreamed of her son becoming a great poet. He in turn clearly loved her: his friend Hanns Otto Munsterer claims that the women in Brecht's later plays can only be fully appreciated when his adoration of his mother is understood. Brecht also had a younger brother, Walter, whose attitude to his famous elder brother seems to have been at best ambiguous, perhaps a mixture of jealousy, mistrust, and admiration.

When the First World War broke out, Brecht was at school. He sighed later that he had been 'lulled to sleep' for nine years there, and had therefore been unable to teach his teachers much, but he had founded a school

Robert Leach, from "Bertolt Brecht," *Makers of Modern Theatre*, pp. 102–124, 146–150. Copyright © 2004 by Taylor & Francis Group. Reprinted with permission.

magazine, performed in his own puppet theatre and had begun to attend the theatre proper in Augsburg. When the war came, like many others he was proudly patriotic, though he later modified this attitude, and when the time came for him to join up, his father did all he could to prevent it. By 1918, however, he had become a medical orderly, a post he described with high humour later to his friend, Sergei Tretyakov:

> *I bound up wounds and painted them with iodine, I administered enemas and gave blood transfusions. If a doctor had said to me: 'Brecht, amputate this leg!' I would have replied: 'As you order, Herr Staff Doctor!' and cut off the leg. If somebody had given the order: 'Brecht, trepan! ' then I would have cut open the skull and poked about in the brain.*

From this time, too, came his *Legend of the Dead Soldier,* a poem which describes how a dead soldier is patched up and marched back to the front.

This is the work of a 'poete maudit', who 'wallowed in' Rimbaud, and mourned Frank Wedekind as 'ugly, brutal [and] dangerous,' when he died in March 1918. The following summer Brecht and a friend spent weeks rambling through the Bavarian countryside, earning their board and lodging by entertaining the customers in wayside inns, as often as not hiking through the night or sleeping rough under the stars. To Arnold Zweig,

Brecht was 'a descendant of the folk singers, [and] the unknown poets of the open road'. For two or three summers after the end of the First World War,

> *or go climbing trees ... Brecht recited funeral orations and devotions ... so grotesque that we doubled up with laughter and rolled around in the reeds. The next day provoked philosophical musings.*

These probably took place in Brecht's attic room. His parents had allowed him the top floor of their house, which had its own entrance, and here the young would-be writer played host to young ladies as well as to his men friends, composed his earliest ballads, and began drafting plays and poems, usually in company with one or more of his delighted and supportive companions.

He also loved the local fairs. 'I keep on spending my evenings mooching around the *Planer*', he notes in his diary, 'where they hammer their nigger minstrel tunes into you till you can't get them out of the creases of your skin'. Brecht also liked the ice cream parlour, where he could flirt with the waitresses and sing his ballads to his own accompaniment, the 'Lachkeller', a pub with entertainment where he met and performed with the comedian, Karl Valentin, and the Blumensale Theatre, where Valentin also appeared. Here the audience sat at tables, the more conveniently to smoke and drink during the acts, which often contained pungent political comment. In these idyllic years, Brecht also discovered love and (not quite the same thing) sex. Throughout his life, his affairs were multifarious, complex, and usually destructive. Like Shakespeare, Wagner, and many other geniuses, his treatment of his lovers was too often disgraceful, especially, as Peter Thomson has pointed out, for one who wrote so often about 'goodness' (though it should be added that *The Good Person of Szechuan,* for instance, is not about 'goodness' in people, but 'not-goodness' in society).

His first great love was Paula Banholzer, 'Bi'. 'A queen is a queen, terror is terror, and Bi is Bi', Brecht wrote, and, when she was naked, he thought her naive as a child and artful as a (film) star. In summer 1918 they became lovers, greatly to their mutual delight, but soon Bi became pregnant, and Frank, Brecht's first child, was born on 31 July 1919. He was cared for largely by foster parents, neither his father nor mother spending much time with him, and ironically when he grew up he was conscripted into Hitler's armed forces and killed in November 1943. Bi and Brecht continued as lovers, but gradually became less passionate, though he remained possessive, and even dedicated *Drums in the Night* to her in 1922. Nevertheless, by then he was involved with other women, most notably Marianne Zoff, an Austrian opera singer, with whom he was living in Munich in March 1921. She too became pregnant, and despite his diary note - 'I can't get

married. I must have elbowroom, be able to spit as I want, to sleep alone, be unscrupulous' - in November 1922 they were married, four months before their daughter, Hanne, was born.

Brecht the young man was a fascinating, charismatic mass of contradictions: a shabby provincial, who yet seemed worldly wise, a wildly romantic cynic, someone who was frequently ill, yet whom many remembered as laughing with gusto, and inspiring laughter in others. He noted in his diary in August 1920: 'I'm continually forgetting my opinions, [and] can't ever make up my mind to learn them off by heart'. In October 1921 he derided Wagner ('Enough to make you sick') one day, and lauded Charlie Chaplin ('The most profoundly moving thing I've ever seen in the cinema') the next.

By then Brecht was working strenuously at becoming a writer. Determinedly, he sought a publisher, or publishers, for his work, which included poems and ballads, short stories, and plays, both full-length and one-act. He shoved typescripts into the hands of those higher on the ladder than himself, such as Lion Feuchtwanger, and gradually he began to make progress. He wrote theatre criticism for the local newspaper, a short story appeared in print, he was offered some directing work, and in 1922 his second play, *Drums in the Night,* was performed successfully at the Munich Kammerspiele. It was published, too, in a volume with the earlier *Baal,* and he was taken onto the staff of the theatre. In November that year Brecht was awarded the prestigious Kleist Prize: recognition that he was a significant new talent in the German theatre. The following year, *Baal* and his third play, *In the Jungle of Cities,* were both produced, and Brecht received, jointly with Lion Feuchtwanger, a commission to adapt Marlowe's *Edward II* for the Kammerspiele. Brecht himself directed it in March 1924 - his first successfully completed professional production. And six months later he moved to Berlin, to take up a post as dramaturg at Reinhardt's Deutsches Theatre.

Now was formed the persona of Brecht the Berliner: combative, sexy, and unpredictable, who was associated equally with 'new drama' and scandal. The artist Wieland Herzfelde remembered 'a very argumentative, very polished, and even sharp-tongued person. He had a passion ... for saying things which shocked'. Arnold Bronnen described Brecht's 'bristly wan face with piercing button-eyes, and unruly bush of short dark hair ... A pair of cheap wire spectacles dangled loosely from his remarkably delicate ears and hung across his narrow pointed nose. His mouth was peculiarly fine, and seemed to hold the dreams which others hold in their eyes.'

His love affairs continued to be complex and extraordinary. By the end of 1924 Marianne Zoff had left Brecht, having found him in bed with Helene Weigel, a beautiful Jewish actress with a successful career, who married Brecht in 1928. They had two children, Stefan, born on 3 November 1924,

and Barbara, born on 18 October 1930. But this should not imply that Brecht was anything like faithful to Weigel. His other lovers in the 1920s included Asja Lacis, a Latvian-born, Russian-trained actress, who informed him of some at least of the excitement of Meyerhold's revolutionary theatre; Marieluisse Fleisser, a significant playwright in her own right, and author of, for example, *Pioneers in Ingolstadt;* and, most significantly, Elisabeth Hauptmann, a would-be writer from a well-off Prussian family, whose fluency in English was to prove decisive to Brecht when she translated Gay's *The Beggar's Opera* for him.

Brecht's first Berlin-created work was *Man is Man* (though he had been toying with a play abuot a character called Galy Gay for years). Written in the closest collaboration with a group of sympathetic friends, including Elisabeth Hauptmann, Bernhard Reich (Asja Lacis's partner), Brecht's school friend Caspar Neher, who designed the first production at Darmstadt on 26 September 1926, and the journalist, Emil Burri, the play is a brilliant *tour de force*, that is still greatly underestimated, lyrical, cynical, theatrical, and funny. Feuchtwanger wrote: 'when the live Galy Gay holds the funeral oration for the dead Galy Gay, I know of no scene by a living author which can equal it in greatness of grotesque-tragic invention and basic grasp'. It is, in fact, Brecht's first 'epic' drama, and some of its awkwardnesses, which do not detract from its dramatic power, come from the fact that Brecht was still formulating what he meant by this term. In May 1939 looking back on this work, he noted in his journal: 'I brought the epic elements "into the business" ready-made from the Karl Valentin theatre, the open-air circus, and the Augsburg Fair. Then there was a film, especially the silents in the early days before the cinema began to copy drrrramatics [sic] from the theatre.'

Equally significant was the new subject matter which so scoured life in the Weimar Republic, and which Brecht was now approaching: capitalism, the market, imperialism, and the relationship between economics and politics. Whether this signified a whole-hearted conversion to Marxism at this time is doubtful, but it does show an attempt to dramatise questions of power, and especially of the creation and workings of specific power structures. His experience of working as a member of a collective at the theatre of the Communist director, Erwin Piscator, at this time also sharpened his thinking, not only about political power, but also about the theatre itself, its function and standing as a social and intellectual institution, whose interests it served, what the role of the audience is or should be, and the place of dramatic literature within it.

These are questions underlying the series of plays Brecht wrote in the late 1920s and early 1930s, known as *Lehrstucke*, which were deliberately created for an alternative 'theatre for instruction'. Their subject is dialectics itself. Spare in form, they use a minimum of naturalistic detail, and employ songs, direct address to the audience, and courtroom scenes where points of view can be argued. They aim to fuse content, form and function, or rather to let the contradictions between these stimulate reflection.

Alongside the *Lehrstücke*, Brecht worked with Kurt Weill to create a series of musical and operatic works, the first and most successful of which was *The Threepenny Opera*, based on Gay's *The Beggar's Opera*, which opened at the Theatre am Schiffbauerdamm in Berlin on 31 August 1928. It was a shimmering success, especially because of its caustic and sentimental ballads which still retain their allure today. Brecht and Weill followed it with the less popular, but still attractive, *Happy End*, and, in March 1930, the major opera, *The Rise and Fall of the City of Mahagonny*. Meanwhile, the rights to film *The Threepenny Opera* had been bought, and Leo Lania, Bela Belasz, and Ladislas Vajda began to adapt the original.[14] But the project went sour, with disagreements, accusations of bad faith, and finally recourse to the courts. Brecht and Weill failed to prevent the film from going ahead, though each received some monetary compensation, and the events provoked Brecht into writing his only completed novel, *Threepenny Novel*, as well as the long theoretical essay 'The Threepenny Lawsuit'.

In January 1933 the work of Brecht and many other progressive or controversial artists was stopped in its tracks. Hitler became German Chancellor. In the last years of the Weimar Republic, and especially after the Wall Street crash of 1929, the quality of life in Germany rapidly deteriorated. Unemployment soared, politics became polarised, and anti-Semitism strode the street in ugly fury. Would Hitler restore sense and stability? The answer came less than a month after he took power: the Reichstag, the nation's parliament, was burned down. Within days, swathes of the country's intellectual and artistic elite had either been arrested or had fled abroad. Brecht was one of the lucky ones. He escaped.

Yet for a writer exile is particularly terrible, for the most basic tool of his trade, his language, is useless to him. And when his homeland is simultaneously being ravaged, as Germany was by Nazism, the loss becomes almost unendurable. Brecht and his family found a home in Denmark, on the island of Fyn, which became their base for nearly six years. It may be added that exile did not quash Brecht's sexual appetite. In Denmark he had at least two significant love affairs, first with Margarete Steffin, whom he had first met in Germany shortly before the Nazis took power and who now became a valued collaborator as well as his lover, and second with Ruth Berlau, a wealthy Danish Communist, who was both a political activist and a determined theatre worker.

The sudden severance from his home, his successful career, and its future possibilities clearly affected Brecht. He worked on a number of plays and other texts, though not with anything like the sharpness which might have been expected from his earlier works, and spent much time

in travel. Sometimes this was in connection with productions of his works, sometimes for meetings or conferences of anti-Fascist writers or other progressive bodies, where he spoke, argued, and listened. Thus, in summer 1933 he was in Paris, and he returned there in the autumn. In 1934 he spent October and November in London. In the spring of 1935 he stayed with Tretyakov in Moscow; he was in Paris again in June, and in New York from October to December. He spent nearly four months of 1936 back in London, and in autumn 1937 and again in spring 1939 he was in Paris.

One of the reasons for his travels was to enable him to take part in the increasingly bitter arguments among progressive and left-wing intellectuals, writers, and artists about the nature of 'Realism', and in particular the Soviet-proclaimed 'Socialist Realism'. Brecht rejected this, and perhaps partly in a deliberate attempt to demonstrate that a much more subtle and challenging form of Marxist art was possible, he turned back to writing plays. The result was the series of dramas which made his name after the Second World War. In 1938 he completed *Fear and Misery of the Third Reich* and the first version of *Galileo*. In 1939 he began work on *The Good Person of Szechuan* (which, however, was not completed until 1941) and wrote *Mother Courage and Her Children*, which received its world premiere in Zurich in April 1941. And in 1940 he completed *Mr Puntila and His Man Matti* and *The Resistable Rise of Arturo Ui*.

In the meantime, world events were again pressing in on Brecht. The increasing likelihood of war in Europe forced him and his family to leave Denmark for Sweden in April 1939, and a year later they were forced further from Europe's epicentre to Finland. Finally, in May 1941, 'changing countries oftener than their shoes', they moved via the Soviet Union to the west coast of the United States. On the way, in Moscow, Margarete Steffin's desperate illness prevented her further travel. Brecht was distraught, and telephoned her from every station along the Trans-Siberian railway, the route of his escape. She died on 4 June. It has been suggested that Brecht should have stayed with her, but he had a passage on the last ship to the west coast of America (and it was going via Manila in the Philippines). Moreover, as Eric Bentley has pointed out, had Brecht spent even a week longer in Moscow, it is likely he would have disappeared into the gulag. Though he muffled his criticism of Stalin's regime in public, he was in no doubt about its reality in the privacy of his diary: 'Literature and art are up the creek, political theory has gone to the dogs, what is left is a thin, bloodless, proletarian humanism propagated by officialdom in an official article.' Later, he noted that 'in Fascism, Socialism is confronted with a distorted mirror-image of itself'. The same month Brecht left the Soviet Union, June 1941, Germany invaded.

Brecht and his family lived in Santa Monica, California, for most of the six years they were in the United States.

Times were not easy, though the physical danger they had endured in Europe from the Nazis was gone. The actor Fritz Kortner referred to Brecht living an 'almost Gandhi-like ascetic existence ' which, however, was punctuated by visits made and received:

> Helene Weigel held open house every Sunday evening. They were very nice occasions socially, unpretentious, warm, with beer and an item or two of Weigel's cooking. Hostess was a very good role for this actress, even if Host was not something her husband could bring himself to be. He would deposit himself in a corner where people had to come and seek him out, whereas she would flit about and make sure that any who felt unwelcome changed their minds.

The move from Europe to America was another destructive upheaval for Brecht, and he recorded in his diary: 'for the first time in ten years, I am not working seriously on anything'. He pondered whether to become an American citizen. In 1944 Ruth Berlau became pregnant. She discovered she also had a stomach tumour which was removed, but the baby, born by caesarean section, did not survive.

Brecht obtained a little work from Hollywood, most notably with Fritz Lang on the script of *Hangmen Also Die,* but he had little else to show for living so close to so many studios. Otherwise, besides one or two adaptations of classics, he wrote most of *The*

Visions of Simone Machard with the also exiled Lion Feuchtwanger, and the following year created *Schweyk in the Second World War*, an ironic sequel to Hasek's masterpiece. Finally, in 1994, with Ruth Berlau, he wrote the brilliant *Caucasian Chalk Circle*. In 1995, Charles Laughton, a significant film star, became entranced with *Galileo*, and he and Brecht began to work to create an English version which would be acceptable to American audiences.

> *The collaboration with Laughton was the classic one of our profession—playwright and actor. At certain points he saw the play collapsing, at which he built himself up like an immoveable mountain of flesh until the required change was identified and made. This stubborn sensitivity proved to be more fruitful than his factual suggestions (which he always offered with the greatest circumspection).*

The production opened in Hollywood on 30 July 1947.

Brecht, however, was hardly able to enjoy this before he was summoned by the House Committee on Un-American Activities to Washington. He appeared before them on 30 October and, controlling his responses by recourse to his familiar cigars, he fenced courteously with the lawyers who tried to extract a commitment to Communism from him. 'Did you write that, Mr Brecht?' the prosecutor asked, having read (badly) a translation of a poem. 'No', replied Brecht,

'I wrote a German poem, but that is very different from this.' The transcript records like a stage direction: '[Laughter.]' The chairman, in dismissing Brecht, assured him that he was 'a good example' to other witnesses. But within little more than twenty-four hours, despite fog almost as thick as the obfuscating cigar fumes he had exhaled in the witness-box, Brecht, with typically heroic cowardice, was flying out of the United States, back towards Europe.

He landed in Switzerland where *Mother Courage and Her Children* had successfully premiered. Teo Otto, stage designer of that *Mother Courage*, noted that 'the years that followed the war were a period of hope clad in rags', a comment which in a way summarises Brecht's own attitude at this time. In Switzerland, his adaptation of *Antigone*, as well as the premiere of *Mr Puntila and His Man Matti* were staged, and he worked on both *The Days of the Commune* and the theoretical statement, *A Short Organum for the Theatre*.

By the end of 1948 he was ready to re-enter the now divided Germany. He came via Czechoslovakia to the Soviet sector of Berlin. It was the time of the Cold War. East and west could not meet. Brecht, though he retained an Austrian passport, became effectively an East (Communist) German. The attraction, above all, was the offer of his own production of *Mother Courage and Her Children,* with his wife, Helene Weigel, in the title role. This opened at the Deutsches Theatre in

Berlin on 11 January 1949, and was a success comparable only with that of *The Threepenny Opera* over twenty years before. Brecht's theatrical future was then cemented with the establishment of the Berliner Ensemble, his own company, a mere month after the Communists proclaimed their sector of Germany the independent German Democratic Republic. And for the rest of its existence, East Germany supported Brecht's theatre to the hilt, through bad times and good. The subsidy was nearly three million marks per annum at the beginning, and it rose from there.

The repressive state and its theatrical jewel did not always co-exist easily. After the death of Stalin, the East Berlin workers revolted. Perhaps they were still infected with the Nazism of yesteryear, but their uprising was brutally crushed by Soviet tanks, and Brecht notoriously wrote a letter apparently supporting the repression. Was his reward the allocation to the Ensemble in March 1954 of the old Theatre am Schiffbauerdamm, where *The Threepenny Opera* had premiered in 1928, and where now his new, perhaps unsurpassed production of *The Caucasian Chalk Circle* received its first performance? Or the Stalin Peace Prize, which he was awarded in 1955? Perhaps it was permission to take his company abroad. In 1954, and again in 1955, they appeared in Paris, where in each year they won First Prize at the Theatre des Nations. And in August 1956 they came to London.

Brecht was still an enigma. It was noticeable that his fierce rationality had become softer, and increasingly tempered by cunning. On the other hand, his position as a moralist was still contradicted by his personal immorality, at least in its sexual dimension. In these Berlin years he found time for new liaisons, most notably with Kathe Reichel and Isot Kilian. Nevertheless, he was no longer the bohemian outsider with a penchant for scandal of earlier years. Teo Otto recalled: 'For all his genius Brecht was endearingly simple; his talk was not aimed at the book of quotations, nor did he ever, in speech or gesture, flirt with posterity. He liked beer, sausages and straightforward conversation, was witty, humorous and a dead shot with words.' Erwin Strittmatter, who only knew him after the war, said simply: 'Since Brecht died I have never again laughed tears.'

In May 1956 Brecht was taken to hospital after a heart attack. That summer he was 'shrunken in body, swollen somewhat in the face, flaccid. And without that familiar and distinctive voice.' In August he returned to rehearsals, and wrote a particularly apposite note of encouragement to the company before they left for London. Any recovery, however, was an illusion. He died of a coronary thrombosis on 14 August 1956.

THE KEY QUESTIONS

German art and culture in the early decades of the twentieth century were dominated by Richard Wagner's idea of the *Gesamkunstwerk*, the total work of art which fused music, poetry, light, scenery, dance, and more into a single overwhelming whole. Beside this were more apparently progressive theatrical forms, like Naturalism and Expressionism, which also offered what was basically an intense experience. And over decades a theatre 'apparatus' had been created in Germany which was capable of 'theatring down' anything which challenged this intensity.

For Brecht, however, a new age had dawned: the 'scientific age', which required thinking theatregoers, not people who were swept away by an overwhelming tide of experienced feeling. For the scientific age was characterised by fluctuating money markets and wheat distribution, the development of petroleum complexes, and so on, which humanity had to master. Artistically, this provided subject matter not easily comprehended by a form developed to enhance a mythical mystique. 'Petroleum resists the five act form', Brecht proclaimed. Moreover, as a Marxist, he was fond of repeating Marx's observation: 'Philosophers have only interpreted the world in various ways; the point, however, is to change it.' Could the theatre help to 'change the world', in Marx's sense? How? How could theatre intervene in the daily affairs of humankind, unveil the commodifi-cations inherent in bourgeois society, show how it is man-made and not eternal? Could theatre not simply interpret the world, but actually help people to change it?

This question, daunting enough in itself, was further complicated, however, by Brecht's insistence that theatre, even as it addressed this task, was to remain 'entertaining', though his concept of 'fun' was something other than Wagnerian self-forgetfulness. In 1939, in a lecture to Scandi-navian students, he demanded:

> *How can the theatre be both instructive and entertaining? How can it be divorced from spiritual dope traffic and turned from a home of illusions to a home of experiences? How can the unfree, ignorant man of our century, with his thirst for freedom and his hunger for knowledge; how can the tortured and heroic, abused and ingenious, changeable and world-changing man of this great and ghastly century obtain his own theatre which will help him to master the world and himself?*

If he could find the answer to this, he would truly create a theatre for 'the children of the scientific age'.

BRECHT'S ANSWERS

Brecht's answers to his key question changed over time, but there is a relentless persistence in his search for what he called 'epic theatre' for most of his working life.

Early in his career, he asserted that 'to expound the principles of the epic theatre in a few catch-phrases is not possible', but even then it was clear to him that it would *report events*, and therefore be dispassionate. In addition, unlike comedy or tragedy, epic would deal with the totality of human relations. But Brecht was careful to place these relations in specific, changing, historical situations upon which they depended. Thus:

By studying people and their interrelations in particular situations, epic would enable opinions to be formed, and criticisms, or judgements, to be made. Thus epic theatre aimed to be influential; it would help to change the world.

This led to an epic form of drama which, in terms of construction, does not lead to an inexorable climax, or revelation, but rather proceeds step by step. If it were a horse race, our eyes would be on the course, not on the finish. It is a montage, in which each scene has a self-contained life, and, like the segments of a worm, each is capable of life even when cut off from its neighbour. It implies, not an ending, but a continuing, for human relations do not just 'end', and opinions and judgements are formed and revised. Thus *The Good Person of Szechuan* concludes with 'A Player' addressing the audience:

What is your answer? Nothing's been arranged.

Should men be better? Should the world be changed?

To help the spectator to a position from which to consider this question, it was necessary for the play to concentrate on *how* things happen. Lion Feuchtwanger wrote in 1928 that Brecht wanted the spectator to 'observe the mechanism of an event like the mechanism of a car'. Then he would be in a position to weigh the evidence and judge it. In 1931 Tretyakov reported Brecht's proposal for a 'panopticum theatre' which would present 'the most interesting trials in human history', such as the trial of Socrates, a witchcraft trial, and so on, and it is no coincidence that so many of Brecht's plays include trials. Towards the end of his life, Brecht wanted to rename epic theatre 'dialectical' theatre because it presented a situation dialectically for discussion and judgement. It also presented it as something which *had happened*. Brecht wanted his theatre to 'historicize' the events portrayed: '*Historicizing* involves judging a particular social system from another social system's point of view': 'Anyone who has observed with astonishment the eating habits, the judicial processes, the love life of savage peoples will also be able to observe our own eating customs, judicial processes and love life with astonishment.' Understanding one system through watching another, or the present through seeing the past, also of course suggests possible futures.

The heart of Brecht's method was the 'alienation' or V-effect. The word 'alienation' in English carries connotations of turning someone away from something, or inhibiting them. Brecht's German original, *Verfremdung*, probably derives from his stay in Moscow at the flat of Sergei Tretyakov, when he came into contact with a number of 'Formalists', most notably Viktor Shklovsky, who believed the purpose of art was to make us see the world afresh. At its most basic, this meant showing, say, the 'stoniness' of a stone. It was a process of seeing anew–what the Russians called *ostrannenie*, 'estranging'—but Brecht added to it something to do with the function of the stone. He asked, was it merely a nuisance, something to stub your toe on, or could it be used to throw at riot-controlling police, or to help build a barricade? This creates a process which involves something more than simply seeing afresh, and it therefore requires its own word, *Verfremdung*. Unfortunately, there is no agreement on an appropriate English equivalent: 'distanciation'? 'defamiliarisation'? It may be best to make do with 'V-effect'. Brecht made a number of attempts to define the V-effect. In *The Messingkauf Dialogues* he wrote: 'It consists in the reproduction of real-life incidents on the stage in such a way as to underline their causality and bring it to the spectator's attention.' He saw Mei Lan-fang's Chinese players and thought their technique embodied the V-effect. He even claimed it was a key to human progress: 'The man who first looked with astonishment at a swinging lantern and instead of taking it for granted found it highly remarkable that it should swing, and swing in that

particular way rather than any other, was brought close to understanding the phenomenon by this observation, and so to mastering it.' The theatre's brightly lit stage is particularly successful in making us 'look again'. Brecht emphasised that not 'looking again', because we think we know something, usually means that we are taking it for granted. 'Habit is a great deadener', as Beckett reminds us in *Waiting for Godot*. It is to combat 'habit' that the V-effect is useful.

It operates when you think of your mother as someone's lover, or your teacher in his underwear. You look at your watch many times every day; yet when did you last 'see' it? Without looking, can you tell what form its numerals take, or if the number of jewels it contains is written on its face? The crude historical pictures hung out at the Bavarian fairs created a V-effect for the stories they illustrated. In the theatre, the effect is obtained when a woman plays a man to point up gender differences; or when or if we saw Romeo forcing money owed to him out of one of his tenants so that he could the better entertain Juliet. The whole barrage of typical 'Brechtian' theatre effects were originally devised to produce the V-effect: the use of placards, the half-curtain, exposing the source of lighting, the direct address to the audience; and so on. Particularly effective is when a character stops speaking and begins to sing, interrupting himself, as it were.

A theatre which 'historicised' and subjected its content to V-effects was not for those who simply wanted their drama 'dished up' for them. That was what Brecht called 'culinary' theatre, where the audience can safely 'hang its brains up in the cloakroom along with its coat'. Initially his alternative vision was a 'smokers' theatre', perhaps like Karl Valentin's Blumensale Theatre, for 'smoking is an attitude highly conducive to observation'. The ideal spectator was one capable of 'complex seeing', who could swim with the river, but also float above it. For his 1931 production of *Man Is Man*, he said he wanted a spectator who would resemble a reader, cross-checking, referring to the equivalent of footnotes, going back and re-reading. He was delighted at one audience discussion of *Mother Courage* in 1949 when a spectator

> singled out the drum scene ... and praised the fact that it was precisely 'the most helpless person who was prepared to help, the same one as had been called a "poor creature" by her brother a few scenes earlier'. What a spectator! He must have made a note of this sentence in the third scene (with annoyance)—in the eleventh he found his answer.

This spectator has in fact been drawn into the productive process of the theatre. His critical response, his aesthetic judgement has been brought into play decisively, so that the play has, in a sense, produced him, just as he has produced the play. This was precisely the two-way, dialectical process Brecht sought.

Implicit in such a response, of course, is enjoyment. Throughout his career Brecht insisted that 'fun' is necessary in the theatre. In 1926 Elisabeth Hauptmann noted that 'if Brecht gets no fun out of what he has created, he immediately goes and changes it'. And this remained his approach. Twenty years later, he stated: 'theatre needs no other passport than fun, but this it has got to have'. Of course, for Brecht, learning was fun, dialectics was fun, and he protested 'against the suspicion that [they are] highly disagreeable, humourless, indeed strenuous affair[s].' He asserted, significantly, that 'the contrast between learning and amusing oneself is not laid down by divine rule'.

THEATRE PRACTICE

For Brecht, 'the proof of the pudding is in the eating'. He often seemed content to accept any theatrical practice which seemed to answer an immediate need of the 'theatre of the scientific age'.

For example, he was not very interested in actor training, and might employ any actor who was intellectually and artistically interested in the problems posed by his epic theatre. Nevertheless he did suggest a number of acting exercises or improvisations for the epic actor, such as adopting different by typical attitudes of smokers, or developing scenes out of simple situations, like, for example, women (or men) folding linen.

Ovservation, Brecht maintained, was the actor's key. He should observe like the scientist who watched the swinging lantern.

> *Above all other arts*
> *You, the actor, must conquer*
> *The art of observation.*
> *Your training must begin among*
> *The lives of other people. Make your*
> *first school*
> *The place you work in, your home,*
> *The district to which you belong,*
> *The shop, the street, the train.*
> *Observe each one you set eyes upon.*
> *Observe strangers as if they were*
> *familiar*
> *And those whom you know as if they*
> *were strangers.*

But merely observing was not enough

> *because the original says what*
> *it has to say with too subdued*
> *a voice. To achieve a character*
> *rather than a caricature, the actor*
> *looks at people as though they were*
> *playing him their actions, in other*
> *words as though they were advising*
> *him to give their actions careful*
> *consideration.*

Consequently, a Brechtian actor will perform many exercises in observation, watching and imitating others, describing for others to imitate, and so on. But the point will be in *presenting* the observed behaviour.

This is implicit in Brecht's most significant acting exercise, the 'Street Scene'. You witness an old man who is crossing the road knocked down by a lorry. Explain what you saw by demonstrating it. First, you show the old man trudging painfully along, puffing, leaning on his stick. You point out that he does not look to see if there is any traffic, but simply steps off the kerb. Then you show the lorry driver, and how he took his eyes off the road to light a cigarette at the critical moment. You demonstrate so that each participant's share of the responsibility will be clear.

You need not be a highly trained actor in order to do this. You can explain that, say, the old man leaned on a stick: you need not actually have a stick. Brecht points out that it may increase the clarity of the demonstration if the acting is not perfect, because it is important that the bystanders—police, other witnesses, etc.—should concentrate on *what happened,* and not be distracted into admiration of the witness's acting skills. Besides, there is no attempt here to create an illusion. This is a report. In no sense are you to 'experience' the action. Your characterisations depend on the events and relevant observable features—did he limp? was his hair too long so it prevented him seeing the approach of the lorry? And so on. You might indulge in a little make-up by, say, ruffling your hair, but only if it is relevant to explaining the event. Do you speak passionately? Not unless there is a particular point to be made by it, and even then you may preface your apparent increase in emotion by acknowledging that 'he got really cross'. Do you 'lose yourself' in the performance? Of course not. Finally, Brecht is eager to point out that this 'theatre of the street' is *useful*. Its purpose is to enable judgement to be made as to the responsibility for the accident. Many things might depend on it, such as the lorry driver's job, or insurance payments, or the building of a pedestrian crossing at this corner. This acting does not spring from the actor's 'soul'; it quotes other people.

One of Brecht's finest plays, *The Measures Taken,* has often been misinterpreted as an apology for Stalinism, or an attack on individualism. In fact, it is not an apology or an attack on anything. It is a *report* of an incident, like the street scene, which then invites us to analyse and judge it. And we must judge the judgement too. The play does not endorse a particular course of action; it opens up something which has happened to questioning. It is helpful if the spectator knows the outcome of the event in advance. Then it is easier to focus on *how* it happened, and what can be done about it. Brecht's adaptation of *Hamlet* for German radio began with Horatio explaining that the listener was *going to* hear of

> carnal, bloody and unnatural acts,
> Of accidental judgements, casual slaughters,
> Of deaths put on by cunning and forc'd cause,
> And, in the upshot, purposes mistook
> Fall'n on the inventors' heads.

Then the play proceeded. In this way, Brecht's theatre provides a contrast to the *intensity* of other systems, and especially of German Expressionism, Stanislavskian naturalism, and Wagnerian feeling.

When it came to production, Brecht often seemed unable to rehearse a play unless there were plenty of people present, any of whom might make suggestions or ask questions. Carl Weber, an assistant director at the Berliner Ensemble, described how, when he appeared at his first rehearsal, he believed the coffee break was in progress so he sat waiting, until someone said: 'Well, now we're finished, let's go home.' Brecht sat in the middle of the stalls, towards the front, and responded volubly to whatever was proceeding, guffawing with laughter, looking puzzled, shouting a suggestion, and occasionally—about twice per production, he calculated—losing his temper. Rehearsals were the means to explore the play. He sought solutions to problems which the play set, collaboratively and in a spirit of enquiry and intellectual adventure. It reminded some visitors of a children's nursery.

Brecht's attitude to his company was unequivocal. According to Weber, 'he truly loved actors, and they returned this love in kind'. They appreciated his desire, granted at the Berliner Ensemble, for very long rehearsal periods—up to, or even longer than, a year—before he felt ready to put his productions before the public. However, his rehearsal process became increasingly formalised after his death, and if the following description seems over-schematic, it is because it draws some aspects from the later Berliner Ensemble model, to focus Brecht's practice.

At the first rehearsal it was usual for Brecht to introduce the work briefly, and make some generalised statements about the play, the story line, its central oppositions and perhaps about how rehearsals were to proceed. The work began with the first 'naive' reading. In this, parts were read round the group. When the speaker changed, the next reader took over, but there was no attempt to match actors to parts. Actors read lightly, with interest, but with no attempt at characterisation or 'drama'. Stage directions, scene headings, and so on, were also read out. The scene (or whole play) was then discussed, often in the manner of the discussion reproduced in *Brecht on Theatre*. If possible it proceeded dialectically, by question and answer: 'What happens in the first scene? Brecht asks. A street is being built, leading to the town. At whose behest? At the behest of the Socialist Unity Party. Brecht says no. Silence . . . Brecht then adds, "That is revealed only in the third scene".' 'What happens?' was the key question. Discussion focused on the story. 'The exposition of the story and its communication by suitable means of alienation constitute the main business of the theatre.' Where? When? Who? What? All specific, concrete questions. Where does it happen? When does it happen? Who is involved? What happens?

Then the answers were evaluated. What is interesting about this play? Why are we proposing to present it? Discussion covered historical, political, social, and moral questions, and finally aesthetics. Whatever was agreed upon here would inform all the work on the play, and had to be accessible ultimately to the audience. These discussions led naturally to the first decisions about settings, costumes, music, and so on.

Brecht, who worked well with designers, especially his friend from school days Caspar Neher, preferred to begin rehearsing without preconceived designs, and encouraged his designer to make initial sketches during the naive readings. These would implicitly include suggestions about characters' postures and possible groupings. Designs begin 'with the people themselves' and 'what is happening to and through them', Brecht insisted. The designer 'provides no "decor", frames and backgrounds, but constructs the space for "people" to experience something in'. Weber pointed out that Brecht wanted above all *a space* to tell his story in, and Thomson uses the German word *Bild*, which means not only picture and frame, but also includes the connotation of understanding, as in the English phrase, to 'get the picture'. With this in mind Brecht's setting for, say, *Mother Courage and Her Children* was deceptively simple: the white, silky curtain at 'half height' across the stage, its draw wires constantly visible to remind us we are watching a play; the revolve built into the stage floor; the hanging military paraphernalia.

No more than these. But Jones points out that the horizontal division of the space by the curtain wires, when the action beneath seems circular, is not accidental: 'Brecht, who believed that the round and round theory was an exploitative myth, presented his fiction within a frame that was horizontally bisected, as if stage reality were dialectical and capable of objectifying and particularizing human actions.' The onstage buildings in this production had a chunky reality, but were incomplete, suggestive rather than real. In the earlier production of *Mother*:

> *the stage was not supposed to represent any real locality: it as it were took up an attitude towards the incidents shown; it quoted, narrated, prepared and recalled. Its sparse indication of furniture, doors, etc, was limited to objects that had a part in the play, i.e. those without which the action would have been altered or halted.*

This production also used projections —pictures and texts—which referred to the great events like war and strikes going on beyond the particular story being told, but affecting its events. The settings, projections, and so on were designed not 'to help the spectator, but to block him; they prevent his complete empathy, interrupt his being automatically carried away'.

TWENTY-FIRST-CENTURY PERSPECTIVES

By the end of the twentieth century, Brecht seemed 'dead' to many. He had acquired the status of 'classic' and his plays, though no doubt interesting, were no more (and no less) relevant to today's politics, societies or aesthetics than were, say, Buchner's Woyzeck or D. H. Lawrence's *The Daughter-in-Law*. He was said to have held and presented a simplified view of life. The Marxism he had espoused all his life had disintegrated in Moscow, and his avant-garde Modernism was outdated and gauche in a time of international mass culture, global consumerism, and the world wide web.

Yet already, for those with their ears to the ground, a new kind of investigation around Brecht was beginning, and in the twenty-first century perhaps a new kind of Brecht is emerging. Note has been taken of the fact that Brecht was an inveterate experimenter—he published his works under the title *Experiments*—and after the 1960s, perhaps, it began to be noticed that his output was considerably more diverse, and more challenging, than a number of 'great plays' fit for national theatres. He wrote stories, plays (of various sorts), novels, poems, songs, diaries, theory, political analyses, cultural commentary, philosophy. His mode of production was fundamentally collaborative, and most typical of his creative work was its characteristic reworking of pre-existing material.

He re-possessed older plays, and was notoriously lax about 'plagiarism', so that he affords a rich mine for diggers after intertextuality.

In addition, Brecht was never happy to consider any work of his 'finished': he wrote and re-wrote tirelessly. His extraordinary rehearsals at the Berliner Ensemble perhaps aspired to be 'endless'. His only certainty was doubt. His work on one level appears extraordinarily 'modern' in that it challenges individual conceptions of identity, and indeed asks what we mean by identity. All of which suggests that he is a remarkably suitable body for dissection by contemporary theorists.

And indeed he had seemed so to some as early as the 1950s. Roland Barthes applauded Brecht's idea of the gest, grappled with his concept of 'demystifying', and pointed out the politics of the sign. For Barthes, Brecht offered a system (a 'readerly' text) which the Structuralist could analyse, while denying the possibility of 'final' meaning (in this sense producing 'writerly' texts). Brecht's irony and his self-reflexivity were further elements Barthes enjoyed, and indeed his *Mythologies* is profoundly Brechtian in its method.

Brecht also provided a paradigm for the emerging Feminist theatre movement. Lizbeth Goodman noticed that just as Brecht's work did not fit the 'apparatus' of German theatre in the 1920s, so Feminist theatre did not fit the theatre apparatus of the western world in the last quarter of the twentieth century. Perhaps as a consequence, his collaborative method was developed most consciously, and most successfully, in woman's groups. His theory, too, helped those feminists who argued that gender is a social construction: Shen Te-Shui Ta played by a man is very different proposition to Shen Te-Shiu Ta played, as is usual, by a woman. And Brechtian historicisation also proved a useful tool for Feminist theatre practice which sought to unearth and deconstruct the oppressed position of women in history. The heart of his writing sometimes seems to parallel, and be extended by, writing by women such as Hélène Cixous, with her facility in exposing contradictions. And Sue-Ellen Case pointed out that Brecht's epic form has an inherently female dimension as compared to the subliminal maleness of tragedy. Where the structure of tragedy is comparable to—even modeled on—the male sexual experience, proceeding from foreplay to arousal to ejaculation, the structure of epic is more like the female experience of multiple consecutive orgasms.

Another challenging theatre project infused with the knowledge and spirit of Brecht was Augusto Boal's 'Theatre of the Opressed'. Taking his cue from Brecht, Boal asserted the manipulative oppression of Aristotelian theatre, from the Greeks to soap operas, and proposed not just a theatre in which the audience could *think* their way out from under this hegemony, but one in which they could *act* against it, in a 'rehearsal of revolution'. Boal's groundbreaking and positive work and ideas have become widely available through a series of thought-provoking books.

Meanwhile, in more academic circles, Brecht has begun to provide unexpected areas for examination. Thus, the old 'three-phase' Brecht, conjured out of a biographical reading (early anarchic works, middle-period austere Marxist *Lehrstucke,* and 'mature' great plays, all knitted up theoretically in *A Short Organum for the Theatre)* was challenged by Elizabeth Wright, who saw his fragments, revisions, and notes as often more revealing than the *Short Organum* and centred a critique in the often disregarded *Lehrstucke.* She showed how the early plays operated deliberately to disrupt and decentre, and this enabled her to deconstruct the conventional boundary between comedy and tragedy. Wright believed that, for various reasons, Brecht's more radical ideas had not fertilised his later work, and that only in the later, less 'tidy' productions of Heiner Muller and Pina Bausch had these ideas begun to bear the appropriate fruit.

Steve Giles deconstructed the *Threepenny* 'Lawsuit' and its ramifications to reveal the genesis and perhaps the significance of Brecht's Marxism, which he also related provocatively to problems associated with the mass media and to post-modern and post-structuralist theory. Fredric Jameson highlighted Brecht's 'showing of showing'. He suggested that the shape of Brechtian thought derived specifically from the acting out of stories, with a V-effect which inevitably leads to 'choosing'. Indeed, the *Lehrstucke* he characterised specifically as 'machines for choosing'. Jameson's Brecht has

something in common with the traditional Buddha, who said:

> *My teaching is a method to experience reality and not reality itself, just as a finger pointing at the moon is not the moon itself. An intelligent person makes use of the finger to see the moon. A person who only looks at the finger and mistakes it for the moon will never see the real moon.*

Sarah Bryant-Bertail attempted a contemporary assessment of 'the Brechtian legacy' which widened the scope of enquiry to include Piscator's 1920s work and also some post-Brechtian stagings by Stein, Mnouchkine, and others. Her work complemented Steve Giles's in its deconstructing of the mass media, especially representations of war and capitalism, and suggested that theatre is perhaps uniquely placed to act as a forum for the critiquing of contemporary crises.

Inevitably, these comments provide only the tiniest peephole into some contemporary philosophical and critical approaches to Brecht. But it is instructive that at last his whole oeuvre is being interrogated, and through it new and fruitful ways of thinking about identity, culture, politics, and society are being found.

FURTHER READING

Brecht's works are published in Berlin and Frankfurt, in Germany, in a series so far stretching to thirty volumes: *Bertolt Brecht Grosse kommentierte*

Berliner und Frankfurter Ausgabe, Berlin and Frankfurt: Aufbau and Suhrkamp.

Methuen has published almost all Brecht's plays in English translation, in a series of eight volumes of the Collected Plays. A ninth volume, containing adaptations, was published in the United States, in 1973, but has not yet appeared in Britain. In addition, various single volumes and other translations of the plays have been published.

Methuen are also responsible for the ongoing publication of Brecht's 'Plays, Poetry and Prose', of which the Collected Plays are a part. This series, originally edited by John Willett and Ralph Manheim, and now by Tom Kuhn, includes four volumes of poetry, one volume of short stories, *Diaries 1920–1922, Journals 1934–1955*, and *Letters 1913–1956*. Brecht's *The Threepenny Novel* was published in England by Penguin in 1961, though the translation first appeared in the United States as *A Penny for the Poor* in 1937.

Methuen have also published significant selections from Brecht's theoretical writings, most notably in:

Kuhn, Tom, and Giles, Steve, Brecht on Art and Politics (first published 2003). Silberman, Marc, *Brecht on Film and Radio* (first published 2000).

Willet, John, *Brecht on Theatre, the Development of an Aesthetic* (first published 1964; reprinted many times).

Methuen also published *The Messingkauf Dialogues* originally in 1965, and it has been reprinted several times since.

Critical analysis and discussion about Brecht is carried on in the annual publication of the International Brecht Society, *The Brecht Yearbook*.

Critical books about Brecht are too many to enumerate, even if one were to confine oneself to books written in English only. Notoriously, there has been something of a 'Brecht industry' in the half century since Brecht himself died. What follows is one reader's selection of the most interesting of these works form the last fifteen years or so:

Brooker, Peter, *Bertold Brecht: Dialectics, Poetry, Politics*, London: Croom Helm, 1988.

Bryant-Bertail, Sarah, *Space and Time in Epic Theatre*, Woodbridge: Camden House, 2000.

Giles, Steve, *Bertolt Brecht and Critical Theory: Marxism, Modernity and the 'Threepenny Lawsuit'*, Bern: Peter Lang, 1998.

Giles, Steven, and Livingstone, Rodney (eds), *Bertolt Brecht: Centenary Essays*, Amsterdam: Rodopi, 1998,

Jameson, Fredric, *Brecht and Method*, London: Verso, 1998

Kleber, Pia, and Visser, Colin, *Reinterpreting Brecht: His Influence on Contemporary Drama and Film*, Cambridge: Cambridge University Press, 1990.

Martin, Carol, and Bial, Henry (eds), *Brecht Sourcebook*, London: Routledge, 2000.

Suvin, Darko, *To Brecht and Beyond: Soundings in Modern Dramaturgy*, Brighton: Harvester, 1984.

Thomson, Peter, and Sacks, Glendyr (eds), *The Cambridge Companion to Brecht*, Cambridge: Cambridge University Press, 1944.

Wright, Elizabeth, *Postmodern Brecht: A Re-presentation*, London: Routledge, 1989.

Expressionism

Expressionism, which began in Europe at the start of the twentieth century, is a style of art and theatre that is greatly influenced by the creators' individual emotions. In the art of Expressionism, strong feelings are projected onto objects, and those objects are then portrayed as modified and distorted by the artist's vision. In this way, Expressionism is a very subjective, intuitive, and personal expression of reality. The goal of Expressionist theatre is not to express or mirror reality. Instead, it aims to present the world from a solely subjective perspective in order to express a message or an emotional experience.

Most Expressionists sought to focus attention on truth by looking at humanity's internal spiritual qualities rather than on the trappings of the externals of life. They rejected Naturalism and Realism because those styles focused attention on the external facets of human existence and suggested that the observable aspects of life represented fundamental truth. The Expressionists argued that reality is alterable and should be changed until it is brought into harmony with humankind's spiritual nature, which they considered to be the only real truth. Since the Expressionists' "truth" could be found only in the spiritual (subjective) realm, it could only be expressed subjectively. Therefore, Expressionist theatre radically distorts reality in order to elicit an emotional effect, evoking moods and ideas in the audience.

Watching an Expressionist play is, at times, like watching a dream or nightmare. The world of the play will likely be radically distorted visually and aurally in order to evoke certain moods or ideas. The Expressionist production will stress the emotional content of the play and the symbolic or abstract depiction of reality. Expressionist plays often dramatize the sufferings and spiritual awakenings of their main characters and the struggle against bourgeois values and authority figures. Dramatic characters in Expressionist theatre tend to be allegorical characters who have lost their individuality and are identified by unspecified labels such as The Man, The Father, etc. These characters are stereotypes who have no psychological depth or individual personality. They merely represent categories of people found in society, not specific, fleshed-out human beings. Like the characters in dreams, they can often seem outrageous, monstrous, and unreal. Expressionist theatre also makes use of crowds who are dispassionate groups, moving rhythmically en masse, often like machines.

The dramatic structure of an Expressionist play is primarily episodic and finds unity from a central idea or argument. The action may represent stages in the hero's life, or it may be a series of visions as seen from his unconscious mind. Because the action tends to be broken into episodes, tableaux, and experiences that each have a meaning of their own, a sense of fragmentation and disconnection is created.

In Expressionist theatre, language is not lifelike or natural. Instead, the playwright often writes with a focus on the rhythm and musicality of the sounds that make up words. It may be unrestrained, enthusiastic, smooth sounding and lyrical, or clipped, short, sharp, and concise. The meaning of the words takes a backseat to the feeling evoked by the sounds and the rhythm of words and the feelings they evoke in the audience. There is also extensive use of pause and silence—sometimes for long periods of time—in counterpoint to speech and sound. This contributes to the dreamlike effect of the production.

The style of acting in an Expressionist play is antithetical to the naturalistic acting found in Realism. In an attempt to avoid the psychological detail of character and intention found in Realism, an actor in an Expressionist play may seem to be overacting, or acting in an exaggerated way. The performance may appear contrived and forced when compared to the representational acting that has come to be known as "good" acting, such as that seen on TV and in film. The viewer must remember that the acting in an Expressionist play is not bad; it is a different style than what he has become accustomed to through the expectations of popular cultural. The actor in an Expressionist play may use broad, mechanical movements, almost like those of a puppet. The actor's movements can be intense, extreme, forceful, even violent. Actors will express powerful emotion and break out into sudden fits of passion, sometimes attacking each other physically. The text may be spoken rapidly, breathlessly, with a staccato rhythm, or languidly. The primary focus is more often on the musicality of the words and the feelings evoked by sound rather than the meaning. And the actor's physical energy and movement will often support and be in concert with the verbal histrionics.

Like the language, design elements in an Expressionist play are non-naturalistic. Distorted line, exaggerated shape, and abnormal coloring are used to lead audiences beyond surface appearance. At times, all aspects of the production are seen through the eyes of the protagonist, whose view of the world might change emphasis and apply a unique interpretation. Designers work together to create a world that is moody, mercurial, nightmarish, or dreamlike. Design elements are selected primarily for their emotional and symbolic qualities. The set will not duplicate the detail of Realistic drama but will utilize simple and precise images that connote the theme of the play. The location of the action is abstract and general. The scenery and costuming are often angular, distorted, and seemingly nonsensical, like a bad dream. Props, if they exist at all, are few and symbolic. The stage lighting is moody and often shadowy and unrealistic, creating visual distortions on the set. All design elements help to create a symbolic and abstract representation of reality that stresses the emotional content of the play, working to focus attention on the inner qualities of humankind—deemed so important by the Expressionists and yet ignored by the technological advances of an increasingly industrialized society.

Surrealism

Surrealism, like Expressionism, began in Europe at the start of the twentieth century, and is a style of art and theatre that is greatly influenced by the creators' individual emotions. It is also a very subjective, intuitive, and personal expression of reality. Surrealism is greatly influenced by Freud's work on the influence of the subconscious mind on human behavior. The Surrealists believe in the great, positive healing power of the subconscious mind. Surrealists argue that the subconscious mind is the source of artistic truth. As proponents of automatic writing, Surrealists promoted drama that embraced spontaneity, originality, and disjointed dreamlike episodes. Their drama abandoned order, clarity, and rational thought in an attempt to entice the revelation of a new kind of truth. The Surrealists rejected Realism in theatre as an imitation of surface reality and, instead, strove to replace it with a theatre of visions that expressed a reality that was more real than what was visible to the naked eye—performance that dealt with inner truth rather than surface appearance.

Anton Artaud was an early Surrealist who believed that theatre should be a mystical and metaphysical experience. He believed that the use of language and rational discourse did not reveal any truth about humankind but, rather, created "falsehoods and illusion" that led humanity farther and farther away from the truth. Artaud created the *Theatre of Cruelty*, a new form of theatre in which emotions, feelings, the abstract, and spiritual aspects of what it is to be human were expressed through movement, not language. Using the body to create a mythological, archetypal, and allegorical vision that was closely related to the world of dreams, performers and the audience were linked in a sort of ritual event in a direct and immediate way through the connection of their unconscious minds through performance.

Surrealist writers and artists explore human dreams and desires in a way that turns logic upside down. They often incorporate dreamlike sequences, and those who use language might integrate innovative comic word play into their performance. There is often no sense of order or rationality to the dramatic structure of the play. Some audiences are shocked by the seemingly uncivilized behavior that they see on stage in a Surrealist play because the actions of the subconscious mind can be seen as very uncivilized and raw. Poet Andre Breton claimed that the foundation of Surrealism is "thought expressed in the absence of any control exerted by reason and outside all moral and aesthetic considerations.

The subconscious experience of Surrealism, when presented on stage, is melancholy in tone and can seem very disjointed in structure. It uses a combination of subject matters. Sometimes there is a discernible unifying idea, but sometimes not. The Surrealists claim to be rediscovering theatre's roots—the mystical and religious ritualistic experience of theatre. This style of theatre is immediate and direct in its connection between performer and spectator. The Surrealists make use of surprise, abstraction, horror, attraction, and the unexpected to move toward a deeper understanding of the subconscious and unlocking the truth that lies there. This truth of the subconscious is more real than anything that can be understood in the external world, according to the Surrealists. It is a truth that, through performance, connects people with something more primal, honest, and true within themselves. They believed that participation in a performance of this type would enable participants to overcome societal traditions and strictures that oppressed the freedom of the individual. One key goal of this type of theatre is to liberate humankind to explore the far reaches of its imagination, dreams, and desires in a completely free and uninhibited way.

CHAPTER TWENTY-SIX

Commedia dell'Arte

WHAT IS COMMEDIA DELL'ARTE?

Commedia dell'Arte is a type of comedy developed in sixteenth- and seventeenth-century Italy. During this period in European theater, plays were classic, stylish, and followed extremely strict rules that were drawn from Aristotle's *Poetics,* known as *the unities.* Whereas Aristotle had observed and commented on his theories concerning what made a good play, this new adherence to the unities was much more authoritative and limiting. Acting troupes and their playwrights in Italy during the sixteenth and seventeenth centuries were also supported by the patronage of the ruling classes, which dictated, to some extent, the characters, themes, and message of plays.

During this period, European secular theatre was also just emerging from a semi-banishment. From the time of the fall of Rome through the Middle Ages, the Catholic Church controlled European society and, therefore, theatre. Church officials banned performances of works written by artists of the pagan societies of the ancient Greeks and Romans. Performances were limited to religious material (primarily stories taken from the Bible), which were performed either in church courtyards or, eventually, as part of the rituals of the mass celebrated within the church buildings.

In part as a reaction to these limitations, Commedia dell'Arte—which in many ways is the exact opposite to this limited- and rule-based theatre—developed. Commedia dell'Arte is filled with characters who are loud, colorful representations of common people. Its performance energy, dynamic characters, fantastical masks and costumes, and bold, improvisational style are in direct contrast to the ordered theatre supported by and performed for the ruling classes in Europe in the seventeenth century. In a Commedia performance, the "rules" of theatre that were strictly adhered to at the time are subverted. Commedia players work from a basic plot—the scenario—within which there are some set speeches and usually some set physical business. The scenario summarizes the situations, complications, and outcome. Actors improvise the dialogue and flesh-out the action. Broad outlines of story remain the same, but details differ at every performance based on audience reaction and the actors' inspiration at the moment.

Many scenarios have survived since the Renaissance. Some are musicals, tragedies, melodramas, but most are comedies, revolving around love affairs, intrigue, disguises, mistaken identity, and cross-purposes. The set business, called *lazzi*, is movement that is very active and broadly physical. It is most often comic characters performing stock bits of clownish business that is sometimes even farcical in nature. With the exception of these set pieces, actors improvise much of the dialogue and action. Plots revolve around everyday domestic conflicts. Plot development is often interrupted for long periods by the *lazzi*.

Commedia dell'Arte actors are complete professionals. Performers train in and then play the same character for years—sometimes a lifetime. Actors become masters at their characters, which promotes ease in improvisation—itself a distinguishing feature of Commedia. Actors develop stage business and dialogue on which they can call as needed. Some comic physical stage business—*lazzi*—are standardized and indicated in the plot outline (*lazzi* of fear, fight *lazzi*, etc.) The actors do not make everything up as they go along; improvisation occurs within a rehearsed framework. In order for the improvisation to be successful, the actors need to keep in mind where the scene is headed and what needs to happen for the plot as a whole to work. They must know the outline of the action and when they insert *lazzi*; they cannot let the piece of comic business go so far as to obscure the plot line. Performances create the impression of spontaneity because the actors are so well-trained and so well-rehearsed.

Unlike in other theatrical styles and traditions, women have always performed in Commedia. When Commedia was created, and for many years after, women did not perform on stage in other theatrical styles. So the novelty of having real women acting added to the appeal.

Each actor in the troupe plays the same stock character in almost every scenario. The actor uses the same costume and mask, reuses the same *lazzi*, and even repeats some of the same dialogue from scenario to scenario.

Unlike other forms of theatre in Renaissance Italy, Commedia was open to the masses. Performances first appeared on simple stages set outdoors. The actor is the heart of Commedia and practically the only necessary element. Commedia companies can play almost anywhere: town centers, courts, indoors, outdoors, improvised stages, or permanent theatres. Scenery is not necessary; the only requirement is a curtain with openings for entrances and exits. Adaptability is one of its major assets. The powerful mix of various theatrical elements—popular themes, complex stories with lots of climax, acrobatic jumps, and mellow love scenes—made it a success. Commedia troupes average ten to 12 players.

Commedia was at its most vigorous and most popular between 1575–1650 but continued to thrive until the last half of the eighteenth century. In all periods of Western culture since the Renaissance, Commedia dell'Arte has been a conscious or subconscious presence. Using sexually-challenging language and physical comedy, Commedia pokes fun at elements of society's respectable values by means of exaggerated styles and insightful character traits. This style of theatre has had a tremendous impact on and is the foundation for the works of Moliere, Punch and Judy puppet theatre, street theatre, improvisational theatre, and all slapstick comedy. Its costumes, masks, and physical comedy have a strong universal appeal. Commedia dell'Arte is still performed by troupes throughout the world today.

Characters

The stock characters of Commedia dell'Arte can be divided into three main categories: the lovers, masters, and servants.

THE LOVERS (INNAMORATI)

The lovers are the most realistic characters. They are young and attractive, do not wear masks, and are dressed in beautiful Renaissance costumes. The lovers are usually the children of the masters. Their love affairs are usually opposed by their fathers and aided by the servants. The lovers bring into the Commedia dell'Arte the romance and domestic conflict around which the action may easily be developed. The Innamorati, whose thwarted passionate love creates the conflict upon which the plot revolves, help the audience to identify with the stories.

THE MASTERS

The masters referred to most often are Pantalone (Il Magnifico), Dottore and Il Capitano.

Il Magnifico/Pantalone

Il Magnifico, best known as Pantalone, is an elderly merchant who is either father to one of the young lovers or a would-be lover himself. He is a Venetian merchant or nobleman who is rich, greedy, miserly, lustful, naive, and paranoid. He believes that people are trying to take his gold from him. Money is his obsession. He finds elaborate ways to hoard it, count it, hide it, manipulate deals with it, and avoid spending it. He is lascivious and thinks he is a master at seducing beautiful young women. He complains about his physical ailments (e.g., aching back, bad knees, gout) that conveniently come and go at his discretion.

Il Dottore (The Doctor)

Il Dottore, usually Pantalone's friend or rival, is a pompous lawyer or academic doctor who likes to show off his bogus knowledge in speeches filled with Latin that is often inaccurate. He is gullible and easily tricked. He is arrogant, ignorant, rather fat, always dresses in black, is well-groomed, rich looking, and talks and talks. Il Dottore professes to know everything but actually knows nothing. He loves to hear himself speak and expounds on answers whether asked or not (but he is always wrong). He is a delightfully pretentious bag of wind. He often creates a break in the action, with empty, prefabricated, and supposedly erudite monologues.

Il Capitano (The Captain)

Originally, *Il Capitano* was one of the lovers, but eventually he was transformed into a cowardly braggart of a soldier who boasts of his accomplishments in love and war, eventually to be debunked in both. He is often an unwanted suitor to one of the young female lovers. He is the foreigner in the scenario, speaking with an accent (or two), who enters to conquer arrogant foes, to rescue young damsels in distress, or to win the hearts of beautiful widows. He is, however, a wimp. He avoids fighting at all costs by deflecting conflicts, feigning death, or outsmarting aggressors. He vainly claims superior physical prowess on the battlefield and in bedchambers all over the world but fails at everything. In his mind, anyone is a fool who cannot recognize his beauty, strength, sensitivity, and foresight. In fact, he is usually penniless and easily intimidated. With his long, pointy moustache, huge sword (never used), and several daggers in his belt, the Captain talks more than he actually fights. In his own mind, he's very brave, but he usually gets scared and flies off stage when Harlequin (see below in "The Servants") enters with his *batocio* (a short wooden club).

THE SERVANTS

The most varied of the Commedia dell'Arte types are the servants. Most troupes include at least two servants, one clever and one witless. The servants figure very prominently in the action; their maneuvering keeps the plot moving as they work to assist or thwart their masters.

Arlecchino (Harlequin, Arlechino, Arlequin)

Arlecchino, best known as Harlequin, is probably the most famous Commedia character. At first a minor character, Arlecchino eventually became the most popular *Zanni* (see below). This character is a mixture of cunning and stupidity and is played by a performer who is a master acrobat and dancer. He is usually at the center of any intrigue in the play. He is eager to please his master or mistress, lives in the present, loves the world that he sees right in front of him, and forgets what is out of sight. His first attention is to food: how to get it, how to savor it, how to preserve it for later. He loves tricks and physical antics (lazzi). He relishes his cleverness at getting out of difficult situations and seldom considers the consequences of his actions until it is too late. Always witty, but never malicious, Arlecchino is sympathetic to everyone's misfortunes. He is ignorant and usually cannot read, which makes him confuse messages sent by the lovers.

Figure 26.1 Alexander Moissi as "Arlecchino." (M. Schwarzkopf / Copyright in the Public Domain.)

But he is quick physically. His actions and moods can change in an instant. He is a poor character who wears a colorful patched costume. (see Figure 26.1.) His costume began as a suit with irregularly placed multicolored patches and evolved into one with a diamond-shaped red, green, and blue pattern.

Zanni (Zany Cornetto)

Zanni, is poor—part of that emigrant population that has to mingle into an hostile environment to survive. This character is desperate and ignorant, but smart in his own way. Everybody makes fun of him, but he often turns the tables on those who do. He's constantly hungry and constantly exploited. The *primo* (first) Zanni is smart while the second Zanni is hopelessly stupid. Zanni is friend/antagonist to Harlequin. They share the basic characteristics of a lack of food and nobility.

Pulcinella (Polichinelle)

Pulcinella is philosophical, eternally melancholic, a poet, and a dreamer. He coasts through problematic situations, lives adventurously, and, in the end, simply avoids any type of difficulty. His winning strategy is a simple philosophy and a positive approach to life. His costume is white and plain. He wears the *coppolone* (sugar loaf hat.) His mask has an enormous hooked nose. He often has a hunched back. Pulcinella is the precursor of the English puppet, Punch.

Brighella

Brighella has the highest status of any of the servants. He is irritable, violent, bad tempered, crafty, quick, unscrupulous, and a womanizer. He is always ready for intrigue, loves to fight, and will actively seek out the next battle. He is often paired with Arlecchino. He thrives on double-dealings, intrigues, and foul play. Sometimes depicted as an innkeeper, shop owner, valet, or soldier, he cunningly separates patrons from their cash and possessions. He is a cynical liar who only looks out for himself, and he is never repentant when caught in wrongdoing. He is sleazy, seductive, and dangerous. He executes his crimes ingeniously, offering assistance to innocents in an effort to win them over and then steal from these unsuspecting victims. Money for him is worth only the pleasure it provides, and he loves nothing but his own pleasure. He is a drunkard and boisterous debaucherer who readily insults anyone weaker.

La Servetta (The Soubrette)

The *Soubrette* is one of those characters who appears in the Commedia dell'Arte in almost all the plays, keeping a low profile at first and gaining more personality with time. She is simple at heart, witty, vain, a chatterer, and a little clumsy. She serves as a *spalla* (counterpoint) to Harlequin or Pantaloon. She does not wear a mask, and her costume is always plain. She is simple, available, easy, loves life, loves intrigue, and enjoys playing games behind other character's backs.

Colombina

Colombina is the Soubrette of the Commedia dell'Arte who gets more personality and a name of her own. She is everything the Innamorata is not: free, insolent, sometimes brilliant, always vain, a chatterer, a gossip, and a lover of intrigue at somebody else's expense. She can be seen as a sort of Harlequin in female clothes. In fact, she appears in some scenarios as Harlequina (Arlecchinetta), with a patched costume duplicate of Harlequin's. She is usually Harlequin's companion and the only woman to sometimes wear a mask on stage. Colombina is, very often, the cause of conflicts between Pantaloon and Harlequin.

SLAPSTICK COMEDY

The term *slapstick comedy* comes from the use of slapsticks by the Zanni—the *batocio* that translates as the bell's clapper or slapstick. What looks like a stick or baton carried by Arlecchino is actually a piece of wood that has been sliced down the middle and hinged at one end. The center piece of wood is hollowed out. Leather is wrapped around the other piece. The *batocio* in Harlequin's hands becomes a stage prop, something that may be used in different ways: mixing something in a pot, as a knife or a spoon in those rare times he is actually eating, as a sword, club, dagger, or bat for fighting with other characters. When hitting someone or something, this specially-designed stick made a slapping sound. This was used in many *lazzi* moments of physical comedy and became associated with physical antics. This device would lend its name to a whole genre of physical farce, "slapstick comedy," which is famous for feigned bodily beatings and physical pranks that are performed to elicit laughter from the audience (as previously discussed in Chapter 25).

PLAYING COMMEDIA

The inspirational actor is content to rely exclusively on his own mood. He refuses to bend his will to the discipline of technique. The inspirational actor proudly claims to have rekindled the flame of improvisation in the theatre. In his naïveté he imagines that his improvisations have something in common with the improvisations of traditional Italian comedy. He does not realise the improvisations of commedia dell'arte have a firm basis of faultless technique. The inspirational actor totally rejects technique of any kind. 'Technique hinders creative freedom' is what he always says.

—MEYERHOLD

STAGING

I write 'playing' rather than 'acting' advisedly. If *commedia dell'arte* were a game it would be an outdoor one. As soon as a few basic skills in acting a Mask have been acquired, I suggest you send it out into the fresh air to play with its friends. The primal energies of Commedia can successfully be released into the nocturnal, darkened rooms we call theatres, but only after their potential has been fully developed in the full light of day. In the end, or rather the beginning, the only way to learn to play Commedia is to go outside, put on a mask, stand on a box and give it a try. Many of an actor's normal preoccupations will immediately be found to be irrelevant. The need to develop further technique becomes real rather than academic. Even if you are only playing in a park to two drunks, a barking dog and a small child who has lost its parents you will learn more about the necessary scale and clarity, immediacy and impetus of Commedia from fifteen minutes of 'having a go' than from fifteen days of self-doubt in a rehearsal room. Further training and practice are then obviously

John Rudlin, from "Playing Commedia," *Commedia Dell'Arte: An Actor's Handbook*, pp. 48–49, 51–62. Copyright © 1994 by Taylor & Francis Group. Reprinted with permission.

essential, but one learns not to undertake the kind of over-specific rehearsal which is inhibiting to spontaneity and liable to create a false text which will let you down in performance.

To play outdoors you will need, apart from masks, costumes and props, at least a mountebank-style platform and a curtain from behind which to enter.

Already there are decisions to be made: how wide, how deep and how high? For the inexperienced it is far better for the acting area to be too small than too large: in a limited space the Masks have to relate to each other visually and make meaningful compositions, and they will also be able to sustain *tempi* more readily. Width is more useful than depth: it takes a lot of experience to work a mask (with its narrow field of vision) for the audience, at the same time as relating to someone playing some distance behind you. It is also easier to create an illusion of space on a crowded stage than to create a crowd from a handful of characters in the middle of indeterminate space.

THE SCENARIO

After a platform and a back curtain you need a scenario, literally 'that which is on the scenery', i.e. pinned up backstage. All it consists of is a plot summary, the bare bones of who does what when. The most readily available scenarios in English are Flaminio Scala's *Il teatro delle favole rappresentative*, but they have been dressed up as

literary creations and are too baroque for contemporary performers to attempt whole. Start with something plainer. For example, here is the first act of a scenario by Basilio Locatelli, *A Play within a Play:*

Pantalone and Arlecchino. Pantalone says that he intends to give his daughter Sylvia in marriage; Pulcinella has asked for her hand and he wants her to accept.

Pulcinella, from the house. He overhears that Pantalone is disposed to give him Sylvia for a wife. *Lazzi.* They come to an agreement on the dowry. Pulcinella calls

Sylvia, from the house. She realises that she will be given in marriage to Pulcinella. She refuses. *Lazzi.* Finally, by dint of threats, Sylvia gives way and touches Pulcinella's hand. Sylvia, rebellious, re-enters the house. Pulcinella says he will go to the office for the marriage contract and will await Pantalone there; he leaves. Pantalone tells Arlecchino to go and warn the comedians and tell the relatives that a comedy will be played and everyone will make merry. Arlecchino goes on his way; so does Pantalone.

Flavio, from the street. He says that, in order to see Sylvia whom he loves, he has left Padua University, where he was sent by his father. Knocking.

Sylvia, from the house. She recognises Flavio, who is incognito, having changed his name since leaving Padua. He is wearing a false beard. Sylvia is in despair because Pantalone, her father, wishes to give her in marriage to Pulcinella. Flavio sorrowfully tells her to be of good heart and he will try to upset all the arrangements. He leaves. Sylvia goes back into the house.

Pantalone, entering from the street, says that the marriage contract has been drawn up and that Pulcinella wants the wedding to be very soon. Enter

Arlecchino and *Il Capitano,* from the street. Arlecchino tells Pantalone that he has informed all the relatives and that he has brought with him the leader of the comedians, Il Capitano. Pantalone asks him what part he plays. Il Capitano says that he plays the part of the Lover. Pantalone laughs at this, saying: 'Look at this ugly mug who plays the Lover!' In the end they agree to play a comedy for 10 scudi; Pantalone gives him a deposit on the price. Il Capitano says he will call his companions, and leaves. Pantalone has all the preparations made and the seats arranged in the open. He says he is looking forward to it. All enter the house.

Pulcinella, from the street. He is filled with joy about the wedding and the festivities. He says he would like his daughter Franceschina to enjoy the wedding. He knocks.

Franceschina, from the house. She has heard that her father, Pulcinella, wants to take a wife without first finding her a husband and wants

her to attend the wedding and the comedy.

Pantalone, Sylvia, and *Arlecchino,* from the house. Pantalone embraces his future son-in-law, Pulcinella, and they make merry. Sylvia, against her will, receives them. Then they sit down, having understood from Arlecchino that the comedians are now ready.

Il Dottore then enters from the street, having come to listen to the comedy. They welcome him and he sits down. After which

Flavio enters from the street and sits himself near the others to hear the comedy. Orders are given for the comedy to begin. Enter

The Prologue, spoken by *Pedrolino.* After some music has been played, he calls for silence, because a comedy will be played *all'improvviso.* Enter

Oratio. He speaks of his love for Isabella, daughter of Il Capitano. He says that he wants to ask her father for her hand in marriage. He knocks.

Il Capitano, from the house, having overheard everything Oratio has said, comes to an agreement with him about the marriage. At this, Sylvia drops a glove.

Flavio immediately runs to pick it up. He kisses it and hands it back to Sylvia. Pulcinella rises, telling Flavio that he will have to settle accounts with him. There is much noise and confusion; everyone runs away, some by the street, others into the houses.

Although not numbered, the scenes are 'French', that is to say separated by changes of personnel onstage. The lay-out is such that an actor can easily see what action he or she is involved in. But there can be quite a panicky queue round the scenario, so I recommend writing down your personal through line for your Mask separately and keeping it handy somewhere else. Domenico Biancolelli (known as Dominique), the Arlequin of the Italian troupe in Paris between 1662 and 1680, seems to have done just that. Here are a couple of examples of his performance notes:

In this scene I call Diamantine and beg her pardon, I say that someone wants to kill me, that she must hide me and that I will tell her all, she says she will shut me in the flour bin, I agree and tell her that I don't want to get in there because if the old cook finds me covered in flour she will take me for a sole and try to fry me.

And:

I arrive on stage. I find Trivelin there on the ground, and thinking him dead I try to pull him to his feet, dropping my wooden sword, which he seizes and uses on my buttocks. I turn without a word, and he gives me a kick in the back and I fall over, get up, pick him up, carry him, and prop him against the right cantonade. I turn away to the footlights, during which time he gets up and sets himself against the left cantonade. This lazzo *is repeated two or three times.*

He includes his own action for each play in the troupe's repertoire, as well as that of other characters onstage at the same time. Sometimes he includes dialogue indications, occasionally whole sections of duologue. There are often insertions at the end of an entry, probably successful additions from later performances. Similarly there is one suggestion of *lazzi* to replace others which have not worked. He is not interested in plot, presumably because he knew he could get that from the scenario.

Scenario, like *commedia dell'arte*, is in fact a term which came into use late in the development of the form; earlier names were *canovaccio, centone, soggetto*, even *commedia*. *Canovaccio* (that which is on the canvas) is the word used by Antonio Fava to mean a short single plot sequence, rather than a three-act structure with sub-plots, and this can be a helpful distinction. For a group starting out it is far better to play a series of unrelated *canovacci* than attempt a full scenario.

The *canovaccio* is a simple synopsis, a technical indication of scenic content, a list of characters and the action to be accomplished by them, perhaps together with some hints about argument and dialogue. A *canovaccio* can be driven by one of three desires: love, money or vengeance, whereas a scenario, if one accepts the working distinction, often includes all three in complications of plot and sub-plot.

In a full scenario, which almost invariably has three acts (among the hundreds of extant scenarios, there are only a handful of five-acters), there needs to be a proposition, a development and a solution within each act, within each scene of each act, and even within its composite dialogues, monologues, *lazzi, burle, concetti,* etc. Again an analogy can be made with Japanese Noh which operates throughout on the principle known as 'Jo, Ha and Kyu', terms which can be roughly translated as Introduction, Exposition and Denouement.

> *These three sections move at an ever-increasing pace and form the basic dramatic, rhythmic, and melodic basis of the Noh. A more literal translation might be 'introduction' (jo), 'breaking' (ha), and 'rapid' (kyu), suggesting some of these performance elements.*

A workable *commedia dell'arte* scenario structure for performance today might, then, look something like this:
ACT I

> *Prologue.* Traditionally prologues had little to do with the actual entertainment, but were stock introductions by one of the characters, often Pantalone, Il Dottore or Colombina (see pp. 131–2). Sometimes they might be given

by a minor character who would not appear in the action itself. For a present-day audience it might be better to have an introduction to all the characters (see Part III, The San Francisco Mime Troupe) or a company song setting the atmosphere and possibly the theme of the piece.

Exposition of events so far: an optional scene played out by the characters as background to the story.

First scene in the present—establishing a simple, uncomplicated normality.

First complications introduced and leading to a cliffhanger—ending on a reaction of surprise and despair.

ACT II
Résumé of first act, possibly as a musical interlude.

Continuation of a series of complications, each building on the other, with attempted solutions breeding even greater problems. And all with increasing tempo.

ACT III
Take up all complications so far and add more.

Another résumé (perhaps a monologue delivered by Il Dottore).

Extreme consequences of complications are reached: a solution is imminent.

The solution—the revelation and unmasking of any disguised characters.

Finale—a joyous celebration, forgiveness all round, possibly after a ritual beating or other comeuppance for Il Capitano or Pantalone.

The whole to last no more than two hours, including intervals which should be musical. Act I should take no more than thirty minutes. The résumés are important: you have to educate a modern audience in the conventions of Commedia at the same time as playing to them. Don't try to be funny all the time! The progress of a good scenario is from the physical to the metaphysical and back again.

As regards content, you may find arranged marriages, masters beating servants, the ridiculing of old age, attempted sexual harassment and other stocks-in-trade of the Renaissance aversive to contemporary sensibilities. By all means look for today's equivalents, and obviously the ones you find will depend to an extent on the political and social standpoint of your troupe—but be careful not to throw Mr Punch out with the baby's bathwater.

NON-IMPROVISED ELEMENTS

The amount of improvisation to be done in performance can be overestimated: all the exits, entrances etc. are fixed by the scenario and used to be gone through beforehand by the choregos or actor-manager (Italian *corago*).

The corago, *the leader or the* maestro, *the one most capable of instructing others, should rehearse the* soggetto *before it is performed so that the actors are familiar with the content of the play, know where to conclude their speeches, and can explore in rehearsal some new witticism or new* lazzo. *The person in charge of the rehearsal does not restrict himself to just reading the scenario, but explains the names and qualities of the characters, the argument of the play, the location of the action, the stage houses, the distribution of the* lazzi *and all the necessary details, taking care of the props required for the play, like letters, purses, daggers and such like, as listed at the end of the scenario.*

Furthermore, the stock-in-trade of each Mask remained the same from one piece to the next, consisting of individual *lazzi* (sight-gags), *burle* (byplay between characters), *battute* (stock repartees) and *concetti* (stock rhetorical passages). Even seemingly improvised dialogue would be more an extemporisation, using known structures or *meccanismi*. Monologues were also stock, taken from the *repertorio* or *zibaldone* (gag-book) kept by the actor for each Mask.

In order to act properly in improvisations, therefore, it is necessary to observe all the rules laid down for written plays. For in this respect neither form of acting is different in the theatre—neither in costume, voice, pronunciation, memory, gestures or acting. All that is necessary is that there be some preparations for acting with greater facility and measure, so that the improvisation conform as much as possible to a well-rehearsed performance.

A modern practitioner, Carlo Mazzone-Clementi, suggests that changes of level are the key to not getting lost:

To perform commedia *properly you must also have a concept of the levels of* commedia *style. Andare a* soggetto, *to go with the subject, is to accept a basic premise and, with your team, create in, around, over, under and through it.* Commedia a braccia, *indicates that the physical activity is measurable 'at arm's length'; in other words that the actors adapt their movements and positions precisely but spontaneously....* Commedia all'improvviso *or 'all of a sudden' means just that: anything goes (or comes!).*

And another level comes from the *aparte* (asides) through which a continuous channel is kept open between some Masks and the audience.

The performance elements which are not to be done 'suddenly', i.e. improvised on the spot, need careful preparation, but not full-scale rehearsal. I recommend 'marking', i.e. going through the motions, but without performance energy,

carrying the mask rather than wearing it, *sotto voce* rehearsals, or even armchair run-throughs where the stating of intentions replaces acting them out—anything, in fact, rather than full-scale repetition of the scenario as if it were a text. The elements need to be kept separate until they are brought together in live performance.

It was further necessary that [you] should stock [your] mind with what the actors called the dote *of a play and with a repertory of what they called* generici. *The* dote *or dowry of a comedy consisted of soliloquies, narratives, dissertations, and studied passages of rhetoric, which were not left to improvisation. These existed in manuscript, or were composed for the occasion. They had to be used at decisive points of the action, and formed fixed pegs on which to hang the dialogue. The* generici *or common-places were sententiou smaxims, descriptions, outpourings of emotion, humorous an fanciful diatribes, declarations of passion, lovelaments, ravings, reproaches, declamatory outbursts, which could be employed ad* libitum *whenever the situation rendered them appropriate. Each mask had its own stock of common topics, suited to the personage who used them. A consummate artist displayed his ability by improving on these, A consummate artist displayed his ability by improving on these, introducing fresh points and features, and adapting them to his own conception of the part.*

These prepared sequences, whatever terms a company may agree to call them by, and whether or not they are stock or have been specially invented for a particular scenario, need to be led up to and away from in performance in such a way that the audience do not notice that they have been prepared.

LAZZI

Such seamlessness is not needed, however, in the playing of *lazzi,* which are inspired by the action but do not further it. *Lazzi,* according to a doubtful etymology, comes from the Tuscan word *lacci,* 'tied', because these tricks are supposed to have tied the action together. Rather they are insertions, most useful when the action is flagging. But the word can also mean 'ribbons', in which case they could be seen as being superfluous but decorative additions. Perhaps the most useful concept implied in this derivation is the idea of tying your shoelaces: you stop what you are doing for a brief moment to do something physical at which long practice has given you skill.

We give the name of lazzi *to those sallies and bits of byplay with which Arlecchino and the other Masks interrupt a scene in progress—it may be by demonstrations of astonishment or fright, or humorous extravagances alien to the matter in hand—after which, however, the action has to be renewed upon its previous lines. In sum they are bits of uselessness which consist only in comic business invented by the actor according to personal genius.*

Lazzi and other flights of fancy should thus always return to their starting point, from which the action then continues as if nothing had happened. However, once an idea has been introduced it can never be worked at a lesser level or dropped without coming to fulfillment—if you start such an interruption, you must finish it, even if the audience are not laughing. The same foes for the introduction of extraneous objects. This is not easy for the person who is being interrupted, who needs to be ready to take the focus back, but not until the byplay is finished.

In fact in performing Commedia, readiness is all: you must be constantly prepared not only to interrupt and be interrupted, but also to be called on even when you are not onstage and you think the scenario is offering you a break. Anyone who is called onstage *must come at once,* and as many times as necessary; for example a master calls for Zanni, sends him off, then keeps stopping him and bringing him back for a further demand or to check that he has remembered the message right.

Being on the *qui vive* all the time can lead to hyperactivity in the inexperienced:

There are in fact two pitfalls that must be avoided—too little ardour, or too much. Some players who are very conscientious, but sadly inhibited, keep to the letter of their part, and throw themselves into it so little that they freeze their protagonist. Others are so impulsive and so uncontrolled that they come on to the stage in a sort of frenzy, and while as soloists they are superlative and often extremely original, they are the despair of their fellow players. For example, they throw that which is needed in the following scene through the window and off the stage in a transport of folly: they carry off the armchair into which the heroine must shortly sink in a swoon; they drink with great gusto the potion that was to be swallowed as a poison by another character, while the unhappy actor who was working up into a wonderful death scene looks everywhere for it with increasing anxiety, and sees himself reduced to cracking his skull against the wall, if he doesn't happen to be wearing a dagger in that scene. The perfect player is he who can give himself up to the excitement of his role without forgetting the least detail, and without ceasing to be aware of what the others are doing or saying, in order to provoke the cue that he needs. He must at one and the same time be the ecstatic character of the comedy and the tranquil actor who watches and guides him.

IMPROVISATION

The amateur actors at Nohant, starting as they did from scratch, made the kind of mistakes that it is helpful to be warned of:

> The strange thing is that, when you begin to improvise, far from having nothing to say, you find yourself overflowing with dialogue and make scenes last too long as a result. The hidden danger in this genre is to sacrifice the development of the basic idea to incidents which stem from it. You must also be very alert, in order not to have several characters speaking at the same time, to the possibility of having to sacrifice what you were going to say as a result of something your partner has said, and also to revitalise the action when you sense him flagging; to bring the scene back to its objective when the others are wandering off the point and to stick to it yourself when your imagination is trying to persuade you to go off into dreamland. In spite of our good intentions, it happened more than once that the voice of those actors who had left the stage and become spectators would bring us to order, shouting 'get back to the scenario'. It was like a bucket of cold water being poured over your head, but we'd promised to obey it, so we obeyed it.

The constant quest in improvisation is for form, not content. The wine is no problem: it is the skin to put it in which is needed if the audience are to be able to drink it. To change the metaphor, a foundation, once established, needs building on, not swapping for another. In fact the audience will not be satisfied until you have reached the chimney pot. As soon as you find a rhythm, a mechanism which works between your Mask and another one, don't lose it: it is more important to develop the form than it is to avoid speaking rubbish. In fact gobbledygook can be extremely useful. In Commedia it is called *grummelot*.

Grummelot

Dario Fo uses this technique a lot, though he calls it *grammelot:*

> Grammelot *is a term of French origin, coined by Commedia players, and the word itself is devoid of meaning. It refers to a babel of sounds which, nonetheless, manage to convey the sense of a speech.* Grammelot *means the onomatopoeic flow of a speech, articulated without rhyme or reason, but capable of transmitting with the aid of particular gestures, rhythms and sounds, an entire rounded speech.*

Fo probably learned of it from Jacques Lecoq who certainly got it from Jean Dasté who had used it with the Copiaus (the touring troupe which emerged from Jacques Copeau's Vieux Colombier School), which called it *grummelot*. At that school it formed the basis of the second phase of improvisation training (the first being the miming of simple dramatic actions). Instead of adding text, Michel Saint-Denis recalls, they then used '*grummelots* which gave—I really mean *gave*—the music of the meaning. The characters were merely indicated; one could recognise the fat woman, the trollop and the shrew, but that was all.'

The technique was originally developed through necessity by the Italian players at the end of the seventeenth century, when they were banished from the Parisian theatres to the fairground booths. Since spoken dialogue was prohibited except on the legitimate stage, they were obliged to turn to oratorio, placards, scrolls and *grummelots*.

In training, once some of the basic physicality of a mask has been discovered, it will naturally want to make sounds, often quite babyish, before words become appropriate. The discovery of a vocal centre, the exploration of its sonority, and the correct mouth shape in relation to the half-mask through which to issue it, should all be developed before the use of actual words. The use of *grummelot* in terms of a country or region of origin can then be a useful next step, throwing in more and more words as the mask develops its particular vocabulary. This is a stage which can then be reverted to in later improvisation when at a loss for words, and which can even have a positive comedic effect when the going gets hectic in performance.

CONCERTED PLAYING

Ensemble work is crucial to the success of a Commedia performance because the very best improviser can only play as well as partners can respond. A chain is only as strong as its weakest link.

> *The Commedia actor never works alone. His virtuoso excursions must never proceed from his own ego. There must be a constant awareness of the whole. He must know and understand his partners, balancing and contrasting them, working together with such sensitivity and unity that we are caught up in their game before we know what has happened. Nonsense is more important than sense.... Trust and confidence, based on real, existing skills and knowledge of one another, must be present in a Commedia company. You are literally all in it together.*

I call this concerted playing after the English concert parties and Pierrot shows of the inter-war years, who used the term to indicate a style of playing with the full company onstage, and also for its musical connotations. In fact a Commedia troupe are almost never all onstage together, except at the end, but nevertheless a sense of collective playfulness and mutual support is necessary throughout and should communicate itself as an atmosphere to the spectator. There is no room on a Commedia platform for a selfish performer:

> *Whoever refers to 'a good actor of the Comédie Italienne' is identifying a player with a personality of his own, one who depends more on the strength of his imagination than on his memory, and one who composes what he performs even as he delivers it; one who knows how to adjust to the player he acts with; one who can, that is, so perfectly marry his own words and actions to the words and actions of his colleague, that he can blend with the action of his companions and react as required, making all believe that his acting was premeditated.*

A good exercise in concerted playing is for a flea to make its way round the company: those laughing at the misery of others soon become afflicted themselves, while all have to keep a single, tiny but highly volatile focus. Eventually it starts to breed, leading to an orgy of frenzied scratching.

MUSIC

It would be strange if an Italian performance genre did not have musicality: in fact it is best not to think of Commedia as being action and dialogue with interposed songs and musical interludes, but as being inherently musical and constantly on the brink of tipping over into operetta. Most of the *zanni* can carry instruments and they should use them to provide an underlying score rather than for punctuation, though they can communicate directly through them rather as Harpo Marx does with his parphorn.

PROPERTIES

Props could be toured by strolling players, whereas settings could not. Actors would therefore be very familiar with the stock they had in their basket and with the comedic potential of each object. These were called *robe per la commedia*, and a typical list of requirements for a scenario reads

> A soldier's helmet
> Sword and buckler for Burratino
> A bucket with water
> A chamber-pot with white wine in it
> A club
> A lady's cloak for Pantalone.

Indeed one way of creating the basis for a scenario is to improvise around some typical props. Ladders, letters, lanterns, syringes for enemas, boxes of jewels, goblets, rings and all kinds of disguising costumes might also be called for. Or the requirements could be simply

> A sign for the inn
> A large travelling bag
> A packet of letters.

Such props should be as authentic as possible, not token or stagy. Objects should only be mimed in *commedia dell'arte* when speculating or fantasising—for example what would happen if Arlecchino were to hang himself, in which case he can mime the rope being thrown over a branch. Never work with the uncontrollable—for example balls or animals, which are likely to create their own chaos.

FINALE

Why Theatre? The Future of the Living Theatre

INTRODUCTION

••• *Art is large and it enlarges you and me. To a shrunk-up world its vistas are shocking. Art is the burning bush that both shelters and makes visible our profounder longings.*

—Jeanette Winterson

I regard the theatre as an art form because I believe in its transformative power. I work in the theatre because I want the challenge of decisiveness and articulation in my daily life. Directing chose me as much as I chose it. We found one another. I like to watch. I like to study. I like to meet people in the charged atmosphere of a rehearsal room or in a theatre.

The theatre has been good to me. It has produced great friendships, love, travel, hard work, fun, terror and pleasure. It has also offered an entire life of study. Study is a fulltime engagement which includes reading books, reading people, reading situations, reading about the past and reading the present. To study, you enter into a situation with your whole being, you listen and then begin to move around inside it with your imagination. You can study every situation you are in. You can learn to read life while life is happening.

A scuba diver lies first in the water and waits until the entire ocean floor below starts to teem with life. Then the swimmer begins to move. This is how I study. I listen until there is movement and then I begin to swim.

I wanted to approach the theatre as an artist does, so I began to study the tools we have inherited and the procedures we use to make work in the theatre. I also studied how artists in other fields do what they do—how they think and how they create. I looked for helpful allies in the artistic process. How do we approach one another in the arena of a rehearsal or on a stage? How do we begin and then how do we go on?

As a director in the theatre I have encountered certain consistent problems that just do not go away. I have found myself repeatedly face to face with issues about violence, memory, terror, eroticism, stereotype, embarrassment and resistance. Rather than avoiding these problems I have found it fruitful to study them. And this study has changed the way I approach all my work in the theatre. The problems became allies.

Artists are individuals willing to articulate in the face of flux and transformation. And the successful artist finds new shapes for our present ambiguities and uncertainties. The artist becomes the creator of the future through the violent act of articulation. I say violent because articulation is a forceful act. It demands an aggressiveness and an ability to enter into the fray and translate that experience into expression. In the articulation begins a new organization of the inherited landscape.

My good friend the writer Charles L.Mee, Jr helped me to recognize the relationship between art and the way societies are structured. He suggested that, as societies develop, it is the artists who articulate the necessary myths that embody our experience of life and provide parameters for ethics and values. Every so often the inherited myths lose their value because they become too small and confined to contain the complexities of the ever-transforming and expanding societies. In that moment new myths are needed to encompass who we are becoming. These new constructs do not eliminate anything already in the mix; rather, they include fresh influences and engender new formations. The new mythologies always include ideas, cultures and people formerly excluded from the previous mythologies. So, deduces Mee, the history of art is the history of inclusion.

National and international cultures as well as artistic communities are currently undergoing gigantic shifts in mythology. Technological and corporate revolutions have already changed the way we communicate, interact, live, make art and articulate our ethics and values. The myths of the last century are now inadequate to encompass these new experiences. We are living in the space between mythologies. It is a a very creative moment, brimming with possibilities of new social structures, alternate paradigms and for the inclusion of disparate cultural influences.

I believe that the new mythologies will be created and articulated in art, in literature, architecture, painting and poetry. It is the artists who will create a livable future through their ability to articulate in the face of flux and change.

And yet, to succeed in this fast-changing world requires action, speed, decisiveness and hard work. To survive, to keep up, to feed a family, to ensure a roof over our heads, it is necessary to act from a very particular personal impulse: the survival instinct. And there is always the danger that this survival mode will dominate the artistic process. Most of the choices that we make in the survival mode issue from a need for security and advancement. But the instinct for security gives access only to a small part of our creative abilities. If we limit our impulses to the survival instinct, our scope and range of artistic work will be limited.

Lewis Hyde in his book entitled *The Gift: Imagination and the Erotic Life of Property* suggests that humans always take action and make decisions from two possible sources: the survival instinct or the gift-giving impulse.

The gift-giving impulse, like the survival instinct, also demands action and decisiveness, but the results differ because the intention that provokes the action has nothing to do with security. The action originates in the impulse to give someone a gift and the urge to create a journey for others outside of their daily experience. This instinct requires generosity, interest in others, and empathy.

Imagine planning a surprise birthday party for a friend. You make decisions about whom to invite and how to astonish and when to reveal, all with a sense of vicarious pleasure and excitement. You are structuring a journey for another person through direct empathy and feeling. The creative action and choices spring from the gift-giving impetus. This kind of impulse also determines how we compose a song, develop a story, design a house and, ideally, how we rehearse a play. We create journeys for others to be received in the spirit of a gift.

To approach the theatre as an art form we must be able to act in this empathetic spirit. But in our new global environment we find ourselves immersed in commerce, in the marketplace and, perhaps because of it, we find ourselves in conflict. In a world of commodities, we are not solely artists, but producers as well. Each of us is a producer and an artist in one and we must take care that one does not overwhelm the other. The producer in us must protect the gift giver and know when and how to give it space and freedom. The gift giver must step aside for the survival instinct in the right moments. The two must have their range and autonomy. How can we survive in the marketplace and still make art? How can we live in this fast and competitive environment and still walk into a rehearsal able to call upon the wild, violent child in us that makes the art poetic and magnificent and dangerous and terrifying? How can we, in a climate racing for survival, generate gifts with presence and generosity?

The study of violence, memory, terror, eroticism, stereotype, embarrassment and resistance has helped me to treat each one as an ally in the creative process. It has been a journey outward towards other cultures, ideas and people. It has given me the courage to welcome the imbalance of our present uncertainties and attempt the violence of articulation in order to actualize the new mythologies of our time.

Selected Bibliography

Allison, Mary Ellen. *A Survival Guide for Stage Managers: A Practical Step-by-step Handbook to Stage Management*. Denver, Colo.: Outskirts Press, 2011.

Artaud, Antonin. *The Theater and Its Double*. New York: Grove Press, 1958.

Ball, William. *A Sense of Direction: Some Observations on the Art of Directing*. New York: Drama Book Publishers, 1984.

Banham, Martin. *A History of Theatre in Africa*. Digitally Printed Version. ed. Cambridge: Cambridge University Press, 2008.

Banham, Martin. *The Cambridge Guide to Asian Theatre*. Reprinted ed. Cambridge: Cambridge Univ. Press, 1999.

Baumer, Rachel Van M. *Sanskrit Drama in Performance*. Honolulu: University Press of Hawaii, 1981.

Bellman, William. *Scene Design, Stage Lighting, Sound, Costume and Make up*. New York, New York: Harper & Row, 1983.

Bogart, Anne. *A Director Prepares: Seven Essays on Art and Theatre*. London: Routledge, 2001.

Brazell, Karen. *Traditional Japanese Theater: An Anthology of Plays*. New York: Columbia University Press, 1998.

Brockett, Oscar G., and Franklin J. Hildy. *History of the Theatre*. 9th ed. Boston: Allyn and Bacon, 2003.

Brook, Peter. *The Empty Space*. New York: Simon & Schuster, 1996.

Brown, John Russell. *The Oxford Illustrated History of Theatre*. New York: Oxford University Press, 2001.

Caffrey, Mary Kate. *The Natural Actor*. Cognella Academic Publishing, 2012.

Carter, Paul Douglas, and Sally Friedman Carter. *Backstage Handbook: An Illustrated Almanac of Technical Information*. 3rd ed. Shelter Island, N.Y.: Broadway Press, 1994.

Catron, Louis E. *The Director's Vision: Play Direction from Analysis to Production*. Long Grove, Ill.: Waveland Press, 2010.

"Classicism In The Theatre." World News. Accessed September 7, 2014. http://wn.com/classicism_in_the_theatre.

"Commedia Bibliography." Accessed September 12, 2014. http://www.commedia-dell-arte.com/bibliography.htm.

"COMMEDIA DELL'ARTE (Italian Comedy)." Commedia Dell'Arte. Accessed September 28, 2014. http://www.delpiano.com/carnival/html/commedia.html.

Corson, Richard, and James Glavan. *Stage Makeup*. 9th ed. Boston, MA: Allyn and Bacon, 2001.

Dolby, William. *A History of Chinese Drama*. London: P. Elek, 1976.

Eaker, Sherry. *The Back Stage Handbook for Performing Artists*. New York: Back Stage Books, 1989.

Fava, Antonio. *The Comic Mask in the Commedia Dell'arte: Actor Training, Improvisation, and the Poetics of Survival*. Evanston, Ill.: Northwestern University Press, 2007.

Gainor, J. Ellen. *The Norton Anthology of Drama*. New York: W. W. Norton & Company, 2009.

Gainor, J. Ellen, Stanton Gainor, and Martin Puchner, eds. *The Norton Anthology of Drama*. Second ed. W. W. Norton & Company, 2013.

Gillette, J. Michael. *Designing with Light: An Introduction to Stage Lighting*. 5th ed. New York: McGraw-Hill, 2008.

Gillette, J. Michael. *Theatrical Design and Production: An Introduction to Scene Design and Construction, Lighting, Sound, Costume, and Makeup*. 7th ed. New York, NY: McGraw-Hill, 2013.

Green, Stanley, and Cary Ginell. *Broadway Musicals: Show by Show*. Eighth ed. Applause Theatre & Cinema Books, 2014.

Gordon, Mel. *Lazzi: The Comic Routines of the Commedia Dell'arte*. New York: Performing Arts Journal Publications, 1983.

Ingham, Rosemary, and Liz Covey. *The Costume Designer's Handbook: A Complete Guide for Amateur and Professional Costume Designers*. 2nd ed. Portsmouth, NH: Heinemann, 1992.

"Invitation to Kabuki - Guidance for Kabuki Appreciation." Accessed October 30, 2014. http://www2.ntj.jac.go.jp/unesco/kabuki/en/index.html.

"Japanese Culture - Entertainment - Bunraku." Accessed August 20, 2014. http://www.japan-zone.com/culture/bunraku.shtml.

"Japanese Culture - Entertainment - Kabuki Theater." Accessed October 30, 2014. http://www.japan-zone.com/culture/kabuki.shtml.

"Japanese Culture - Entertainment - Noh Theater." Accessed October 7, 2014. http://www.japan-zone.com/culture/noh.shtml#kyogen.

Jones, John Bush. *Our Musicals, Ourselves: A Social History of the American Musical Theater*. Hanover: Brandeis University Press, Published by University Press of New England, 2003.

Jones, Robert Edmond. *The Dramatic Imagination: Reflections and Speculations on the Art of the Theatre*. New York: Routledge, 2004.

"KABUKI WEB." Accessed October 2, 2014. http://www.kabuki-bito.jp/eng/top.html.

Kelly, Thomas A. *The Back Stage Guide to Stage Management: Traditional and New Methods for Running a Show from First Rehearsal to Last Performance*. 3rd ed. New York: Backstage Books, 2009.

Keene, Donald, and Keizo Kaneko. *Nô and Bunraku: Two Forms of Japanese Theatre*. New York [u.a.: Columbia Univ. Press, 1990.

Kenrick, John. *Musical Theatre a History*. Pbk. ed. New York: Continuum, 2010.

Mackerras, Colin. *Chinese Theater: From Its Origins to the Present Day*. Honolulu: University of Hawaii Press, 1983.

Marasinghe, E. W. *The Sanskrit Theatre and Stagecraft*. Delhi, India: Sri Satguru Publications, 1989.

Mehta, Tarla. *Sanskrit Play Production in Ancient India*. Delhi: Motilal Banarsidass Publishers, 1995.

Mordden, Ethan. *Anything Goes: A History of American Musical Theatre*. 1st ed. Oxford University Press, 2013.

Nicoll, Allardyce. *The World of Harlequin, a Critical Study of the Commedia Dell'arte*. Cambridge [Eng: University Press, 1963.

"NOH & KYOGEN -An Introduction to the World of Noh & Kyogen-." Accessed October 20, 2014. http://www2.ntj.jac.go.jp/unesco/noh/en/index.html.

"Noh Plays." Accessed October 28, 2014. http://etext.lib.virginia.edu/japanese/noh/index.html.

Ortolani, Benito. *The Japanese Theatre: From Shamanistic Ritual to Contemporary Pluralism*. Rev. ed. Princeton, N.J.: Princeton University Press, 1995.

Pecktal, Lynn. *Designing and Drawing for the Theatre*. New York: McGraw-Hill, 1995.

Pilbrow, Richard. *Stage Lighting*. Rev. ed. New York: Drama Book Specialists, 1979.

Raoul, Bill. *Stock Scenery Construction Handbook*. 2nd ed. Louisville, KY: Broadway Press, 1999.

Richmond, Farley P. *Kutiyattam Sanskrit Theater of India*. Ann Arbor, Mich.: Univ. of Michigan Press, 2000.

Rudlin, John. *Commedia Dell'Arte in the 20th Century: Handbook*. Routledge, 1994.

Stanislavsky, Konstantin, and Jean Benedetti. *An Actor's Work: A Student's Diary*. London: Routledge, 2008.

Stempel, Larry. *Showtime: A History of the Broadway Musical Theater*. New York, NY: W.W. Norton &, 2010.

Tarlekar, Ganesh Hari. *Studies in the Nātyaśāstra: With Special Reference to the Sanskrit Drama in Performance.* 2nd Rev. ed. Delhi: Motilal Banarsidass, 1991.

"The Barbara Curtis Adachi Bunraku Collection." Bunraku:Brownstein. Accessed November 11, 2014. http://bunraku.cul.columbia.edu/bunraku/pages/brownstein.

"The Barbara Curtis Adachi Bunraku Collection." Bunraku:Early. Accessed September 28, 2014. http://bunraku.cul.columbia.edu/bunraku/pages/early.

"The Barbara Curtis Adachi Bunraku Collection." Bunraku:Music. Accessed September 28, 2014. http://bunraku.cul.columbia.edu/bunraku/pages/music.

Siu, Wang. *Chinese Opera: The Actor's Craft.* 1st ed. Hong Kong University Press, 2014.

Stern, Lawrence. *Stage Management.* 8th ed. Boston: Pearson/Allyn & Bacon, 2006.

Wickham, Glynne. *A History of the Theatre.* 2nd ed. Oxford: Phaidon, 1992.

Wilson, Edwin. *Anthology of Living Theater.* 3rd ed. Boston: McGraw Hill, 2008.

Wilson, Edwin, and Alvin Goldfarb. *Living Theatre: History of the Theatre.* 6th ed. New York: McGraw-Hill, 2012.

Xu, Chengbei. *Peking Opera.* Updated ed. Cambridge: Cambridge University Press, 2012.

Zarrilli, Phillip B. *Theatre Histories: An Introduction.* 2nd ed. New York: Routledge, 2010.

CPSIA information can be obtained
at www.ICGtesting.com
Printed in the USA
LVOW02s0750311215
468478LV00003B/3/P

9 781631 890529